Uenerabili patri & semp uiro Rob. olim pan couus
ecclie. suus tuz dict^ dunsiensis u bonuz q^ mdo dut. & eo
pleniare. Post qua bono omine de rua Wint ecclia caruuia
pfectus es. intu^ z sepe delibau subueq sic pbectu recu fome
temasuu. certo au^ iusus^ q^ aget. q^uu uiuez. dno cella Car/
ruise celsioz suo zcelo marmoz claust^ Wint. Noluut & ruode uoto meo
carissace. bem. z iuuisa solus uenissem. tu tbi me dno. fuerut q; qui
mecu ueriant tu cu recessus. q^ eu illis uelle displicauz. fuore q; u dict
erroze tage th secundo. Vidi Aps nos q^ alibi u mdam. q^ uo corudam q^
mus mitari potam. qm decez. In quibet cellaru uirarum z unu hostru
ex instituto q^ nos apure licez ad placus. s; p illud exire u licez. n tm
ita. u mu pedu cu lumen cella siup remaneam. Egrediat^ uno pede q
uoluerit siup alto remandoz i cella. Magnu z pfundu sacmentu debe
hostiu habe q^ pareaz. z q^ mote z exire u liceat. Oz uoz z aliud. Cibz
bouis vpalib; habudamez ralgm enchil habitoz roia possidimez. filii
misediores hoib; z huaniozes plenissima ad nos uuroe karitate habm
ves karitatis effectu dimidiatu ad aduenas. Uidetoz sui poridia dam^
hospitalib;. Otroz z vruu. Viri miutres nos exc^ sectin secto acsingla/
rib; omi ues gestas scius u suus z quus pscias sm^ qm biam.

THE CHRONICLE

OF

RICHARD OF DEVIZES

CONCERNING THE DEEDS OF
RICHARD THE FIRST,
KING OF ENGLAND.

ALSO

RICHARD OF CIRENCESTER'S

DESCRIPTION OF BRITAIN.

———

TRANSLATED AND EDITED

BY J. A. GILES, LL.D.
LATE FELLOW OF C. C. COLL. OXFORD.

———

LONDON:
JAMES BOHN, 12, KING WILLIAM STREET, STRAND.
MDCCCXLI.

LONDON:
WILLIAM STEVENS, PRINTER, BELL YARD,
TEMPLE BAR.

TO THE RIGHT REVEREND

EDWARD,

LORD BISHOP OF LLANDAFF,

THIS TRANSLATION OF

RICHARD OF DEVIZES,

IS RESPECTFULLY INSCRIBED,

BY HIS LORDSHIP'S

OBEDIENT AND HUMBLE SERVANT,

J. A. GILES.

TABLE OF CONTENTS.

———◆———

PREFACE.

———•———

THIS volume contains a valuable Chronicle of
King Richard's expedition to the Holy Land, by
Richard of Devizes, translated for the first time
from the original Latin, recently published by the
English Historical Society, and a reprint of the
former translation of Richard of Cirencester. Of
the former of these chroniclers nothing more is
known than the information which he has himself
given in his preface. It is, therefore, useless on
the present occasion to indulge in conjecture, or
to amplify what is so scanty. Of the latter a
notice reprinted from the former London edition
(8vo. 1809) will be found in page 81. It has
been a question whether the work is a genuine
production of Richard of Cirencester, who has

written other works sfill extant. It is, therefore, repeated here on its own merits, of which the reader will be the judge. The original Latin has been added, as it is not likely to be republished in a separate form.

PROLOGUE.

To the Venerable Father Robert, his very good Lord, formerly Prior of the Church of Winchester, health to persevere in the good work he has begun, his faithful servant, Richard, surnamed of Devizes, sends greeting :

§ 1. AFTER you had happily proceeded to the Charter House (*at Witham*) from our church of Winchester, much and often did I desire to follow you who had thus departed, peradventure to remain with you, but certainly to behold what you were about, how you lived, and whether the Carthusian cell is more exalted and nearer heaven than the cloister of Winchester. It pleased God at length to satisfy my wish. I came, and oh that I had come alone! I went thither making the third, and those who went with me were the cause of my return. My desire displeased them, and they caused my fervor, I will not say error, to grow cold. I saw with you that which elsewhere I had not seen, which I could not have believed, and which I could not sufficiently admire. In each of your cells there is one door according to custom, which you are permitted to open at pleasure, but to go out by it is not permitted, except so much as that one foot should always remain in the

B

cell, within the threshold. The brethren may step out with one foot, whichever they please, but the other must remain in the cell. A great and solemn oath is to be taken that the door by which it is not permitted to enter or depart should be kept open. I am astonished also at another thing ; abounding in all the good things of this world, as having nothing, yet possessing all things, more compassionate and humane than all men, having thé most perfect love one to another, you divide the affection of charity to strangers, you bless without giving supplies to your guests. Nor do I less admire in the third place, that living to yourselves apart out of society, and singly, you understand all the great things achieved in the World as they happen, and even sometimes you know them prior to their being accomplished. Do not, however, consider it want of respect in me to your more than Pythagoræan taciturnity, if I shall dare presume to address men of so great gravity, and so arduous profession, rather with the trifles of the world than mere idle gossip.

§ 2. Nevertheless, although, as it is thought, the Omniscient God is with you and in you, and through Him you know all things, and not from man, nor yet by man, you were pleased, as you said, that my essay would be a solace to you, inasmuch as in the first place I should write to you a history of the fresh changes, which the world has produced, turning squares into circles, (more especially since your transmigration to the celled heaven, by means of which the world may appear more worthless to you, having its fickleness before your eyes,) and, secondly, that a well-known hand might recal to you the memory of one beloved.

Oh! what delight! if that holy spirit, if the angel of the Lord, if the deified man who is become already of the number of the gods, should deign to remember me before the great God, me, who am scarcely worthy to be accounted a man. I have done that which you desired, do that which you have promised. And that the little book may have a commencement of some importance, I have begun a little higher than was stipulated, making our Royal house, troubled like that of Œdipus, the bounds of my work, commencing at the latter part, not daring to hope to unravel the whole. Why, and how, and when, the father may have crowned his son; how great things and of what importance thence ensued; who and how often and what regions they embroiled; with what success they all ended I have left to those who produce greater works: my narrative serves only for the living.

RICHARD OF DEVIZES.

---

§ 3. Now in the year of our Lord's incarnation 1189, Richard, the son of King Henry the Second by Eleanor, brother of Henry the Third, was consecrated king of the English by Baldwin, archbishop of Canterbury, at Westminster, on the third of the nones of September (3 Sept.). On the very day of the coronation, about that solemn hour, in which the Son was immolated to the Father, a sacrifice of the Jews to their father the devil was commenced in the city of London, and so long was the duration of this famous mystery, that the holocaust could scarcely be accomplished the ensuing day. The other cities and towns of the kingdom emulated the faith of the Londoners, and with a like devotion despatched their blood-suckers with blood to hell. In this commotion there was prepared, although unequally, some evil against the wicked, everywhere throughout the realm, only Winchester alone, the people being prudent and circumspect, and the city always acting mildly, spared its vermin. It never did anything overspeedily; fearing nothing more than to repent, it considers the result of every thing before the commencement. It was unwilling, unprepared, to cast up violently through the parts the indigestion by which it was oppressed to its bodily peril, and it was careful for its bowels, in the mean time temperately concealing its

[margin notes:] A. D. 1189, Richard's coronation. Henry, son of King Henry II., is frequently styled Henry the Third, in the early Chronicles. Jews, so called probably from their usurious practices.

uneasiness, until it should be possible for it, at a convenient time for cure, to cast out the whole cause of the disease at once and once for all.

§ 4. Not without the anxious solicitude and amazement of many a bat was seen, in the middle and bright part of the day, to flutter through the monastery, inconveniently recircling in the same tracks, and especially around the king's throne.

§ 5. William de Longchamp, who had been the chancellor of the Earl of Poitiers before his accession, when the earl was crowned king, considered his office to have profited as much for the better, as a kingdom is superior to an earldom.

§ 6. A circumstance happened on the self-same day of the coronation in Westminster Abbey, a presage of such portentous omen, as then was hardly allowable to be related even in a whisper. At Complin, the last hour of the day, the first peal that day happened to be rung, neither by any agreement, nor even the ministers of the church themselves being aware of it, till after it was done; for Prime, Tierce, Sext, Nones, and the solemn service of Vespers and two Masses were celebrated without any ringing of peals.

Fines levied on Stephen de Marzai, otherwise called Stephen de Turonis,

Stephen de Marzai, seneschal of Anjou, under the king lately deceased, he great and mighty, singularly fierce, and the master of his lord, being taken and cast in chains, was dragged to Winchester, where being made a gazing-stock to angels and to men, emaciated with woeful hunger, and broken with the weight of his irons, he was constrained to the payment of thirty thousand pounds of money of Anjou, and the promise of fifteen

and Ralph de Glanville.

thousand pounds, for his ransom. Ralph de Glanville, Justiciary of the realm of England and the king's eye, a man not inferior to Stephen, except in manners and riches, being deprived of authority and given into custody, redeemed merely his liberty to go and come for fifteen thousand pounds of silver. And whereas this

name Glanville had been so great the day before, a name
as it were above every name, so that whosoever, to
whom it should be given by the Lord, would converse
among princes, and would be adored by the people, yet
the next morning there remained not one in the land
who could be called by this name. That was the ruin
of those two, to wit, of Stephen and Ralph, which also
it is certain has been the ruin of thousands before them,
and which hereafter may ruin others, namely, a sus-
picion arising from the confidence of their former lord.

§ 8. John the king's brother, who alone of the sons *John's power.*
of his mother Queen Eleanor survived his brother, besides the earldom of Mortain, which by his father's gift
he had long enjoyed, was so greatly enriched and increased in England by his brother, that both privately
and publicly it was affirmed by many that the king had
no thoughts of returning to the kingdom, and that his
brother, already no less powerful than himself, if he
should not restrain his innate temper, would, impelled
by the desire of sovereignty, endeavour to drive him
vanquished from the realm.

§ 9. The time of commencing his journey pressed *Richard raises funds for the cru-sade.*
hard upon King Richard, as he, who had been first of
all the princes on this side the Alps in the taking up
of the cross, was unwilling to be last in setting out. A
king worthy of the name of king, who, in the first year
of his reign, left the kingdom of England for Christ,
scarcely otherwise than if he had departed never to
return. So great was the devotion of the man, so
hastily, so quickly and so speedily did he run, yea fly, to
avenge the wrongs of Christ. However, whilst he kept
the greater matter in his mind, giving himself in some
little measure to deliberation for the kingdom, having
received power from the Pope that he might withdraw
the cross from such of his own subjects, as he should
desire, for the government of his kingdom, he first
appointed Hugh Pudsey, bishop of Durham, to be Chief

Justice of the whole realm, and with design, as is
thought by many, further creating him a young Earl of
Northumberland out of an old bishop, the custody of as
many castles as he liked being yielded to him, he diligently cleared from his coffers ten thousand pounds of
silver. Geoffrey Fitz Peter, William Briwere, and
Hugh Bardulf being permitted to remain at home, the
cross being withdrawn from them, the king's treasurer
transferred the whole collections of the three as three
nuts into the Exchequer. All the sheriffs of the kingdom on any trivial accusation falling under the king's
displeasure, were deprived of their unlucky power, and
scarcely permitted to see his face, even by the mediation
of inestimable treasure. Ralph de Glanville, than whom
none of his time was more subtile whilst he was in
power, now being reduced to a private person by his
prince, was so stupified through grief, that his son-in-
law Ralph de Ardenne utterly lost, by reason of his
careless talk, whatever he had previously acquired by
the judgment of his mouth. He too himself, because
he was an old man, and not able to bear fatigue, if he
had been willing to give the king that little which remained after the payment of the fine, as a gratuity,
would easily have obtained a remission of the peril of
the journey. The king received security from the tributary kings of the Welsh and of the Scots, that they
would not pass their borders for the annoyance of England during his absence.

§ 10. Godfrey, son of that renowned Richard de
Luci, Richard (Fitz Neale) the Treasurer, Hubert Walter, and William de Longchamp, four men of no
small virtue, and of no mean praise, were elected at
Pippewelle to the four vacant sees, viz. Winchester,
London, Salisbury, and Ely. They all obtained sufficient canonical nomination, and especially the elect of
Winchester, who obtained his nomination to the dignity
on the seventeenth of the kalends of October (Sept. 15),

Consecrates bishops.

while the election of the other three was delayed till the
morrow, the king consenting and the archbishop con-
firming what was done, although at the first he would
rather have had it somewhat otherwise: concerning
which it wonderfully happened that he who had been
nominated to one of the sees by the archbishop's means,
died that very day. William, bishop elect of Ely, retained the king's seal on the payment of three thousand
pounds of silver, although Reginald the Italian had bid
one thousand more. The bishops elect of Winchester
and Salisbury were consecrated at Westminster, by
Baldwin, archbishop of Canterbury, on the eleventh of
the kalends of November (Oct. 22). On that day,
Hugh de Nonante, bishop of Coventry, laid his complaint before the archbishop and bishops assembled at
the consecration of the bishops elect, against his monks
of Coventry, for having laid violent hands on him and
drawn his blood before the altar. He had also expelled
the greater part of the congregation before his complaint, nor did he cease from his importunity, until he
had obtained the sanction of all the bishops in attesta-
tion to the Pope against the monks.

§ 11. Godfrey, bishop of Winchester, mindful of his Richard
profession, suing for the restoration of the possessions raises money.
of his church, which had been taken away, as no one
had any right of replevin against the church of Winchester with respect to its two manors, namely Meones
and Weregrave, recovered them by judicial decree,
three thousand pounds of silver being privately given to
the king. Nor did the considerate man omit at the
same time to pay a fine to the king for the indemnity of
the church's treasure, for his patrimony, for the county
of Hampshire and for the custody of the castles of
Winchester and Porchester. And because the time for
the payment of so much money was nigh at hand, as he
could not pass over the day fixed for the payment without detriment to the whole business, and he could find

no nearer resource under heaven, although against his
will, he laid his hand on the treasure of his church, to
restore which, however, he obliged himself and his successors, providing security to the convent by the testimony of a sealed bond. A man of such courtesy and
moderation, who not even when angry ever did any
thing to those who were under him, but what savoured
of mildness : truly of His family, and one of His familiars,
of Whom it is said, under Whom to live is to reign.

§ 12. The king readily disburthened all, whose money
was a burden to them, such powers and possessions as
they chose being given to anybody at pleasure; wherewith also on a time an old acquaintance in the company joking him, he broke off with this evasion, "I
would sell London if I could find a chapman." Many
a one might have been forewarned by that expression,
had it been uttered sooner, not to learn to be a wise
merchant, after the English proverb, " by buying for a
dozen, and selling for one and a half."

IN THE YEAR OF THE LORD MCXC.

12th Decem-
ber, 1189.
A. D. 1190.
§ 13. In the year from the incarnation of the Lord
1190, the king crossed the channel to Neustria (Normandy), the care of the whole kingdom being committed
to the chancellor.

Richard, bishop elect of London, and William of
Ely, were consecrated by Archbishop Baldwin at Westminster, the second of the kalends of January (Dec. 31,
1189).   William de Mandeville, earl of Albemarle,
being seized with delirium in an acute semitertian fever,
died at Gisorz : whose relict, a woman almost a man,
who was deficient in nothing masculine but manhood,
William de Fortibus, a knight a thousand times approved in arms, received to wife by King Richard's gift,
together with all the honours of her former husband.

Proceedings
of the chan-
cellor.
§ 14. William, bishop of Ely, and the king's chancellor, by nature a second Jacob, although he did not

wrestle with the angel, a goodly person, making up in
mind for his shortness in stature, secure of his master's
love, and presuming on his favour, because all power
was, is, and will be impatient of a partner, expelled
Hugh de Pusac from the Exchequer, and barely leaving
him even his sword with which he had been invested
as an earl by the king's hand, after a short time, deprived him of the honour of his earldom also.   And lest
the bishop of Durham alone should bewail his misfortunes, the villain, who was now more cruel than a wild
beast, and spared nobody, fell upon the bishop of Winchester also.   The custody of the castles and county is
taken away from him, nor is he even permitted to enjoy
his own patrimony.   The kingdom is disturbed, and the
discontented are charged with disaffection to the king.
Everybody crosses the sea to importune the king against
the tyrant, but he having crossed first of all, briefly related before the king a partial account of his entire proceeding and expulsion; by whom also he was fully instructed in all things to be done; he thus foiled the
adverse wishes of his rivals, and was on his return before
those who assailed him could obtain admission to the
king's presence.   So he returns to the English not less
powerful and prosperous, than one who has accomplished
all things whatsoever he desired.   The king having returned from Gascony where he had forcibly put down the
thieves, and captured the holds they had occupied, all those
whom the chancellor had injured assembled before him,
who satisfying every one as then to each seemed good,
sent them all back to the chancellor with such letters as
they then desired.   John, bishop of Norwich, being also
one of those who threatened Saladin, amply furnished for
his journey and the cause, whilst proceeding on his way
in the borders of Burgundy, fell among robbers, who
took from him all his substance; and, as he had no
means left wherewith he might proceed, he turned his
course towards the Pope, and when with his insinuation

he had bemoaned his mischance and poverty to him, the
clemency of the holy see dismissed him home, absolved
from his vow.

The chan-
cellor seizes
the bishop
of Durham. § 15. The bishop of Winchester, being affected with a
serious disease, remained some time beyond the sea. The
bishop of Durham in haste proceeded direct to London,
but not being received by the barons of the Exchequer,
he hastily, as if sure to triumph, pursues his way after
the chancellor, who at that time had gone on an expedition towards Lincoln: whom having overtaken, he
saluted in the king's name, not freely nor without a
frown, and then questioned him seriously concerning the
affairs of state, and, indeed, as if he would not suffer
anything to be done without his consent. He neglected
fine language and long words, and while he boasted too
much of power not yet received, not considering with
whom he was speaking, he loosely uttered whatever he
ought to have kept secret. At the conclusion of his
address, the staff is put forth to silence talk, the king's
solemn act much to be reverenced is exhibited for reci-
tal. The mountains travail, the silly mouse is produced.
The observance of strict silence is enjoined during the
king's mandate; all were hushed, and attentive held
their tongues. The epistle is read in public, which
would have been much more to be feared if it had
not been so soon read; he (Longchamp) well able to
conceal his device, shrewdly deferred to answer what he
had heard till the seventh day, appointing their place
of conference at Tickhill. On the day appointed the
bishop of Durham comes to the castle, and his attendants being commanded to wait for him before the gates,
he goes in to the chancellor quite alone; he who before
had held his peace, speaks first, and compels the deceived to recite with his own mouth letters he had
obtained after the former against whatever he had
hoped. As he was preparing to answer, he added,
" The other day while you were speaking it was time

for me to be silent, now that you may discern why I
have taken a time for speaking, you being silent; as
my lord the king lives, you shall not depart hence until
you have given me hostages for all the castles which you
hold being delivered up to me, for I do not take you as
a bishop a bishop, but as a chancellor a chancellor!"
The ensnared had neither the firmness nor the oppor-
tunity to resist; the hostages are given, and at the term
assigned the castles are given up for the restoring of
the hostages.   William, bishop of Worcester, who succeeded next to Baldwin, went the way of all flesh.

§ 16. The lord bishop of Winchester, at length re- Besieges
Gloucester
covering in Neustria, and also desiring to receive back castle.
the things taken from him, recrossed with all the speed
he could, and found the chancellor besieging the castle
of Gloucester.   Whose arrival being known, the chancellor goes forth to meet him as he comes, and having
heartily embraced and kissed him, says, " You have
come at a most desirable time, dear friend! are we to
prosecute the siege or desist?"   To whom the bishop re-
plies, " If you desire peace, lay down arms."   He, quick
of apprehension, perceived the force of the words, and
commanded the heralds to sound the retreat; he also
restored to the bishop his patrimony without dispute,
but that only.   All the others, who had crossed the sea
against the chancellor, profited less than nothing.
William, legate of the apostolic see, held a council at
Westminster, in which, lest there should be nothing
done to be reported of him hereafter, he sentenced all
religion to be expelled from Coventry cathedral, and pre-
bendary clerks to be substituted in place of the monks.

§ 17. William, the wonderful bishop of Ely, chan- Appointed
papal le-
cellor of the king, Justiciary of the kingdom, of three- gate.
fold charge and threefold title, that he might use both
hands as the right, and that the sword of Peter might
succour the sword of the ruler, took upon himself the
office of legate of all England, Scotland, Wales, and

Ireland, which he obtained from the Pope at the instance of the king, who would not otherwise set out, by Reginald, bishop of Bath. Therefore successful in every office which he craved, he passed to and fro through the kingdom with the rapidity of a flash of lightning.

The King of Darkness, that old Incendiary, having added fresh fuel, fanned the ancient spark between the church of Salisbury and the monastery of Malmesbury into renewed flames. The abbot is roused not now to make the profession of pontiff, but to disavow the very title of the bishop as well as his crosier. Royal letters to the chancellor were obtained, by which the abbot should be compelled to respond at law to the motions of the bishop. Nor did the man whose affairs were at stake forget himself, no peril could ever overtake him unprovided, who never knew the loss of anything through sloth. He repelled one nail by another, being presented by the king with letters invalidating the former letters. The chancellor having perceived the shameful contrariety of the mandates of his prince, lest the king's fame should be injured by the fact, if he proceeded in the cause, deferred all process of both the one party and the other till the king's return.

§ 18. King Richard exacted an oath from his two brothers, John his own brother and Geoffrey a bastard, that they would not enter England within three years from his departure, the three years to be reckoned from the day of his starting from Tours ; through the entreaties of his mother, however, dispensing so far concerning John, that passing into England with the chancellor's approbation, he should abide his judgment, and at his pleasure he should either remain in the kingdom, or live in exile.

Queen Eleanor's dowry was recognized throughout the king's territories by a solemn act, and delivered up to her, so that she who had before lived on the Exchequer might thenceforward live on her own.

The king's fleet, having left its own shores, sailed round Spain, and from the ocean having entered the Mediterranean, which further on is called the Grecian Sea, by the Straits of Africa, is steered on to Marseilles, *i. e. of Gibraltar.* there to await the king.

The king of France and the king of England, having held a council at Tours and again at Vezelay, and confirmed the treaty between themselves and their kingdoms, and having settled and disposed of all things on both sides according to their pleasure, depart from each other with their respective armies. The Frenchman, being subject to sickness at sea, marches by land to Sicily; the Englishman, on the contrary, about to proceed by sea, comes to Marseilles to his ships. Baldwin, archbishop of Canterurby, and Hubert Walter, bishop of Salisbury, being the only bishops of all England who accomplished their vows, follow the king to Sicily, and arrive first in the land of Juda.

§ 19. The monks of the order of Cluni were not wont to supplant one another in their priories and government either by entreaty or bribes, and although some of them have sometimes attempted something of that sort, that however we have seen visited with condign punishment. There was a certain venerable man elected prior of Montacute solely on account of his worth, Josceline by name, in whom you could discern nothing but what was praiseworthy. To supplant this so good a man there came a certain one, whose name it is not necessary to mention, one of his false brethren, with letters, obtained by great cunning from the abbot of Cluni, by which it was commanded that the prior should resign to the bearer of the present letters and the congregation receive him for their prelate. The prior by some means foreknew what commodity the dealer had come to seek, wherefore, without awaiting the mandate, he vacated his seat in the chapter, and, the congregation being present, addressed him, " Friend, for what art thou come ?" He, having tarried long that he might appear unwillingly to receive that, which he had come to take by violence, at length betook himself to his seat, and anon imprecated himself, saying, " O thou who with unalterable purpose governest the world, whose power takes its pastime in human affairs, who puttest down the mighty and exaltest the humble ! O thou just Judge Jesu Christ, if wrongfully I here preside, without delay and manifestly do thou vouchsafe to show !" Behold the miracle ! On that same day he lost his speech; on the next his life; on the third, being consigned to the earth, he learnt by experience, and taught by example, that sordid plunder is never followed by prosperous results.

A certain monk of Glastonbury, in hopes of promotion, courted Earl John with many presents, but just as he should have come to receive it, a certain beam having suddenly given way, fell in his face, so that bruised and wholly disfigured, he lost both his eggs (*qy.* expectations) and his money together.

§ 20. The ships which the king found already prepared on the shore were one hundred in number, and fourteen busses, vessels of great magnitude and admirable swiftness, strong vessels and very sound, whereof this was the equipage and appointment. The first of the ships had three spare rudders, thirteen anchors, thirty oars, two sails, three sets of ropes of all kinds, and besides these double whatever a ship can want, except the mast and the ship's boat. There is appointed to the ship's command a most experienced steersman, and fourteen subordinate attendants picked for the service are assigned him. The ship is freighted with forty horses of value, trained to arms, and with arms of all kinds for as many horsemen, and forty foot, and fifteen sailors, and with an entire year's provisions for as many men and horses. There was one appointment for all the ships, but each of the busses received a double appoint-

Description of Richard's fleet.

ment and freight. The king's treasure, which was very great and inestimable, was divided amongst the ships and busses, that if one part should experience danger, the rest might be saved. All things being thus arranged, the king himself, with a small household, and the chief men of his army, with his attendants, having quitted the shore, advanced before the fleet in galleys, and being daily entertained by the maritime towns, taking along with them the larger ships and busses of that sea, arrived prosperously at Messina. So great was the splendour _{He arrives at Messina,} of the approaching armament, such the clashing and _{Sept. 23.} brilliancy of their arms, so noble the sound of the trumpets and clarions, that the city quaked and was greatly astounded, and there came to meet the king a multitude of all ages, people without number, wondering and proclaiming with what exceeding glory and magnificence that king had arrived, surpassing the king of France, who with his forces had arrived seven days before. And forasmuch as the king of France had been already received into the palace of Tancred, king of Sicily, within the walls, the king of England pitched his camp without the city. The same day the king of France, know- _{His proceedings there.} ing of the arrival of his comrade and brother, flies to his reception, nor could their gestures sufficiently express in embraces and kisses how much each of them rejoiced in the other. The armies cheered one another with mutual applause and intercourse, as if so many thousand men had been all of one heart and one mind. In such pastimes is the holiday spent until the evening, and the weary kings departing, although not satiated, return every one to his own quarters. On the next day the king of England presently caused gibbets to be erected without the camp to hang thereon thieves and robbers. The judges delegated spared neither sex nor age ; the cause of the stranger and the native found the like law and the like punishment. The king of France, whatever transgression his people committed, or whatever

c

offence was committed against them, took no notice and
held his peace; the king of England esteeming the
country of those implicated in guilt as a matter of no
consequence, considered every man his own, and left no
transgression unpunished, wherefore the one was called
a Lamb by the Griffones, the other obtained the name
of a Lion.

He is Insult-
ed by Tan-
cred,
§ 21. The king of England sent his messengers to the
king of Sicily, demanding Johanna his sister, formerly
queen of Sicily, and her dowry, with a golden seat and
the whole legacy which King William had bequeathed to
his father, King Henry, namely, a golden table of twelve
feet in length, a silk tent, a hundred of the best galleys
with all their necessaries for two years, sixty thousand
silinas of wheat, sixty thousand of barley, sixty thousand of wine, four and twenty golden cups, and four and
twenty golden dishes. The king of Sicily, setting little
by the demands of the king of the English, and still
less considering his own exigencies, sent him back his
sister with the ordinary furniture of her bed, having
given her, however, with royal consideration, a thousand
thousand Terrini for her expenses. On the third day
following, the king of England, having passed over the
great river Del Far, which separates Calabria from
Sicily, entered Calabria in arms, and took therein the
well fortified town which is called La Banniere, and having expelled the Griffones, established his sister there,
and secured the place with an armed garrison. Again
the king took a very strong castle, which is called the
Griffones' Monastery, on the same river Del Far, situated
between La Banniere and Messina, and fortified it when
taken; and having without mercy despatched by various
tortures the Griffones who had resisted, caused them to
be exhibited as a gazing-stock to their friends. Wido
king of Jerusalem, sent word to Philip king of the
French, and Richard king of the English, whilst winter-
ing in Sicily, that the residue of the Christians who lay

before Acre, would, on account of their weakness and the violence of the pagans, either be obliged to depart or perish, unless very shortly sustained. To aid whom, the kings sent forward Henry count of Champagne, and Baldwin archbishop of Canterbury, and Hubert bishop of Salisbury, and Ralph de Glanville, with a strong army; of whom Archbishop Baldwin and Ralph de Glanville died at the siege of the city, which the Latins call Acre and the Jews Accaron, while the kings still remained in Sicily.

§ 22. The Griffones, before King Richard's arrival in Sicily, were more powerful than all the mighty of that region, and having moreover always hated the people beyond the Alps, and now irritated by recent occurrences more inveterate than ever, kept the peace with all who claimed the king of France for their master, but sought to wreak the entire vengeance of their wrongs on the king of the English and his tailed followers, for the Greeks and Sicilians followed that king about and called them tailed English. Thereupon all intercourse with the country is denied the English by proclamation; they are murdered both day and night by forties and fifties wherever they are found unarmed. The slaughter was daily multiplied, and it was madly purposed to go on until they should either destroy or put them all to flight. The king of England, excited by these disorders, raged like the fiercest lion, and vented his anger in a manner worthy that noble breast. His fury astounded his nearest friends, and his whole court the famous princes of his army sat around his throne, each according to his rank, and if any one might dare to raise his eyes to look him in the face, it would be very easy to read in the ruler's countenance what he silently considered in his mind. After a long and deep silence, the king disburdened his indignant lips as follows. *and the Greek inhabitants of Sicily. The origin of this joke is unknown.*

§ 23. "O my soldiers! my kingdom's strength and crown! who have endured with me a thousand perils, *His speech.*

c 2

you, who by might have subdued before me so many
tyrants and cities, do you now see how a cowardly rabble
insults us? Shall we vanquish Turks and Arabs? shall
we be a terror to nations the most invincible? shall
our right hand make us a way even to the ends of
the world for the cross of Christ? shall we restore the
kingdom to Israel, when we have turned our backs before vile and effeminate Griffones? Shall we, subdued
here in the confines of our own country, proceed further,
that the sloth of the English may become a by-word to
the ends of the earth? Am I not right then, O my
friends, in regarding this as a new cause of sorrow?
Truly, methinks I see you deliberately spare your pains,
that perchance you may the better contend with Saladin
hereafter. I, your lord and king, love you; I am soli-
citous for your honour; I tell you, I warn you again
and again, if now you depart thus unrevenged, the mention of this base flight will both precede and accompany
you. Old women and children will be raised up against
you, and assurance will yield a double energy to every
enemy against the runaways. I know that he who saves
any one by constraint, does the same as kill him; the
king will retain no man against his will. I am unwilling to compel any one of you to stay with me, lest the
fear of one should shake another's confidence in the
battle. Let every one follow what he may have chosen,
but I will either die here or will revenge these wrongs
common to me and you. If hence I depart alive, Saladin will see me only a conqueror; will you depart, and
leave me your king alone to meet the conflict?"

Its effect.　§ 24. The king had scarcely well concluded his
harangue, when all his brave and valiant men burst out,
troubled only that their lord appeared to mistrust his
men. They promise that they will comply from their
souls with whatever he shall enjoin; they are ready to
penetrate mountains and walls of brass, should he but
give a nod: all Sicily, at his command alone, shall be

subjected to him by their labour; if he should but desire
it, as far as the Pillars of Hercules shall be steeped in
blood. As the clamour, hushed by the ruler's gravity, His plans
subsided, " I am pleased," said he, " with what I hear; sina.
you refresh my spirits by your readiness to cast off your
disgrace. And, as delay has always been hurtful to
those who are prepared, we must make haste, so that
whatever we design may be sudden. Messina shall be
taken by me in the first place, the Griffones shall either
ransom themselves, or be sold. If King Tancred do
not more speedily satisfy me for my sister's dowry and
the legacy of King William, which falls to me in right
of my father, after the depopulation of his kingdom, he
shall be compelled to restore them fourfold. Whatever
belongs to the inhabitants shall be a prey for every body
to whom it shall fall; only with my lord the king of
the French, who lodges in the city, and with all his
followers, shall perfect peace be preserved. Let two
thousand bold knights, the choice of the entire army, Literally,
and a thousand foot, archers, be made ready within two have not their
days. Let the law be enforced without remission; let boots.
the footman, who flies full speed, lose his foot, the knight
be deprived of his girdle. Let every man, according to
military discipline, be disposed in line in exact array,
and on the third day, at the sound of the horn, let them
follow me. I will head them and show them the way
to the city!" The assembly separated with the greatest applause; the king, having relaxed the sternness of
his countenance, was seen returning thanks for their
good-will with his wonted affability of expression.

§ 25. It wonderfully fell out that not even the king's Delayed by
enemy could pretend that his cause was unjust. On the an embassy.
third day on which the army was to have been led forth Oct. 4.
to battle, very early in the morning, Richard archbishop
of Messina, the archbishop of Montreal, the archbishop
of Pisa, Margaritus Admiralis, Jordan de Pin, and many
other of King Tancred's familiar friends, having taken

with them Philip king of the French, the bishop of
Carnot, the duke of Burgundy, the counts of Nevers
and Perch, and many followers of the king of France,
also, the archbishops of Rouen and Auch, the bishops
of Evreux and Bayonne, and all who were supposed
to have any influence with the English, came reverently to the king of England, that they might cause
satisfaction for all his complaints to be given to his
content.   The king, after long and earnest solicitation,
is prevailed on by the entreaty of such honourable men,
and commits the matter to be settled by their arbitration.   They would consider well the enormity of what
he had had to brook, and would provide that the satisfaction should be answerable to the offence.   Whatever
their general deliberation should have determined to be
sufficient, would be satisfactory to him, if only, from that
very moment, none of the Griffones would lay hands
on his men.   Those who had come, were even more
astonished than rejoiced at this unhoped-for clemency,
and giving him at once what he had last propounded,
they retired from the king's presence, and were assembled at some distance to treat of the rest.

Messina be-
sieged by
Richard;
§ 26. The king's army having on the previous day
been numbered according to the aforementioned order,
was with solemn silence in arms before the camp, awaiting the herald, from the rising of the sun, and the
framers of the peace, not so easily coming to a deter-
mination, had protracted the day till full the third hour,
when behold, suddenly and unexpectedly, there was
proclaimed by a voice, too distinctly heard, before the
gates, "To arms, to arms, men! Hugo Brunus is taken
and being murdered by the Griffones, all he has is being
plundered, and his men are being slaughtered."   The
cry of the breach of peace confounded those who were
treating for the peace, and the king of France broke
forth in the following speech : " I take it that God has
hated these men, and hardened their hearts that they

may fall into the hands of the destroyer:" and having
quickly returned, with all who were with him, to the
king's pavilion, he found him already girding on his
sword, whom he thus briefly addressed: " I will be a
witness before all men, whatever be the consequence,
that thou art blameless, if at length thou takest arms
against the cursèd Griffones." When he had said this,
he departed; those who had accompanied him followed,
and were received into the city. The king of England
proceeds in arms; the terrible standard of the dragon
is borne in front unfurled, while behind the king the
sound of the trumpet excites the army. The sun shone
brightly on the golden shields, and the mountains were
resplendent in their glare; they marched cautiously and
orderly, and the affair was managed without show. The
Griffones, on the contrary, the city gates being closed,
stood armed at the battlements of the walls and towers,
as yet fearing nothing, and incessantly discharged their
darts upon the enemy. The king, acquainted with
nothing better than to take cities by storm and batter
forts, let their quivers be emptied first, and then at
length made his first assault by his archers who pre-
ceded the army. The sky is hidden by the shower of
arrows, a thousand darts pierce through the shields
spread abroad on the ramparts, nothing could save the
rebels against the force of the darts. The walls are left
without guard, because no one could look out of doors,
but he would have an arrow in his eye before he could
shut it.

§ 27. In the mean time, the king with his troops, and cap-
without repulse, freely and as though with permission, tured.
approached the gates of the city, which with the application of the battering ram he forced in an instant, and
having led in his army took every hold in the city, even to
Tancred's palace and the lodgings of the French around
their king's quarters, which he spared in respect of the
king his lord. The standards of the victors are planted

on the towers through the whole circuit of the city, and
each of the surrendered fortifications he entrusted to
particular captains of his army, and caused his nobles to
take up their quarters in the city.   He took the sons of
all the nobility both of the city and surrounding country
as hostages, that they should either be redeemed at the
king's price or the remainder of the city should be
delivered up to him without conflict, and he should take
to himself satisfaction for his demands from their King
Tancred.   He began to attack the city about the fifth
hour of the day, and took it the tenth hour; and having
withdrawn his army, returned victorious to his camp.
King Tancred terrified at the words of those who announced to him the issue of the transaction, hastened
to make an agreement with him, sending him twenty
thousand ounces of gold for his sister's dowry, and other
twenty thousand ounces of gold for the legacy of King
William and the observance of perpetual peace towards
him and his.   This small sum is accepted with much
ado and scornfully enough, the hostages are given back,
and peace is sworn and confirmed by the nobles of both
nations.

§ 28. The king of England, now having little confidence in the natives, built a new wooden fort of great
strength and height by the walls of Messina, which, to
the reproach of the Griffones, he called "Mategriffun."
The king's valour was greatly extolled, and the land kept
silence in his presence.   Walter, who from a monk and
prior of St. Swithin's church at Winchester, had been
advanced to be abbot of Westminster, died on the fifth

Sept. 27.   of the calends of October.

Queen Elea-   § 29. Queen Eleanor, a matchless woman, beautiful
nor arrives
in Sicily.   and chaste, powerful and modest, meek and eloquent,
which is rarely wont to be met with in a woman, who
Eleanor,   was advanced in years enough to have had two husbands
Queen of
Lewis and   and two sons crowned kings, still indefatigable for every
Henry, mo-
ther of Henry   undertaking, whose power was the admiration of her age,
and Richard.

having taken with her the daughter of the king of the Navarrese, a maid more accomplished than beautiful, followed the king her son, and having overtaken him still abiding in Sicily, she came to Pisa, a city full of every good, and convenient for her reception, there to await the king's pleasure, together with the king of Navarre's ambassadors and the damsel. Many knew, what I wish that none of us had known. This same queen, in the time of her former husband, went to Jerusalem. Let none speak more thereof; I also know well. Be silent.

IN THE YEAR OF THE LORD MCXCI.

§ 30. The first conference between the earl of Mortain, the king's brother, and the chancellor, respecting the custody of certain castles and the money out of the exchequer conceded to the earl by his brother, was held at Winchester on Lætare Hierusalem. A. D. 1191. 4 March.

Robert, prior of St. Swithin's at Winchester, having left his priory and forsaken his profession, cast himself into the sect of the Carthusians at Witham, for grief, (or shall I say for devotion?)

Walter, prior of Bath, with a like fervour or distraction, had before presumed the self-same thing, but once withdrawn, he seemed as yet to think of nothing less than a return.

§ 31. The king, although he had long ago sworn to the king of France that he would accept his sister as a consort, whom his father King Henry had provided for him, and for a long time had taken care of, because he was suspicious of the custody had of her, contemplated marrying the princess his mother had engaged. And that he might accomplish the desire without difficulty, with which he vehemently burned, he consulted the count of Flanders, a most eloquent man, and one who possessed an invaluable power of speech, by whose mediation the king of France released the king of England from his oath to marry his sister, and quit- Richard's marriage with Philip's sister broken off.

claimed to him for ever the whole territory of Vægesin and Gisorz, having received from him ten thousand pounds of silver.

Philip and Richard leave Sicily.
§ 32. The king of France, with his army, departing for Jerusalem before the king of England, put to sea March 30. the third of the calends of April. The king of England, about to leave Sicily, caused the fort which he had built to be taken down, and stowed the whole of the materials in his ships to take along with him. Every sort of engine for the attack of fortifications, and every kind of arms which the heart of man could invent, he had all ready in his ships. Robert, son of William Fitz Ralph, was consecrated for the bishopric of Worcester by William de Longchamp, as yet legate, at Canterbury, on the May 5. third of the nones of May. The convent of Canterbury deposed their prior, whom Archbishop Baldwin had set over them, and substituted another in the place of the deposed.

The archbishop of Rouen returns into England,
§ 33. Walter, archbishop of Rouen, because, as is usual with the clergy, he was pusillanimous and timorous, having bidden adieu to Jerusalem from afar, resigned unasked all indignation against Saladin, and gave to the king all the provision he had brought for attacking him, and the cross; whilst, forgetting shame, he pretended, with that devotion which diffidence, the most wretched of mothers, brought forth, that pastors of the church should rather preach than fight, and that it is not meet for a bishop to wield other arms than those of virtue. But the king, to whom his money appeared more necessary than his personal presence, as if convinced by the overpowering argument, approved the allegations, and having arranged concerning the three years' contribution that he should furnish of a certain number of men and horses, sent him back again into England with his letters to William the Chancellor; this being added at the end of the letters for honour and for all, that the chancellor should use his

counsel in affairs of state. The king, having gained experience from the proceedings of this archbishop, purified his army, not permitting any one to come with him, but such as could bear arms, and with a ready mind would use them; nor did he suffer those who returned to take back with them their money, which they had brought thus far, or their arms. The queen also, his mother, who had been received with all honour, as it was meet, and after affectionate embraces had been led forth with great splendour, he caused to return with the archbishop; having retained for himself the princess whom he had sought, and entrusted her to the safe custody of his sister, who had now returned to the camp to meet her mother.

§ 34. John, bishop of Exeter, closed his last day.

Savaricus, archdeacon of Northampton, being also one of the many who had followed the king of England out of England to Sicily, was supplied by the king with letters patent, in the presence of the king's mother, to the justiciaries of England, containing the king's assent, and something more than an assent, that he should be promoted to whatever vacant diocese he could be elected to. These honourable acquisitions Savaricus sent to his kinsman the bishop of Bath, into England, but he himself retired to Rome as one who had been best known among the Romans.

§ 35. Richard king of England, in letters destined with letters of recommendation from Richard. for England, taking leave of his whole kingdom, and giving strict injunction for the chancellor to be honoured by all, his fleet more to be prized for its quality than its numbers being in readiness, with a chosen and brave army, with his sister Johanna and the princess he was to marry, with all things which could be necessary for those going to war or going to set out on a long journey, set sail on the fourth of the ides of April. In the fleet, 10 April. moreover, there were one hundred and fifty-six ships, four and twenty busses, and thirty and nine galleys; the sum of the vessels two hundred and nineteen.

His beha-
viour.

§ 36. The archbishop of Rouen came to England to
the chancellor, by whom he was received and treated
honourably, and much better than the king had commanded.   Others also followed with many mandates,
in all of which the conclusion was, that the chancellor
should be obeyed by all.   To his brother John especially, he sent word by every messenger, that he should
adhere to the chancellor, that he should be a support to
him against all men, and that he should not violate the
oath he had given him.   The king of England sent orders
to the chancellor, and to the convent of Canterbury, and
to the bishops of the province, that they should canonically and jointly provide for the metropolitan see,
because, Baldwin being dead, it had been bereft of its
prelate ; for the abbacy, however, of Westminster, now
vacant, it is permitted to the chancellor alone to ordain
as he pleases.   There happened an eclipse of the sun
about the third hour of the day : those who were ignorant
of the causes of things were astonished, that in the middle of the day, no clouds obstructing the sun, the sun's
rays should give a much feebler light than usual ; but
those whom the motion of the universe occupies, say
that the making deficiencies of the sun and moon does
not signify anything.

Promotes the
disagreement
between the
chancellor
and Earl
John.

§ 37. John, the king's brother, who had long kept
his ears open for it, when he knew for certain that his
brother had turned his back on England, presently
perambulated the kingdom in a more popular manner,
nor did he forbid his followers calling him the king's
heir.   And as the earth is dreary in the sun's absence,
so was the face of the kingdom altered at the king's
departure.   The nobles are all stirred up in arms, the
castles are closed, the cities are fortified, entrenchments
are thrown up.   The archbishop of Rouen, not foresee-
ing more of the future than the fuel of error which was
praised, knew well how so to give contentment to the
chancellor, that at the same time he might not displease

his rivals. Writs are privately despatched to the heads
of the clergy and of the people, and the minds of every
body are excited against the chancellor. The knights of
parliament willingly, though secretly, consented, but the
clergy, more fearful by nature, dared not swear obedi-
ence to either master. The chancellor, perceiving these
things, dissembled, disdaining to know that any one would
presume any how to attempt anything against him.

§ 38. At length the pot is uncovered; it is an- The chancel-
nounced to him, that Gerrard de Camville, a factious the castle of
man and reckless of allegiance, had done homage to Lincoln.
Earl John, the king's brother, for the castle of Lincoln,
the custody whereof is known to belong to the inheritance of Nicholaa, the wife of the same Gerrard, but
under the king. The deed is considered to infringe
upon the crown, and he resolves to go and revenge its
commission. So having quickly collected a numerous
army, he came into those parts, and having first made
an attack against Wigmore, he compelled Roger de
Mortimer, impeached for a conspiracy made against the
king, with the Welch, to surrender the castles, and
abjure England for three years. As he departed, he was
blamed by his associates for want of courage, because,
while supported by the numerous soldiery of the castles,
and abounding in advantages, he had given way, without a blow, at the bare threats of the priest. Reproof
was too late after the error; Roger leaves the kingdom,
and the chancellor gives orders to besiege Lincoln. Gerrard was with the earl; and his wife Nicholaa, proposing
to herself nothing effeminate, defended the castle like a
man. The chancellor was wholly busied about Lincoln,
whilst Earl John occupied the castle of Nottingham and
that of Tickhill, both very strong, the warden being
compelled to the surrender by fear alone. He proceeded, moreover, to send word to the chancellor that
he must raise the siege, or otherwise he would avenge
the cause of his vassal. That it was not proper to take

from the loyal men of the kingdom, well known and free, their charges, and commit them to strangers and men unknown. That it was a mark of his folly that he had entrusted the king's castles to such, because they would expose them to adventurers. That if it should go with every barbarian with that facility, that even the castles should be ready at all times for their reception, that he would no longer bear in silence the destruction of his brother's kingdom and affairs.

Conduct of the arch-bishop of Rouen. § 39. The chancellor, incredibly troubled at these threats, having summoned before him the peers and chiefs of the army, begins, " Never trust me if this man seeks not to subjugate the kingdom to himself; what he presumes is exorbitant, even if he had a right to wear the crown by annual turns with his brother, for Eteocles has not yet completed a full year in his government." He uttered many words of anguish after this manner ; and then again having taken heart, as he was greater in moral courage than in physical, conceiving great things in his mind, he sent the archbishop of Rouen to the earl, demanding in an imperative manner that he should deliver up the castles, and that he should answer before the court of King's Bench for the breach of his oath to his brother. The archbishop, skilful in working with either hand, praised the constancy of the chancellor ; and having proceeded to the earl, after the delivery of the mandates, he whispered in his ear, that whatever others might say, he should dare something great, worthy of Gyara and the dungeon, if he desired to be anything. In public, however, he advised that the earl and the chancellor should agree to an interview, and that a reference to arbitration should end their disagreement.

An interview agreed upon. § 40. The earl, greatly exasperated at the impropriety of the mandates, was so altered in his whole body that a man would hardly have known him. Rancour made deep furrows in his forehead, his flaming eyes glistened, paleness discoloured the rosy complexion of his face, and I know what would have become of the chancellor, if in that hour of fury he had fallen as an apple into his hands while frantically raging. His indignation increased so much in his stifled breast, that it could not be kept from bursting out at least in part. "This son," said he, "of perdition, the worst of the evil ones, who first borrowed from the pleasantry of the French, and introduced among the English, the preposterous practice of kneeling, would not harass me, as you perceive, if I had not refused to learn the new craft offered to me!" He would fain have said more, whether true or false, but recalling his presence of mind, and repressing his rage, "If I have spoken amiss," said he, "O archbishop, I ask pardon." After these frivolous expressions, they applied themselves to the weighty matters. They consulted about the demands of the chancellor; and the counsel of the archbishop, that there should be a meeting of them both, was agreed to, about the middle of the day. The day was fixed for the fifth of the calends 28 July. of August; the place without Winchester. The chancellor allowed what they had settled to stand, and, having broken up the siege, returned to London.

§ 41. The earl, however, fearing his craftiness, brought Preparatory thither four thousand Welsh, that, if the chancellor arrangements. should endeavour to take him during the truce, they, being placed in ambush close beside the conference, might thwart his endeavours by a sally. Moreover, he commanded that it should be summoned, and required that every one of his men and others his adherents should be prepared to go to battle, should attend him at the place and on the day of the engagement, so that as the interview between himself and the lord of the whole land had been undertaken, at least he might escape alive, if he, who was more than a king, though less in his eyes, should transgress against the law, or should not consent to an arrangement. The chancellor, however, on the

other hand, commanded that one third of the soldiery
with all the arms of all England should proceed to Winchester by the day appointed; moreover, at the expense
of the king's revenue he also hired some Welsh, that
if it should come to a contest with the earl, he might
have an equal array, and javelins threatening javelins.

The meeting. § 42. They came to the interview as was before
agreed on, and it happened to terminate better than was
feared. The agreement, moreover, made between the
earl and the chancellor was thus and in this way provided. First of all were named the three bishops of
Winchester, London, and Bath, in whose fidelity each
party considered himself secure. The bishops chose for
the chancellor's part the three earls of Warren, of
Arundel, of Clare, and certain other eight by name.
For the earl's part, Stephen Ridel the earl's chancellor,
William de Venneval, Reginald de Wasseville, and certain other eight by name. These all, some beholding
some touching the holy Gospels, swore that they would
provide satisfaction between the earl and the chancellor
concerning their quarrels and questions, to the honour of
both parties and the peace of the kingdom. And if
hereafter any disagreement should happen between
them, they would faithfully end it. The earl also and
the chancellor swore that they would consent to whatever
the aforesaid jury should settle; and this was the provision. Girard de Camville, being received into the
chancellor's favour, the custody of the castle of Lincoln
was reserved to him in peace and safety; the earl gave
up the castles which he had taken, and the chancellor
having received them, gave them over to the king's faithful
and liege men, namely, to William de Wenn, the castle
of Nottingham, and to Reginald de Wasseville the castle
of Tickhill; and each of them gave an hostage to the
chancellor, that they would keep those castles in the
safe peace and fidelity of their lord the king, if he
should return alive. If, however, the king should die

before his return, the aforesaid castles should be delivered
up to the earl, and the chancellor should restore the hostages. The constables of the castles of the earl's honours
should be changed by the chancellor, if the earl should
show reason for their being changed. The chancellor, if
the king should die, should not seek the disherison of the
earl; but should promote him to the kingdom with all
his power. Concluded solemnly at Winchester, on the
seventh of the kalends of May. 25 April.

§ 43. The chancellor, by wonderful importunity and Affairs of Westminster.
earnestness, persuaded first a part of the monks, and
afterwards the whole congregation of Westminster,
to permit his brother, a monk of Cadomo, to profess
a cohabitation in Westminster, and to be elected by all
for their abbot for his profession and cohabitation on a
day appointed; and that this election should not be
broken, security was taken by a bond, with the church's
seal affixed as a testimony.

§ 44. Geoffrey, a brother of King Richard and Earl Geoffrey, archbishop of York, prepares to visit England.
John, but not by their mother, who had been conse-
crated archbishop of York at Tours, by the archbishop
of Tours, by the pope's command, continually solicited
by message John the king's brother and his own, that
at the least, it might be permitted him to return to
England; and having obtained his consent, he prepared
to return. The intercourse of the brothers did not
escape the chancellor's knowledge, who providing lest
their natural genuine perverseness should increase, commanded the keepers of the coasts, that wherever that
archbishop, who had abjured England for the three
years of the king's travels, should disembark within the
bounds of the kingdom, he should not be permitted to
proceed, but by the will of the jury, to whose award the
earl and the chancellor had taken oath to stand concerning every thing that should happen.

§ 45. A certain Robert, prior of Hereford, a monk Death of Robert, abbot of Muchelney.
who did not think very meanly of himself, and gladly

D

forced himself into other people's business that he might
intermix his own, had gone into Sicily to the king on the
chancellor's messages ; where after the rest he did not
forget his own interests ; and having by some means or
other worried every body, succeeded in obtaining the
abbacy of Muchelney to be granted to him and confirmed by the king. Into possession of which, by the
chancellor's means, he entered, against the will of the
convent, neither canonically, nor with a benediction ;
and presently on the first day, at the first dinner, by
greedily partaking of fresh eels without wine, and more
than was proper, he fell into a languor, which the food
undigested and lying heavily on an inflamed stomach,
brought on. And lest the languor should be ascribed
to his gluttony, he caused the monks of that place to be
slandered of having given him poison.

§ 46. Geoffrey, archbishop of York, presuming upon
the consent of his brother Earl John, his shipping being
ready, came to Dover ; and presently having landed, first
sought a church for prayer. There is there a priory of
monks of the profession of Canterbury, whose oratory
he entered with his clerks to hear mass, and his household was intent about unlading the ships. No sooner
had the whole of his goods been landed, than suddenly
the constable of the castle caused whatever he thought
was the archbishop's to be brought into the town, understanding more in the command of his lord the chancellor than he had commanded. Certain also of the
soldiers, armed under their tunics, and girt with swords,
came into the monastery, that they might apprehend
the pontiff ; whom when he saw, their intention being
foreknown, he took a cross in his hands, and first
addressing them and extending his hands towards his
followers, he says, " I am the archbishop ; if ye seek
me, let these go their way." And the soldiers reply,
" Whether you be an archbishop or not, it is nothing
to us ; one thing we know, that you are Geoffrey, the

*Geoffrey,
archbishop
of York,
seised by the
chancellor.*

son of King Henry, whom he begot on some strange
bed, who before the king, whose brother you make
yourself, have forsworn England for three years; if you
are not come into the kingdom as a traitor to the kingdom; if you have brought letters of absolution, either
say, or take the reproach." Then said the archbishop,
" I am not a traitor, neither will I show you any letters." They then laid their hands on him there before
the very altar, and violently dragged him out of the
church against his will, and resisting, but not with
force; who immediately being set without the threshold,
excommunicated by name those who had laid hands on
him, both present and whilst they were still holding him;
nor did he receive the horse that they offered him that
he might ride with them to the castle, because it was
the property of the excommunicated. And so, outraging
humanity, they dragged him on foot by the hands, and
carrying the cross, all through the mud of the streets
to the castle. After this they desired of their own good
will to deal humanely with their captive, bringing him
some of the best provisions which they had prepared for
themselves; but he, being firmly resolved, by what he
had now suffered, rejected their victuals as if it were
an offering to idols, and refused to live on any thing
but his own. The report spread over the kingdom more
rapidly than the wind, those who had followed their lord
at a distance came after, relating and complaining to all
that the archbishop, the king's brother, thus landed, had
been so treated and detained in prison.

§ 47. The archbishop was already three days in cus- *The chan-
tody, and the chancellor, as soon as the case was made* *cellor ex-*
cuses his
known to him, restored to him all his goods, and set *conduct.*
him at liberty to depart whithersoever he should desire.
He wrote, moreover, to Earl John, and to all the bishops,
asserting, with an oath, that the aforesaid man had suffered the above-written injuries without his knowledge.
The excuse profited little, because the occasion, which

had been long sought and which spontaneously offered itself against him, was most eagerly and tenaciously laid hold of.   The authors of this daring act, who laid hands on the archbishop, as well as those who consented thereto, were all specially excommunicated in every church of the whole kingdom, that at least the chancellor, who was hateful to everybody, might be involved in the general malediction.

Earl John summons a meeting.

§ 48. Earl John, gnashing his teeth with anger against the chancellor, whom he hated, brought a weighty complaint before all the bishops and lords of the kingdom, of the infringement of the convention by the adverse party, by the arrest of his brother, to his own dishonour.   The jurors are summoned and are sworn to stand by their plighted promise, and to bring it to pass as quickly as possible, that the perjurer and breaker of his faith should repair what he had done amiss by giving ample satisfaction.   The affair, hitherto confined to trifles, now bears a serious aspect ; the chancellor is summoned by the powerful authority of all his and the earl's mediators, to meet him and answer to the earl's accusations, and to submit to the law, the place at Lodbridge, the day the third of the nones of

5 October.

October.

The chancellor comes to London.

§ 49. The earl, with the greatest part of the nobility of the kingdom all favouring him, had awaited the chancellor two days at the place of meeting, and on the third, in the morning, he sent on certain of his followers to London, still waiting at the place of meeting in case he who was expected should either dare or deign to come.   The chancellor, dreading in himself the earl, and being suspicious of the judges, delayed to come to the place for two days ; on the third, (because as every one feels conscious in his mind, so does he conceive in his breast both hope and fear for his deeds,) half-way between hope and fear, he attempted to go to the meeting.   And behold! Henry Biset, a faithful man of his, who had seen the above-mentioned party of the earl's friends passing on, putting frequently the spur to his horse, comes to meet the chancellor, and tells him that the earl, before daylight, had gone in arms to take London; and who was there, on that day, that did not take every thing as gospel, which that honourable man told them? but yet he was not guilty of falsehood, because he thought that what he had said was true. The chancellor, deceived, as all men are liable to be, immediately caused all the force that was with him to arm; and thinking that he was following close upon the earl, came before him to the city. The citizens being asked by him, for the earl was not yet come, that they would close the gates against him when he should come, refused, calling him a disturber of the land, and a traitor. For the archbishop of York, conscious of what would happen, whilst he was tarrying there some days, that he might see the end of the matter, by continual complaints and entreaties had excited them all against him; and then, for the first time, perceiving himself betrayed, he betook himself to the Tower, and the Londoners set a watch, both by land and water, that he might not escape. The earl, having knowledge of his flight, following him up with his forces, was received by the joyful citizens with lanterns and torches, for he came to town by night; and there was nothing wanting in the salutations of the flattering people, save that barbarous Chaire Basileus! which is, " Hail, dear lord!"

§ 50. On the next day, the earl and all the nobles of the land assembled in St. Paul's church, and first of all was heard the archbishop of York's complaint; after that, whosoever had aught against him was admitted. The accusers of the absent had an attentive and diligent hearing, and especially Hugh, bishop of Coventry, so prolix in words, who the day before had been his most familiar friend, who, as the worst pest is a familiar

A meeting in St. Paul's church.

enemy, having harangued more bitterly and perversely
than all the rest, against his friend, did not desist until
it was said by all, " We will not have this man to reign
over us." So the whole assembly, without any delay,
elected Earl John, the king's brother, chief justiciary of
the whole kingdom, and ordaining that all the castles
should be delivered to the custody of such as he should
choose, they left only three of the weakest, and lying at
a great distance from each other, to the now merely
nominal chancellor. The chief justice after the earl, the
justices itinerant, the barons of the exchequer, the constables of castles, all new, are appointed afresh. Amongst
others then gainers, both the bishop of Winchester received the custodies which the chancellor had taken from
him, without diminution, and the lord bishop of Durham
received the county of Northumberland.

The result communicated to the chancellor. § 51. That unlucky day was declining towards evening,
when four bishops and as many earls, sent on the part of
the assembly to the chancellor, explained to him, to the
letter, the acts of the whole day. He was horror-struck
at such unexpected presumption and arrogance, and, his
vigour of mind failing, he fell to the earth so exhausted,
that he foamed at the mouth. Cold water being
sprinkled on his face, he revived, and having risen on
Una salus victis nullam sperare salutem. his feet, he addressed the messengers with a stern countenance, saying, " There is one help for the vanquished,
to hope for no help. You have conquered and you have
bound incautiously. If the Lord God shall grant me to
see my lord the king with my two eyes, be sure this day
has shone inauspiciously for you. As much as in you lay,
you have now delivered to the earl, whatever was the
king's in the kingdom. Say to him, Priam still lives.
You, who forgetful of your still surviving king, have
elected to yourselves another to be lord, tell to that
your lord, that all will turn out otherwise than he supposes. I will not give up the castles, I will not resign
the seal." The messengers, having returned from him,

related to the earl what they had received, who ordered the Tower to be more closely besieged.

§ 52. The chancellor was sleepless the greater part He resolves to surrender. of the night (because he who does not set his mind on honest studies and pursuits, will toss about wakeful through hate or love); and at the same time his people disturbed him more than his conscience, falling prostrate at his feet, and entreating with tears that he would yield to necessity, and not stretch forth his arms against the torrent. He, though harder than iron, is softened by the piteous counsel of those who were weeping round him; again and again having fainted with grief, at last, he with much ado assented that that should be done, which, being entirely destitute of aid, he was compelled to do. One of his brothers, and three, not ignoble, of his adherents, being permitted, not commissioned, announced to the earl at that time of night, that the chancellor, with what readiness it does not matter, was prepared to do and suffer whatever had been determined. He should avoid delay, because it has always been injurious for those who are prepared to defer. It should be done the next day, lest the wind should so veer, that it might be deferred for a year. These return to the Tower, and before day, the earl made known to his adherents that these things had passed.

§ 53. Meanwhile, the rising dawn left the ocean, and A meeting between the earl and the chancellor. the sun having now appeared, the earl, with his whole troop, withdrew to the open field, which is without London towards the east; the chancellor went thither also, but less early than his adversaries. The nobles took the centre, around whom was next a circle of citizens, and beyond an attentive populace, estimated at ten thousand men. The bishop of Coventry first attacked the chancellor, rehearsing the several accusations of the preceding day, and ever adding something of his own. " It is not," said he, " either fit or bearable that such gross incapacity of one, should so often cause so many noble

and honourable men, and from such remote parts, to
assemble for nothing. And since it is better to be troubled once for all, than always, I will conclude all in few
words. It does not please, because it is not convenient,
that you should any longer bear rule in the kingdom.
You will be content with your bishopric, and the three
castles with which we have indulged you, and the shelter
of a great name. You will in the next place give
hostages for giving up all the other castles, and for not
seeking increased power or making tumults, and afterwards you will be able to depart freely whithersoever you
may desire." Many spoke much in favour of this, none
against ; the lord of Winchester, although he was more
eloquent than most of them, alone observed continued
silence. At length the chancellor, scarcely permitted
to speak, exclaimed, "Am I always to be a hearer only?
and shall I never answer? Before all things, know ye
each and every one, that I feel myself guilty of nothing
that I should fear the mouth of any of you. I solemnly
declare that the archbishop of York was taken, without
either my knowledge or my will; that I will prove in
the civil courts if you will, or in the ecclesiastical.
Respecting the deficiencies of the king, if I have done
anything amiss in that matter, Geoffrey Fitz-Peter, William Briwere, and Hugh Bardolf, whom I received from
the king as councillors, would, if it were permitted them
to speak, give satisfaction for me. Why and in what
I have spent the king's treasure, I am ready to give
account to the utmost farthing. I do not refuse to give
hostages for delivering up the castles, though in this
I ought rather to fear the king; yet as I must, I must.
The name which you are not able to take away, and I am
still to bear, I do not set light by. In short, I give
you all to know, that I depose myself from no administration given me by the king. You, being many, have
besieged me alone; you are stronger than I, and I, the
king's chancellor and justiciary of the kingdom, am con-

Semper ego auditor tantum? Nunquamne reponam?

demned against all form of law; it is through necessity
I yield to the stronger." The sun declining to the west,
put an end to the allegations of the parties; the two
brothers of the chancellor that was, and a certain third
person, his chamberlain, who had also been his secretary,
were received in hostage. The assembly is dissolved,
the keys of the Tower of London being given up on the
sixth of the ides of October. The chancellor started Oct. 10.
for Dover, one, to wit, of the three castles of which
mention was made; and the earl delivered, to those he
chose and whom he trusted most, all the fortresses of
the land which had been given up to him.

§ 54. Messengers are immediately despatched to the The chancellor's proceed-
Land of Promise, to the king himself, both by the con- ings.
demned and the condemners, each by his own party, sufficiently instructed to accuse or excuse. The chancellor,
being uncomfortable here under the appellation of his
lost authority, and the recollection of his present state,
whilst he endeavoured by all means to elude the prohi-
bition of his going abroad, got scoffed, not uniformly, nor
once only. I will not recount how he was taken and
detained, both in the habit of a monk and in that of a
woman, because it is enough and more than enough to
recollect what inestimable property and immense treasures the Flemish stripped him of, when at length he
arrived in Flanders. His passage over being known,
whatever revenue he had possessed in England was confiscated. A most dreadful contention is carried on between the mighty. The chancellor suspends his diocese
which had been taken from him, and he denounces his
anathema upon all those who trespassed against him.
Nor was the archbishop of Rouen more remiss in the
same way, for in revenge for his presumptuous excommunication of the exchequer barons, he commanded it
to be announced throughout Normandy that William de
Longchamp should be held as excommunicated. He was,
however, unwilling to seem to fear the malediction,
uttered against the invaders of the aforesaid bishopric,

nor did he believe that the sentence of a fugitive prelate could find its way before his Majesty's throne. So the face of the church of Ely was disfigured, they ceased throughout the diocese from every work of the Lord, the bodies of the dead lay unburied by all the ways. In Normandy, the like being returned, none under the archbishop's authority communicated with the chancellor; on his entry every church was suspended, and on his departure all the bells were rung, and the altars where he officiated cast down.

The papal legates suspend Normandy.

§ 55. Two legates despatched into France by the Pope, at the instigation, though secret, as is reported, of the king of the French, came to Gisorz to visit Normandy, which they understood was a chief part of the kingdom of the French; but both the constable of the castle and the seneschal of Normandy would not admit them, excusing themselves with this shadow of a reason, that the visitation of any province should not be made unless with the approbation or in the presence of the lord of the land; all the kings of the English, and particularly Richard, being especially indulged with this privilege by the holy see. No allegation, whether real or probable, availed with the legates; their almost divine power rose and swelled with rage, though against those who heeded them not: the contemned authority of Roman majesty is exercised; they lay aside high flown sentences and long words. They threaten their adversaries with much bitterness; but, however, as they had not to plead with boys, the castle gates being shut against them, they stood without the doors. But their solace was not wanting, though they were repulsed. They reached with their power, where they could not approach in person. They excommunicated by name the constable of Gisorz and the seneschal of Normandy, there present, and suspended the whole of Normandy from every administration of the rites of the church. It was necessary to yield to their power; the church was silent immediately, and so remained the space of three weeks, until, the

Pope being supplicated, both the sentence against those named was remitted, and the suspension given out against Normandy. The book of liberty was restored to Normandy, and the voice of gladness, and the legates were prohibited to set foot therein.

§ 56. The Westminster monks, who before those days Monastic affairs. had so greatly excelled in magnanimity, that they would not stain their deeds for death itself, as soon as they saw a new era, changed also with the time, putting behind their backs whatever they had covenanted with the chancellor for his brother; with the connivance of the earl, they elected the prior of their house to be abbot, who also received immediately the benediction and staff from the bishop of London. The chancellor's brother, who by agreement should have been elected abbot, seeing the convent break their engagement, troubled thereat, departed with his half-modesty, carrying off with him, however, the bond of security, having made an appeal prior to the second election before legitimate witnesses, that nothing should be done against his stipulated promotion.

The monks of Muchelney, after the example of those of Westminster, though not altogether in a similar way, expelled their principal, I do not know whether abbot or abbot elect, whom they had been forced to accept, casting forth the straw of his bed after him, and thrust him with much insult out of their island to the four winds of Heaven.

§ 57. The archbishop of Rouen being constituted by Election of the arch-bishop of Canterbury. the earl justiciary of the kingdom, and supreme over affairs, having convoked, at Canterbury, the clergy and people, as the king himself had enjoined him, directed them to proceed to the election of an archbishop. The bishops of London and Winchester, however, were not · present, being detained at London by the king's business, and the question being broached among the bishops who had assembled, which of them should be esteemed the greater, whose the election ought to be, as the two aforesaid of chief dignity were absent, the prior of Canterbury solving the point of difficulty, made all equal in choosing a pontiff, and proceeding forth in public with his monks, in the face of the whole church, elected, as archbishop, Reginald, bishop of Bath, from the midst of the clergy.

His death. § 58. Reginald, elect of Canterbury, who would have proceeded to Rome for his pall, had the Fates permitted, having completed the solemnities which are usually celebrated for the elect at Canterbury, came to set things in order in the diocese of Bath, which he greatly loved, and by which he was more beloved. It is reported also, that he had obtained, as he desired, the assent of the prior and convent for electing and substituting in his place, Savaricus, archdeacon of Northampton, and had received the security. Returning from thence, he fell sick by the way, and was laid up very ill at his manor of Dokemeresfeld; and seeing nothing more likely to happen to him than death, he took the habit of a monk at the hands of his prior Walter, then tarrying with him, and receiving it, spoke these words, " God willed not that I should be archbishop, and I will not; God willed that I should be a monk, and I will !" Moreover, being in the last extremities, he took the king's letters to the justices, for conceding to Savaricus whatever diocese he should be elected to, and gave them to the prior of Bath, that by the authority of this instrument he might the sooner be promoted. Then having accomplished all things which relate to faith and penitence devoutly and with a sane mind, he fell asleep in the Lord on Dec. 26. the seventh of the calends of January. His

EPITAPH.

And epitaph.

Dum Reginaldus erat bene seque suosque regebat;
Nemo plus quærat; quicquid docuit faciebat.
Sancti Swithuni nisi pratum præripuisset

Hunc de communi mors tam cito non rapuisset.
Sed, quia pœnituit, minuit mors passa reatum;
Fecit quod potuit, se dedidit ad monachatum.

Whilst Reginald lived, he well governed both himself and his men. Let no one ask more; whatsoever he taught, he practised. If he had not grasped at Saint Swithin's pasture, death would not have snatched him so soon from the public. But, because he was penitent, a premature death diminished his supposed guilt; he did what he could, he dedicated himself to the monastic life. The translation.

Walter, prior of Bath, and his convent without the clergy, elected to themselves for their future bishop Savaricus, archdeacon of Northampton, who was absent, and as yet ignorant of the decease of his fellow pontiff, and although the clergy resisted, they carried it out.

§ 59. The fleet of Richard, king of the English, put out to sea, and proceeded in this order. In the fore- front went three ships only, in one of which was the queen of Sicily and the young damsel of Navarre, probably still a virgin; in the other two, a certain part of the king's treasure and arms; in each of the three, marines and provisions. In the second line there were, what with ships and busses and men of war, thirteen; in the third, fourteen; in the fourth, twenty; in the fifth, thirty; in the sixth, forty; in the seventh, sixty; in the last, the king himself followed with his galleys. There was between the ships, and between their lines, a certain space left by the sailors at such interval, that from one line to another the sound of the trumpet from one ship to another, the human voice, could be heard. This also was admirable, that the king was no less cheerful and healthy, strong and mighty, light and gay, at sea, than he was wont to be by land. I conclude, therefore, that there was not one man more powerful than he in the world, either by land or sea. Disposition of Richard's fleet.

§ 60. Now, as the ships were proceeding in the aforesaid manner and order, some being before others, two
of the three first, driven by the violence of the winds,
were broken on the rocks near the port of Cyprus; the
third, which was English, more speedy than they, having
turned back into the deep, escaped the peril. Almost
all the men of both ships got away alive to land, many
of whom the hostile Cypriotes slew, some they took
captive, some, taking refuge in a certain church, were
besieged. Whatever also in the ships was cast up by
the sea, fell a prey to the Cypriotes. The prince also
of that island coming up, received for his share the gold
and the arms; and he caused the shore to be guarded by
all the armed force he could summon together, that he
might not permit the fleet which followed to approach,
lest the king should take again what had been thus
stolen from him. Above the port, was a strong city,
and upon a natural rock, a high and fortified castle.
The whole of that nation was warlike, and accustomed
to live by theft. They placed beams and planks at the
entrance of the port, across the passage, the gates
and entrances; and the whole land, with one mind,
prepared themselves for a conflict against the English.
God so willed, that the cursed people should receive the
reward of their evil deeds by the hands of one who would
not spare. The third English ship, in which were the
women, having cast out its anchors, rode out at sea, and
watched all things from opposite, to report the misfor-
tune to the king, lest haply, being ignorant of the loss
and disgrace, he should pass the place unrevenged.
The next line of the king's ships came up after the other,
and they all stopped at the first. A full report reached
the king, who, sending heralds to the lord of the island,
and obtaining no satisfaction, commanded his entire
army to arm, from the first even to the last, and to get
out of the great ships into the galleys and boats, and

follow him to the shore. What he commanded, was immediately performed; they came in arms to the port. The king being armed, leaped first from his galley, and gave the first blow in the war; but before he was able to strike a second, he had three thousand of his followers with him striking away by his side. All the timber that had been placed as a barricade in the port was cast down instantly, and the brave fellows went up into the city, as ferocious as lionesses are wont to be when robbed of their young. The fight was carried on manfully against them, numbers fell down wounded on both sides, and the swords of both parties were made drunk with blood. The Cypriotes are vanquished, the city is taken, with the castle besides; whatever the victors choose is ransacked, and the lord of the island is himself taken and brought to the king. He, being taken, *Isaac's submission.* supplicates and obtains pardon; he offers homage to the king, and it is received; and he swears, though unasked, that henceforth he will hold the island of him as his liege lord, and will open all the castles of the land to him, make satisfaction for the damage already done, and further bring presents of his own. On being dismissed after the oath, he is commanded to fulfil the conditions in the morning.

§ 61. That night the king remained peaceably in the *Treachery,* castle; and his newly sworn vassal flying, retired to another castle, and caused the whole of the men of that land, who were able to bear arms, to be summoned to repair to him, and so they did. The king of Jerusalem, however, that same night, landed in Cyprus, that he might assist the king and salute him, whose arrival he had desired above that of any other in the whole world. On the morrow, the lord of Cyprus was sought for and found to have fled. The king, seeing that he was abused, and having been informed where he was, directed the king of Jerusalem to follow the traitor by land with the half of the army, while he conducted the other part

by water, intending to be in the way, that he might not
escape by sea. The divisions reassembled around the
city in which he had taken refuge, and he, having sallied
out against the king, fought with the English, and the
battle was carried on sharply by both sides. The English would that day have been beaten, had they not
fought under the command of King Richard. They at
length obtain a dear-bought victory, the Cypriote flies,
and the castle is taken. The kings pursue him as before, the one by land, the other by water, and he is
besieged in the third castle. Its walls are cast down by
engines hurling huge stones; he, being overcome, pro-
mises to surrender, if only he might not be put in iron
and punish-
ment. fetters. The king consents to the prayers of the sup-
plicant, and caused silver shackles to be made for him.
The prince of the pirates being thus taken, the king
traversed the whole island, and took all its castles, and
placed his constables in each, and constituted justiciaries
and sheriffs; and the whole land was subjected to him in
everything just like England. The gold, and the silk,
and the jewels from the treasures that were broken open
he retained for himself; the silver and victuals he gave
to the army. To the king of Jerusalem also he made a
handsome present out of his booty.

Richard mar-
ries Beren-
garia. And because Lent had already passed, and the lawful
time of contract was come, he caused Berengaria,
daughter of the king of Navarre, whom his mother had
brought to him in Lent, to be affianced to him in the
island.

Captures a
Saracen ship, § 62. After these things, having taken again to the
ships, whilst sailing prosperously towards Acre, he falls
in with a merchant ship of immense dimensions, destined
by Saladin to the besieged, laden with provisions and
full of armed soldiers. A wonderful ship, a ship than
which, with the exception of Noah's ark, we do not read
of any having been greater. The intrepid king here
rejoices, because every where he meets with a fit object

for valour; he, first of his warriors, having summoned
to his, the galleys of his followers, commences the naval
action with the Turks. The ship was fortified with
towers and bulwarks, and the desperate fought furiously,
because "the only hope for the conquered is to have
nothing to hope for." The assault was dreadful and the
defence stout; but what is there so hard, that the sturdy
man who stoutly perseveres shall not subdue? The followers of Mahomet are vanquished; that ship the queen Mocomicolæ.
of ships is shattered and sunk, as lead in the mighty
waters, and the whole property perished with its pos-
sessors.

The king proceeding thence came to the siege of and arrives at
Acre, and was welcomed by the besiegers with as great Acres.
joy, as if it had been Christ that had come again on
earth to restore the kingdom of Israel. The king of the
French had arrived at Acre first, and was very highly
esteemed by the natives; but on Richard's arrival, he
became obscured and without consideration, just as the
moon is wont to relinquish her lustre at the rising of
the sun.

§ 63. Henry, count of Champagne, whose whole store His liberality
that he had brought both of provision and money was to Henry,
now wasted, comes to his king. He asks relief, to count of Champagne.
whom his king and lord caused to be offered a hundred
thousand of Paris money, if, in that case, he would be
ready to pledge to him Champagne. To that the count
replied, " I have done what I could and what I ought,
now I shall do what I am compelled by necessity; I
desired to fight for my king, but he would not accept of
me, unless for my own; I will go to him who will accept
me: who is more ready to give than to receive." The
king of the English, Richard, gave to Henry, count of
Champagne, when he came to him, four thousand bushels
of wheat, four thousand bacons, and four thousand
pounds of silver. So the whole army of strangers out
of every nation under heaven bearing the Christian

E

name, who had already assembled to the siege long before the coming of the kings, at the report of so great a
largess, took King Richard to be their general and lord;
the Franks only who had followed their lord remained
with their poor king of the French.

His exploits.   § 64. The king of the English, unused to delay, on
the third day of his arrival at the siege, caused his
wooden fortress, which he had called " Mate Grifun"
when it was made in Sicily, to be built and set up, and
before the dawn of the fourth day the machine stood
erect by the walls of Acre, and from its height looked
down upon the city lying beneath it; and there were
thereon by sunrise archers casting missiles without intermission on the Turks and Thracians.   Engines also
for casting stones, placed in convenient positions, bat-
tered the walls with frequent volleys.   More important
than these, sappers making themselves a way beneath
the ground, undermined the foundations of the walls;
while soldiers bearing shields, having planted ladders,
sought an entrance over the ramparts.   The king himself was running up and down through the ranks, directing some, reproving some, and urging others, and thus
was he every where present with every one of them, so
that whatever they all did, ought properly to be ascribed
to him.   The king of the French also himself did
not lightly assail them, who made as bold an assault
as he could on the tower of the city which is called
Cursed.

§ 65. The renowned Carracois and Mestocus, after
Saladin the most powerful princes of the heathen, had
at that time the charge of the besieged city, who after
a contest of many days, promised by their interpreters
the surrender of the city, and a ransom for their heads;
but the king of the English desired to subdue their
obstinacy by force; and wished that the vanquished
should pay their heads for the ransom of their bodies,
but, by the mediation of the king of the French, their

life and indemnity of limbs only was accorded them, if, after surrender of the city and yielding of every thing they possessed, the Holy Cross should be given up.

§ 66. All the heathen warriors in Acre were chosen Acre taken. men, and were in number nine thousand. Many of whom, swallowing many gold coins, made a purse of their stomachs, because they foresaw that whatever they had of any value would be turned against them, even against themselves, if they should again oppose the cross, and would only fall a prey to the victors. So all of them come out before the kings entirely disarmed, and outside the city without money are given into custody; and the kings, with triumphal banners having entered the city, divided the whole with all its stores into two parts between themselves and their soldiers; the pontiff's seat alone its bishop received by their united gift. The captives, moreover, being divided, Mestocus fell by lot to the portion of the king of the English, and Carracois, as a drop of cold water, fell into the burning mouth of the thirsty Philip, king of the French.

§ 67. The duke of Austria, who was also one of the Richard offends the ancient besiegers of Acre, followed the king of the duke of Austria. English as a participator in the possession of his portion, and because, as his standard was borne before him, he was thought to take to himself a part of the triumph; if not by command, at least with the consent, of the offended king, the duke's standard was cast down in the dirt, and to his reproach and ridicule trampled under foot by them. The duke, although grievously enraged against the king, dissembled his offence, which he could not vindicate; and having returned to the place where he had carried on the siege, betook himself that night to his tent, which was set up again, and afterwards as soon as he could returned to his own country full of rancor.

§ 68. Messengers on the part of the captives having Beheads his prisoners. been sent to Saladin for their ransom, when the heathen could by no entreaty be moved to restore the Holy Cross, the king of the English beheaded all his, with the exception of Mestocus only, who on account of his nobility was spared, and declared openly without any ceremony that he would act in the same way towards Saladin himself.

Jealousy between him and Philip. § 69. A certain Marquess of Montferrat, a smooth-faced man, had held Tyre, which he had seized on many years ago, to whom the king of the French sold all his captives alive, and promised the crown of the region which was not yet conquered; but the king of the English withstood him to the face. "It is not proper," said he, "for a man of your reputation to bestow or promise what is not yet obtained; but further, if the cause of your journey be Christ, when at length you have taken Jerusalem, the chief of the cities of this region, from the hand of the enemy, you will without delay or condition restore the kingdom to Guy, the legitimate king of Jerusalem. For the rest, if you recollect, you did not obtain Acre without a participator, so that neither should that which is the property of two be dealt out by one hand." Oh, oh, how fine for a godly throat! The marquess, bereft of his blissful hope, returns to Tyre, and the king of the French, who had greatly desired to strengthen himself against his envied ally by means of the marquess, now fell off daily; and this added to the continual irritation of his mind,—that even the scullion of the king of the English fared more sumptuously than the cupbearer of the French. After some time, letters were forged in the tent of the king of the French, by which, as if they had been sent by his nobles out of France, the king was recalled to France. A cause is invented which would necessarily be respected more than it deserved; his only son, after a long illness, was now despaired of by the physicians; France exposed to be desolated, if, after the son's death, the father (as it might fall out) should perish in a foreign land. So, frequent council being held between the kings hereupon, as they were both great and could not dwell together, Abraham remaining, Lot departed from him. Moreover, the king of the French, by his chief nobles, gave security by oath for himself and his vassals, to the king of the English, that he would observe every pledge until he should return to his kingdom in peace.

§ 70. On that day the commonalty of the Londoners *Meeting at London.* was granted and instituted, to which all the nobles of the kingdom, and even the very bishops of that province, are compelled to swear. Now for the first time London, by the agreement conceded to it, found by experience that there was no king in the kingdom, as neither King Richard himself, nor his predecessor and father Henry, would have suffered it to be concluded for one thousand thousand marks of silver. How great evils forsooth may come forth of this agreement, may be estimated by the very definition, which is this. The commonalty is the pride of the common people, the dread of the kingdom, the ferment of the priesthood.

§ 71. The king of the French, with but few followers, *Affairs of Palestine.* returning home from Acre, left at that place the strength of his army to do nothing, to the command of which he appointed the bishop of Beauvais and the duke of Burgundy. The English king, having sent for the commanders of the French, proposed that in the first place they should conjointly attempt Jerusalem itself; but the dissuasion of the French discouraged the hearts of both parties, and dispirited the troops, and restrained the king, thus destitute of men, from his intended march upon that metropolis. The king, troubled at this, though not despairing, from that day forth separated his army from the French, and directing his arms to the storming of castles along the sea-shore, he took every fortress that came in his way from Tyre to Ascalon, though after hard fighting and deep wounds. But to Tyre he deigned not to go, because it was not in the compass of his part of the campaign.

A. D. 1192.
Miscella-
neous trans-
actions.

§ 72. Philip, king of the French, having left his companion Richard, king of the English, in the territory of
Jerusalem amongst the enemies of the cross of Christ,
returned to France, without obtaining either the libera-
tion of the Holy Cross or of the Holy Sepulchre. Godfrey, bishop of Winchester, restored to his church a
great part of the treasure, which, as is related above, he
January. had appointed, on the third of the kalends of February.
The feast of the Purification of the Blessed Mary was
1 February. celebrated on the very Sunday of Septuagesima at Winchester. But the Sunday had nothing belonging to
Sunday but its memory at vespers and matins, and
the morning mass. One full hide of land at the manse
which is called Morslede, of the village of Ciltecumba,
was let to a certain citizen of Winchester of the name
of Pentecuste, to hold for twenty years for the annual
and free service of twenty shillings, without the privity
of the convent.

§ 73. Queen Eleanor sailed from Normandy and
landed at Portsmouth on the third of the ides of
11 February. February. The chancellor repaired to the king of the
French, and deposed before him his complaint relative
to the loss of his treasures in Flanders, but he got
nothing more there than what makes men ridiculous.

The king of the French caused all manner of arms
to be fabricated both day and night throughout his
whole realm, and fortified his cities and castles, as was
thought, by way of preparation for a struggle against
the king of the English, if he should return from his
journey. Which being known in the territories of the
king of the English, his constables throughout Normandy, Le Mans, Anjou, Tours, Bourges, Poitou, and
Gascony, of themselves fortified every place that could
be fortified in the fullest manner. Moreover, the son
of the king of Navarre, to spite the French, ravaged
the country about Toulouse. A certain provost of the

king of the French, desiring to become greater than his
forefathers, set up a castle on the confines of Normandy
and France, where there had never yet been any fortification; which, ere it was built, the Normans, by the
impulse of their natural anger, totally overthrew, and
tore the provost himself to pieces.

§ 74. Queen Eleanor, a lady worthy of repeated Queen Eleanor interests
herself in fa-
vour of the
inhabitants
of Ely. mention, visited certain houses appertaining to her
dower within the diocese of Ely. To meet her there
came out of all the hamlets and manors, wherever she
passed, men with women and little children, not all of
the lowest class, a piteous and pitiable company, with
their feet bare, their clothes unwashed, and their hair
unshorn. They speak in tears, for which, for very grief,
they had failed to utter words, nor was there need of an
interpreter, as more than they desired to say might be
read in the open page. Human bodies lay unburied
every where throughout the country, because their
bishop had deprived them of sepulture. The queen, on
understanding the cause of so great severity, as she was
very compassionate, taking pity on the people's misery
for the dead, immediately neglecting her own, and following other men's matters, repaired to London; she
entreated, nay, she demanded, of the archbishop of
Rouen, that the confiscated estates of the bishop should
be restored to the bishop, and that the same bishop
should in the name of the chancery be proclaimed absolved from the excommunication denounced against
him, throughout the province of Rouen. And who
could be so harsh or obdurate that that lady could not
bend him to her wishes? She, too, forgetful of nothing,
sent word into Normandy to the lord of Ely, of the
public and private restitution which she had obtained
for him, and compelled him to revoke the sentence of
excommunication he had pronounced against the exchequer barons. So by the queen's mediation there was
peace between the implacable, though their vexation

was apparent, as the disaffection of their minds, contracted in their former hatred, could not be changed, without each giving some utterance to his feelings.

John, when about to embark for Normandy,

§ 75. Earl John, sending messengers to Southampton, commanded shipping to be made ready for him to depart, as was thought, to the king of the French; but the queen his mother, fearing lest the light-minded youth, by the counsels of the French, might go to attempt something against his lord and brother, with anxious mind takes in hand with her utmost ability to divert the intention of her son. The fate of her former sons, and the untimely decease of both under their oppressing sins, recurring to her mind, moved, or rather pierced, the maternal bowels of compassion. She desired that their violence might be enough, and that at least, good faith being kept amongst her younger children, she, as their mother, might end her days more happily than had fallen to the lot of their deceased

is prevented by his mother.

father. So having assembled all the peers of the realm, first at Windsor, secondly at Oxford, thirdly at London, and fourthly at Winchester, she with her own tears and the entreaties of the nobles with difficulty obtained that he would not cross the sea for this time. The earl, therefore, being in effect frustrated of his proposed passage, did what he could that way, and received the castles from the king's constables of Windsor and Wallingford, whom he had secretly called to him; and having received them, he delivered them over to his lieges to keep for him.

Council held at London.

§ 76. By command of the archbishop of Rouen, there assembled at London the pillars of the church, the oracles of the laws, to discuss either something or nothing, as it often falls out, in matters of state. There was but one mind among all, to convene Earl John for the pre-occupation of the castles; but, because no one of them durst commit himself to another, every one desired in himself that the question should be proposed rather by a deputy than by his own mouth. So whilst they all clamour to this end, and with this purpose, Æacus alone is wanting, to whom they all simultaneously agreed to resort; but even whilst among other matters they only casually discoursed of the late chancellor, behold! again is Crispinus at hand. The messengers of the chancellor, now again legate, enter the assembly, saluting the queen who was present, and all the rest, whom by chance they found together, on the part of their lord who had safely arrived the day before at Dover. The last clause of the mandates prohibited him from following up the ministration of his legation. Long were they all silent, and greatly astonished, intently kept their peace. At length it came to be the vote of all, that they should humbly entreat him to be their dictator and lord, whom they had assembled to judge as a perjurer and transgressor against their lord. So many of the nobles, of whom one was Echion, are sent, and that repeatedly, to Earl John, then staying at Wallingford, and laughing at their conventions. Humbly, and without austerity, they beg that he would hasten to meet the goat. "Lord!" say they, "he wears horns, beware!"

§ 77. The earl, not greatly moved, long suffered himself to be reverently entreated, but at length, satiated with the honour offered him, he came to London with the last intercessors, whom he most loved, sufficiently taught to answer to every question that might chance to be asked. The court rises up and compliments him on his entry, no order either of age or rank being observed; every body that ·first can, first runs to meet him, and desires himself to be first seen, eager to please the prince, because to have been acceptable to the great is not the last of praises. The leaders were at a stand Of the castles, no mention is made; the whole discussion and consultation was about the chancellor. Should the earl advise, all are ready to proscribe him. They strive

The influence of Earl John.

by all means to soften the earl to consent, but they had a wild beast on their right hand. The earl, on being asked to answer, briefly declares, " The chancellor fears the threats of none of you, nor of you altogether, nor will he beg your love, if only he may succeed to have me alone his friend. He is to give me seven hundred pounds of silver by the seventh day, if I shall not have meddled between you and him. You see I am in want of money. To the wise, a word is sufficient." He said, and withdrew, leaving the conclusion of his proposition in the midst. The court, placed in a great strait, strained its counsel : it appeared expedient to every one to propitiate the man with more than was promised ; the gift or loan of the money is approved, but not of their own, and so in the end it all falls upon the treasury of the absent king. Five hundred pounds of silver sterling out of the exchequer are lent to the earl by the barons, and letters to their liking against the chancellor are received. Nor is there delay; the queen writes, the clergy write, the people write, all unanimously advertise the chancellor to bolt, to cross the sea without delay, unless his ears are ticklish to hear rumours, unless he wishes to take his meals under the charge of armed soldiers.

§ 78. The chancellor stood aghast at the severity of the mandates, and was as pale as one who treads a snake with his bare feet. But, on retiring, is reported to have made only this manly reply:—" Let all who persecute me, know they shall see how great is he whom they have offended. I am not destitute of all counsel, as they reckon. I have one who serves me as a fine ear by true despatches. ' As long as I am an exile,' said he, ' patiently endure the things which you suffer. Every land is a home to the brave, believe one who has found it so by experience ; persevere and preserve your life for a better day. A grateful hour, which is not hoped for, will overtake both you and me. Unlooked for, I shall return and triumph over my enemies, and again shall my

His reflections.

victory make thee a citizen in my kingdom, forbidden
thee, and now not obeying me; haply it may hereafter
be gratifying to us to reflect on this event.'"

§ 79. Because Winchester ought not to be deprived
of its due reward for keeping peace with the Jews, as in
the beginning of this book is related, the Winchester
Jews, (after the manner of the Jews,) studious of the
honour of their city, procured themselves notoriety by
murdering a boy in Winchester, with many signs of
the deed, although, perhaps, the deed was never done.
The case was thus :—A certain Jew engaged a Christian
boy, a pretender to the art of shoe-making, into the
household service of his family. He did not reside there
continually to work, nor was he permitted to complete
anything great all at once, lest his abiding with them
should apprise him of the fate intended for him ; and, as
he was remunerated better for a little labour there, than
for much elsewhere, allured by his gifts and wiles, he
frequented the more freely the wretch's house. Now,
he was French by birth, under age, and an orphan, of
abject condition and extreme poverty. A certain French
Jew, having unfortunately compassionated his great
miseries in France, by frequent advice persuaded him
that he should go to England, a land flowing with milk
and honey ; he praised the English as liberal and boun-
tiful, and that there no one would continue poor who
could be recommended for honesty. The boy, ready to
like whatever you may wish, as is natural with the
French, having taken a certain companion of the same
age as himself, and of the same country, got ready to set
forward on his foreign expedition, having nothing in his
hands but a staff, nothing in his wallet but a cobbler's
awl.

§ 80. He bade farewell to his Jewish friend ; to whom
the Jew replied, " Go forth as a man. The God of my
fathers lead thee as I desire." And having laid his
hands upon his head, as if he had been the scapegoat,

Story of a boy killed by the Jews of Winchester.

after certain muttering of the throat and silent impre-
cations, being now secure of his prey, continued,—
" Be of good courage ; forget your own people and
native land, for every land is the home of the brave,
as the sea is for the fish, and as the whole of the wide
world is for the bird. When you have entered England,
Character of
London. if you should come to London, you will quickly pass
through it, as that city greatly displeases me. Every
race of men, out of every nation which is under heaven,
resort thither in great numbers ; every nation has introduced into that city its vices and bad manners. No one
lives in it without offence ; there is not a single street in
it, that does not abound in miserable obscene wretches ;
there, in proportion as any man has exceeded in wickedness, so much is he the better. I am not ignorant of
the disposition I am exhorting ; you have in addition
to your youth, an ardent disposition, a slowness of
memory, and a soberness of reason between extremes.
I feel in myself no uneasiness about you, unless you
should abide with men of corrupt lives ; for from our
associations, our manners are formed. But let that be
as it may. You will come to London. Behold, I warn
you, whatever of evil or of perversity there is in any,
whatever in all parts of the world, you will find in that
city alone. Go not to the dances of panders, nor mix
yourself up with the herds of the stews ; avoid the talus
and the dice, the theatre and the tavern. You will find
more braggadocios there than in all France, while the
number of flatterers is infinite. Stage players, buf-
foons, those that have no hair on their bodies, Gara-
mantes, pickthanks, catamites, effeminate sodomites,
lewd musical girls, druggists, lustful persons, fortune-
tellers, extortioners, nightly strollers, magicians, mimics,
common beggars, tatterdemalions,—this whole crew has
filled every house. So if you do not wish to live with
the shameful, you will not dwell in London. I am not
speaking against the learned, whether monks or Jews ;

although, still, from their very dwelling together with such evil persons, I should esteem them less perfect there than elsewhere.

§ 81. " Nor does my advice go so far, as that you should betake yourself to no city; with my counsel you will take up your residence nowhere but in a town, though it remains to say in what.   Therefore, if you should land near Canterbury, you will have to lose your way; if even Canterbury. you should but pass through it.   It is an assemblage of the vilest, entirely devoted to their, I know not whom, but who has been lately canonized, and had been the archbishop of Canterbury, as every where they die in open day by the streets for want of bread and employ- ment.   Rochester and Chichester are mere villages, and Rochester. they possess nothing for which they should be called cities, Chichester. but the sees of their bishops.   Oxford, scarcely, I will Oxford. not say satisfies, but sustains, its clerks.   Exeter sup- Exeter. ports men and beasts with the same grain.   Bath is Bath. placed, or rather buried, in the lowest parts of the valleys, in a very dense atmosphere and sulphury vapour, as it were at the gates of hell.   Nor yet will you select your habitation in the northern cities, Worcester, Chester, Worcester. Hereford, on account of the desperate Welchmen. Chester. York abounds in Scots, vile and faithless men, or rather York. rascals.   The town of Ely is always putrefied by the sur- Ely. rounding marshes.   In Durham, Norwich, or Lincoln, Durham, there are very few of your disposition among the power- Norwich, ful; you will never hear any one speak French.   At Bristol, there is nobody who is not, or has not been, a Bristol. soapmaker, and every Frenchman esteems soapmakers as he does nightmen.   After the cities, every market, village, or town, has but rude and rustic inhabitants. Moreover, at all times, account the Cornish people for Cornwall. such as you know our Flemings are accounted in France. For the rest, the kingdom itself is generally most favoured with the dew of heaven, and the fatness of the earth ; and in every place there are some good, but much

fewer in them all than in Winchester alone.

§ 82. " This is in those parts the Jerusalem of the Jews, in it alone they enjoy perpetual peace ; it is the school of those who desire to live well and prosper. Here they become men, here there is bread and wine enough for nothing. There are therein monks of such compassion and gentleness, clergy of such understanding and frankness, citizens of such civility and good faith, ladies of such beauty and modesty, that little hinders but I should go there and become a Christian with such Christians. To that city I direct you, the city of cities, the mother of all, the best above all. There is but one fault, and that alone in which they customarily indulge too much. With the exception I should say of the learned and of the Jews, the Winchester people tell lies like watchmen, but it is in making up reports. For in no place under heaven so many false rumours are fabricated so easily as there ; otherwise they are true in every thing. I should have many things too still to tell you about business ; but for fear you should not understand or should forget, you will place this familiar note in the hands of the Jew my friend, and I think, too, you may sometime be rewarded by him." The short note was in Hebrew. The Jew made an end of his speech, and the boy having understood all things for good, came to Winchester.

§ 83. His awl supplied him, and his companion as well, with food, and the cruel courtesy and deceitful beneficence of the Jew was by the letter unfortunately obtained to their relief. Wherever the poor fellows worked or eat apart by day, they reposed every night in one little bed in the same old cottage of a certain old woman. Days follow days, and months months, and in the same way as we have hitherto so carefully described, our boys hasten the time of their separation that they may meet again. The day of the Holy Cross had

arrived, and the boy that same day, whilst working at
his Jew's, being by some means put out of the way, was
not forthcoming.   Now the passover, a feast of the
Jews, was at hand.   His companion, during the evening, greatly surprised at his absence, not returning home
to bed, was terrified that night with many visions and
dreams.   When he had sought him several days in all
corners of the city without success, he came to the Jew
and simply asked if he had sent his benefactor any-
where; whom when he found violently enraged above
his general disposition, from having been so courteous
the day before, having noticed the incoherence of his
words and change of countenance, he presently fired up,
and as he was of a shrill voice and admirable readiness
of speech, he broke out into abuse, and with great
clamour challenged him with taking his companion
away.   " Thou son of a sordid harlot," said he, " thou
robber, thou traitor, thou devil, thou hast crucified my
friend.   Alas, me ! wherefore have I not now the
strength of a man !   I would tear you to pieces with my
hands."   The noise of his quarrelling in the house is
heard in the street, Jews and Christians come running
together from all quarters.   The boy persists, and now,
deriving courage from the crowd, addressing those present, he alleged his concern for his companion as an
excuse.   " O you good people," said he, " who are
assembled, behold if there is any sorrow like my sorrow.
That Jew is a devil; he has stolen away my heart from
my breast—he has butchered my only companion, and I
presume, too, that he has eaten him.   A certain son of
the devil, a Jew of French birth, I neither know nor am
acquainted with; that Jew gave my comrade letters of
his death-warrant to that man.   To this city he came,
induced, or rather seduced.   He often gave attendance
upon this Jew, and in his house he was last seen."   He
was not without a witness to some points, in as much as
a Christian woman, who, contrary to the canons, had

nursed up the young Jews in the same house, constantly
swore that she had seen the boy go down into the Jew's
store, without coming up again. The Jew denies it—
the case is referred to the judges. The accusers are
defective; the boy because he was under age, the woman
because the service of Jews had rendered her ignomi-
nious. The Jew offered to clear his conscience of the
evil report. Gold contented the judges. Phineas gave
and pleased, and the controversy ceased.

The bishop
of Chester
persecutes
the monks of
Coventry. § 84. The bishop of Chester, who, from his detestation
of religion, had expelled the monks from Coventry,
entirely broke down all the workshops there were in the
monastery, that by the altered appearance of the place,
all remembrance of its past state might be taken away
from posterity. And further, lest the ruins of the walls
should some day bespeak their author, the church of the
place, which had not been finished, was found a ready
plea, and having bestowed the materials upon it, without charge, he began to build. Moreover, he appointed
the masons and plasterers their hire out of the chattels
of the monastery. He selected two principal manors of
the monks for his own proper use; this arrangement
being made for their abuse—that wherever he should
eat, some special delicacy provided out of the issues of
the aforesaid manors should be presented to him to eat,
that he might glory in the victory, and might batten, as
it were, on the viscera of the monks, whom he had by
his wickedness overcome. But all the rest of their revenues he allotted to the prebends, some of which he conferred and settled for ever on the Romish church,
appropriated to certain cardinals of the apostolic see,
appointing them and their canonical successors in the
same titles to be canons of the church of Coventry,
that if by any chance there should be any delay to the
transactions before the Pope, he should make the whole
court the more ready in the defence of his part; he
conferred the other prebends on others, but not one on

any whom he did not know for certain to be an advocate
of no religion. They built eagerly, even the absent
canons, around the church·spacious and lofty villas, perhaps for their own use, if even once in their lives any
chance should offer a cause for visiting the place. None
of the prebendaries regularly resided there any more
than they do elsewhere ; but doing great things for the
gates of palaces, they have left to poor vicars induced by
a trifling remuneration to insult God, to them have they
intrusted the holy chant and vanquished household gods
and bare church walls.

§ 85. This forsooth is true religion ; this should the
church imitate and emulate. It will be permitted the
secular canon to be absent from his church as long as
he may please, and to consume the patrimony of Christ
where, and when, and in whatsoever luxuries he may
list. Let them only provide this, that a frequent voci-
feration be heard in the house of the Lord. If the
stranger should knock at the doors of such, if the poor
should cry, he who lives before the doors will answer,
(he himself being a sufficiently needy vicar,) "Pass on,
and seek elsewhere for alms, for the master of the house
is not at home." This is that glorious religion of the
clerks, for the sake of which the bishop of Chester, the
first of men that durst commit so great iniquity, expelled
his monks from Coventry. For the sake of clerks irre-
gularly regular, that is to say of canons, he capriciously
turned out the monks ; monks who, not with another's,
but with their own mouth praised the Lord, who dwelt
and walked in the house of the Lord with unanimity all
the days of their life, who beyond their food and raiment
knew nothing earthly, whose bread was always for the
poor, whose door was at all times open to every traveller :
nor did they thus please the bishop, who never loved
either monks or their order. A man of bitter jocularity,
who even though he might sometimes spare, never
ceased to worry the monks. O what a fat morsel,

F

and not to be absorbed, is a monk! many a thousand has
that bit choked, while the wicked at their death have
had it for their viaticum. If as often as a monk were
calumniated and reproached he were consumed, all religion would be absorbed before many ages. At all times
and in every place, whether the bishop spoke in earnest
or in jest, a monk was some part of his discourse. Nor
did the expulsion of his own monks satisfy him, but ever
after, true to himself, he continued censuring the monks
as before. But as he could not desist from speaking of
them, lest he should incur the opprobrium of a detrac-
tor, if in their absence he should carp at their order, he
resolved to keep some monk abiding with him in his
court; that his conversation about them might be made
less offensive, by the presence and audience of one of
them. So he took as his quasi chaplain, a certain monk,
scarcely of age, but yet who had professed at Burton,
whom to the scandal of religion he generally took about
with him. O excess of sorrow! Even among the angels
of God is found iniquity. The monk, wise and prudent,
seduced to the delusion, hardened his forehead as a harlot, that he a monk should not blush when monks were
reviled. Alas! how great a thirst for roving and
riding! Hear me and attend a little; you shall see
how the riding of this rider concluded. On a certain
day, as the bishop was standing over his workmen at
Coventry, his monk attending close by his side, on
whom the bishop familiarly resting, said, " Is it not
proper and expedient, my monk, even in your judgment,
that the great beauty of so fair a church, that such a
comely edifice, should rather be appropriated to gods
than devils?" And while the monk was hesitating at
the obscurity of the words, he added, " I," said he,
" call my clerks gods, and monks devils!" And presently putting forth the forefinger of his right hand
towards his clerks, who were standing round him, continued, " I say ye are gods, and ye are all the children

of the Highest!" And having turned again to the left, concluded to the monk, " But ye monks shall die like devils ; and as one and the greatest of your princes ye shall fall away into hell, because ye are devils upon earth. Truly if it should befal me to officiate for a dead monk, which I should be very unwilling to do, I would commend his body and soul not to God, but to the devil !" The monk, who was standing in the very place that the monks had been plundered of, did not refute the insult on the monks, and because on such an occasion he was silent, met, as he deserved, with the reward of eternal silence being imposed upon him. For suddenly a stone falling from the steeple of the church, dashed out the brains of the monk who was attending on the bishop, the bishop being preserved in safety for some greater judgment.

§ 86. The king of the English, Richard, had already completed two years in conquering the region around Jerusalem, and during all that time there had no aid been sent to him from any of his kingdoms. Nor yet were his only and uterine brother, John, earl of Mortain, nor his justiciaries, nor his other nobles, observed to take any care to send him any part of his revenues ; but they did not even think of his return. However, prayer was made without ceasing by the church to God for him. The king's army was decreased daily in the land of promise, and besides those who were slain with the sword, many thousands of the people perished every month by the too sudden extremities of the nightly cold and the daily heat. When it appeared that they would all have to die there, every one had to choose whether he would die as a coward or in battle. On the other side, the strength of the Gentiles greatly increased, and their confidence was strengthened by the misfortunes of the Christians ; their army was relieved at certain times by fresh troops; the weather was natural to them ; the place was their native country ; their labour, health ;

Richard's exploits in Palestine.

Condition of his army.

their frugality, medicine. Amongst the Normans, on the contrary, that became a disadvantage which to the adversaries brought gain. For if our people lived sparingly even once in a week, they were rendered less effective for seven weeks after. The mingled nation of French and English fared sumptuously every day, and (saving the reverence of the French) even to loathing, at whatever cost, while their treasure lasted; and the well known custom of the English being continually kept up even under the very clarions and the clangor of the trumpet or horn, they gaped with due devotion while the chalices were emptied to the dregs. The merchants of the country, who brought the victuals to the camp, were astonished at their wonderful and extra-ordinary habits, and could scarcely believe even what they saw to be true, that one people, and that small in number, consumed threefold the bread and a hundred-fold the wine more than that whereon many nations of the Gentiles had been sustained, and some of those nations innumerable. And the hand of the Lord was deservedly laid upon them according to their merits. So great want of food followed their great gluttony, that their teeth scarcely spared their fingers, as their hands presented to their mouths less than their usual allow-ance. To these and other calamities, which were severe and many, a much greater was added by the sickness of the king.

Richard's Illness.

§ 87. The king was extremely sick, and confined to his bed; his fever continued without intermission; the physicians whispered that it was an acute semiter-tian. And as they despaired of his recovery even from the first, terrible dismay was spread from the king's abode through the camp. There were few among the many thousands who did not meditate on flight, and the utmost confusion of dispersion or surrender would have followed, had not Hubert Walter, bishop of Salis-bury, immediately assembled the council. He obtained by forcible allegations that the army should not break up, until a truce were demanded of Saladin. All well armed stand in array more steadily than usual, and with a threatening look concealing the reluctance of their mind, they feign a desire for battle. No one speaks of the indisposition of the king, lest the secret of their intense sorrow should be disclosed to the enemy; for it was thoroughly understood that Saladin feared the charge of the whole army less than that of the king alone; and if he should know that he was dead, he would instantly pelt the French with cow-dung, and intoxicate the best of the English drunkards with a dose which should make them tremble.

§ 88. In the mean time, a certain Gentile, called Saffatin, came down to see the king, as he generally did; he was a brother of Saladin, an ancient man of war, of remarkable politeness and intelligence, and one whom the king's magnanimity and munificence had charmed even to the love of his person and favour of his party. The king's servants greeting him less joyfully than they were accustomed, and not admitting him to an interview with the king, " I perceive," said he, by his interpreter, " that you are greatly afflicted, nor am I ignorant of the cause. My friend, your king, is sick, and therefore you close his doors to me." And falling into tears with his whole heart, he exclaimed, " O God of the Christians, if thou be a God, do not suffer such a man, so necessary to thy people, to fall so suddenly!" He was entrusted with their avowal, and thus spoke on, " In truth I forewarn you, that if the king should die while things stand as they are at present, all you Christians will perish, and all this region will in time to come be ours without contest. Shall we at all dread that stout king of France, who before he came into battle was defeated? Whose whole strength, which three years had contributed, the short space of three months consumed. Hither will he on no account return any

Saffatin's speech in praise of Richard.

more; for we always esteem this as a sure token (I am not speaking craftily, but simply,) that those whom at first we think cowardly, we ever after find worse. But that king, of all the princes of the Christian name, whom the round circle of the whole world encompasses, is alone worthy of the honour of a captain and the name of a king, because he commenced well, and went on better, and will be crowned by the most prosperous result, if only he shall remain with you a short time.

§ 89. "It is not a new thing for us to dread the English, for fame reported to us his father to be such, that had he come even unarmed to our parts, we should all have fled though armed, nor would it have appeared inglorious to us to be put to flight by him. He our terror, a wonderful man in his day, is dead; but, like the phœnix, renewed himself, a thousand times better, in his son. It was not unknown to us how great that Richard was, even while his father lived; for all the days of his father, we had our agents in those parts, who informed us both of the king's deeds, and of the birth and death of his sons. He was justly beloved for his probity by his father above all his brothers, and preferred before them to the government of his states. It was not unknown to us that when he was made duke of Aquitaine he speedily and valiantly crushed the tyrants of the province, who had been invincible before his grandfather and great grandfather;—how terrible he was even to the king of France himself, as well as to all the governors of the regions on his borders. None took of his to himself, though he always pushed his bounds into his neighbours'. It was not unknown to us, that his two brothers, the one already crowned king, the other duke of Bretagne, had set themselves up against their dear father, and that he ceased not to persecute them with the rigour of war, till he had given them both eternal repose, vanquished as they were by the length of the prosecution. Besides, as you will the more wonder

at, we know all the cities of your parts by name; nor
are we ignorant that the king of your country was
beaten at Le Mans through the treachery of his own
people; that he died at Chinon, and was buried at
Fontevraud.

§ 90. " It is not through ignorance that I do not
relate who made himself the author of such unusual and
mighty slaughter against us.   O! if that Richard,
whom although I love yet I fear, if he were despatched
out of the way, how little should we then fear, how very
little should we make account of that youngest of the
sons, who sleeps at home in clover! It was not unknown to us, that Richard, who nobly succeeded his
great father in the kingdom, immediately set forward
against us even in the very year of his coronation. The
number of his ships and troops was not unknown to us
before his setting forth. We knew, even at the very
time, with what speed he took Messina, the well fortified city of Sicily, which he besieged; and although
none of our people believed it, yet our fears increased,
and fame added false terrors to the true.

§ 91. " His valour, unable to rest in one place, proceeded through a boundless region, and everywhere left
trophies of his courage. We questioned among ourselves
whether he made ready to subdue, for his God, the land
of promise only, or, at the same time to take the whole
world for himself. Who shall worthily relate the cap-
ture of Cyprus? Verily had the island of Cyprus been
close to Egypt, and had my brother Saladin subdued it
in ten years, his name would have been reckoned by the
people among the names of the gods. When, however,
we at last perceived that he overthrew whatever resisted
his purpose, our hearts were melted as the hoar frost
melts at the appearance of the approaching sun, for as
much as it was said of him that he ate his enemies alive.
And if he were not presently, on the very day of his arrival before Acre, received freely into the city with

open gates, fear alone was the cause. It was not from
their desire to preserve the city, but through dread of
the torments promised them and their despair of life
that they fought so bravely, or rather desperately, fearing this more than death, endeavouring this by all
means, namely, that they should not die unrevenged.
And this was not from sheer obstinacy, but to follow up
the doctrine of our faith. For we believe that the spirits of the unavenged wander for ever, and that they are
deprived of all rest. But what did the rashness and
timidity of the devoted profit them? Being vanquished
by force, and constrained by fear to surrender, they
were punished with a more lenient death than they had
expected. And yet, oh! shame on the Gentiles! their
spirits wander unavenged! I swear to you by the Great
God, that if, after he had gained Acre, he had immediately led his army to Jerusalem, he would not have
found even one of our people in the whole circuit of the
Christians' land; on the contrary, we should have offered
to him inestimable treasure, that he might not proceed,
that he might not prosecute us further.

§ 92. "But, thanks be to God! he was burdened with
the king of the French, and hindered by him, like a cat
with a hammer tied to its tail. To conclude, we, though
his rivals, see nothing in Richard that we can find fault
with but his valour; nothing to hate but his experience
in war. But what glory is there in fighting with a sick
man? And although this very morning I could have
wished that both you and he had all received your final
doom, now I compassionate you on account of your
king's illness. I will either obtain for you a settled
peace with my brother, or at the least a good and du-
rable truce. But until I return to you, do not by any
means speak of it to the king, lest, if he should be excited, he may get worse, for he is of so lofty and impatient a disposition, that, even though he should needs
presently die, he would not consent to an arrangement,

without seeing the advantage on his side!" He would
have spoken further, but his tongue, languishing and failing for sorrow, would not continue his harangue, so with
his head resting in his clasped hands he wept sore.

§ 93. The bishop of Salisbury, and such of the most Truce granted by Saladin
trusty of the king's household as were present, who to the English.
had secretly deliberated with him upon this subject, re-
luctantly consented to the truce which before they had
determined to purchase at any price, as if it had been
detested, and not desired by them. So their right hands
being given and received, Saffatin, when he had washed
his face, and disguised his sorrow, returned to Jerusalem,
to Saladin. The council was assembled before his brother, and after seventeen days of weighty argument, he
with difficulty succeeded in prevailing on the stubborn-
ness of the Gentiles to grant a truce to the Christians.
The time was appointed and the form approved. If it
please King Richard, for the space of three years, three
months, three weeks, three days, and three hours, such
a truce shall be observed between the Christians and the
Gentiles, that whatever either one party or the other in
anywise possesses, he shall possess without molestation
to the end; it will be permitted during the interval,
that the Christians at their pleasure may fortify Acre
only, and the Gentiles Jerusalem. All contracts, com-
merce, every act and every thing shall be mutually carried on by all in peace. Saffatin himself is despatched
to the English as the bearer of this decree.

§ 94. Whilst King Richard was sick at Jaffa, word Richard's
recovery.
was brought him that the duke of Burgundy was taken
dangerously ill at Acre. That day was the day for the
king's fever to take its turn, and through his delight at
this report, it left him. The king immediately with
uplifted hands imprecated a curse upon him, saying,
" May God destroy him, for he would not destroy the
enemies of our faith with me, although he had long
served in my pay." On the third day the duke died; as

soon as his decease was known, the bishop of Beauvais, having left the king with all his men, came in haste to Acre; the French out of all the towns assembled before him, all but Henry, count of Champagne, King Richard's nephew by his sister. And the bishop being made their leader and bully, set forth a proclamation and commanded them all to return home.

The French
return home. § 95. The fleet was made ready, and the glorious prince retreating from the East with his cowardly troop, sails over the Etruscan sea. Having landed on the German coast, he spread abroad among the people, during the whole of his journey, that that traitor the king of England, from the first moment of his arrival in Judea, had endeavoured to betray his lord the king of the French to Saladin; that, as soon as he had obtained Tyre, he caused the marquess to be murdered; that he had despatched the duke of Burgundy by poison; that at the last he had sold generally the whole army of the Christians who did not obey him. That he was a man of singular ferocity, of harsh and repulsive manners, subtle in treachery, and most cunning in dissimulation. That on that account the king of the French had returned home so soon; that on that account the French who remained, had left Jerusalem unredeemed. This report gained strength by circulation, and provoked against one man the hatred of all.

Philip plots
against
Richard. § 96. The bishop of Beauvais having returned to France, secretly whispered in the king's ear, that the king of England had sent assassins to France who would murder him. The king, alarmed at that, appointed, though against the custom of his country, a chosen body guard; he further sent ambassadors to the emperor of Germany with presents, and carefully persuaded his imperial majesty to a hatred of the king of England. So it was enjoined by an imperial edict, that all cities and princes of the empire should take the king of the English by force, if by chance in his return from

Judea he should happen to pass through their countries, and present him to him alive or dead. If any one spared him, he should be punished as the public enemy of the empire. All obeyed the emperor's charge; and especially that duke of Austria whom the king of England had dismissed at Acre.

§ 97. Henry, count of Champagne, now the only one of the French nobles left in Judea, returned to the king of the English, to Jaffa; and when he announced to him both the death of the duke of Burgundy and the departure of the French, the hope of the king so revived, that he presently experienced a perfect convalescence with a healthy perspiration. And having resumed his strength of body more by the high temper of his mind than by repose or nourishment, he issued a command through the whole coast from Tyre to Ascalon, that all who were able to serve in the wars should come to the service at the king's charges. There assembled before him a countless multitude, the greater part of whom were foot; which being rejected as they were useless, he mustered the horse, and scarcely found five hundred knights and two thousand shield-bearers whose lords had perished. And not mistrustful on account of their small number, he being a most excellent orator, strengthened the minds of the fearful in a seasonable harangue. He commanded that it should be proclaimed through the companies that on the third day they must follow the king to battle, either to die as martyrs or to take Jerusalem by storm. This was the sum of his project, because as yet he knew nothing of the truce. For there was no one who durst even hint to him, who had so unexpectedly recovered, that which, without his knowledge, they had undertaken through fear of his death. However, Hubert Walter, bishop of Salisbury, took council with Count Henry concerning the truce, and obtained his ready concurrence in his wishes. So having deliberated together by what stratagem they might be able without danger to hinder such

Richard prevented from attacking Jerusalem.

a hazardous engagement, they conceived one of a thousand, namely, to dissuade the people if possible from the
enterprise. And the matter turned out most favourably;
the spirit of those who were going to fight had so greatly
failed, even without dissuasion, that on the appointed
day, when the king according to his custom leading the
van, marshalled his army, there were not found of all the
knights and shield-bearers above nine hundred. On
account of which defection, the king, greatly enraged, or
rather raving, and champing with his teeth the pine rod
which he held in his hand, at length unbridled his indig-
His speech. nant lips as follows:—"O God!" said he, "O God, my
God, why hast thou forsaken me? For whom have we
foolish Christians, for whom have we English come hither from the furthest parts of the earth to bear our
arms? Is it not for the God of the Christians? O fie!
How good art thou to us thy people, who now are for thy
name given up to the sword; we shall become a portion
for foxes. O how unwilling should I be to forsake thee
in so forlorn and dreadful a position, were I thy Lord
and advocate as thou art mine! In sooth, my standards
will in future be despised, not through my fault but
through thine; in sooth, not through any cowardice of
my warfare, art thou thyself, my King and my God,
conquered this day, and not Richard thy vassal."

He sanctions   § 98. He said, and returned to the camp extremely
the truce
with Saladin. dejected; and as a fit occasion now offered, Bishop Hubert and Henry, count of Champagne, approaching him
with unwonted familiarity, and as if nothing had yet
been arranged, importuned under divers pretexts the
king's consent for making such overtures to the Gentiles
as were necessary. And thus the king answered them:
"Since it generally happens that a troubled mind rather
thwarts than affords sound judgment—I, who am greatly
perplexed in mind, authorize you, who have as I see a
collected mind, to arrange what you shall think most
proper for the good of peace." They having gained

their desires, chose messengers to send to Saffatin upon
these matters; Saffatin, who had returned from Jerusalem, is suddenly announced to be at hand; the count
and the bishop go to meet him, and being assured by
him of the truce, they instruct him how he must
speak with the lord their king. Saffatin being admitted
to an interview with the king as one who before had
been his friend, could scarcely prevail with the king not
to make himself a sacrifice, and to consent to the truce.
For so great were the man's strength of body, mental
courage, and entire trust in Christ, that he could hardly
be prevailed upon not to undertake in his own person a
single combat with a thousand of the choicest Gentiles,
as he was destitute of soldiers. And as he was not permitted to break off in this way, he chose another evasion, that, after a truce of seven weeks, the stipulations
of the compact being preserved, it should remain for him
to choose whether it were better to fight or to forbear.
The right hands are given by both parties for faithfully
observing this last agreement; and Saffatin, more honoured than burthened with the king's present, goes back
again to his brother, to return at the expiration of the
term for the final conclusion or breaking off of the above
truce.

§ 99. Richard, king of England, held a council at His arrange-
Acre, and there prudently regulating the government of leaving
that state, he appointed his nephew, Henry, count of Palestine.
Champagne, on whom he had formerly conferred Tyre,
to be captain and lord of the whole land of promise.
Only he thought proper to defer his consecration as
king till haply he might be crowned at Jerusalem.
King Richard now thinking to return home, when with
the assistance of Count Henry he had appointed chosen
men for all the strongholds that had been taken in his
territories, found Ascalon alone without ward or in-
habitant for want of people. Wherefore taking pre-
caution that it might not become a receptacle of the

Gentiles, he caused the ramparts and fortifications of the castle to be cast down. The seventh day of the seventh week appeared, and behold Saffatin, with many mighty ones who desired to see the face of the king, drew near; the truce was confirmed on both sides by oath, this being added to that which had been previously settled, that during the continuance of the truce no one, whether Christian or Gentile, should inhabit Ascalon, and that the whole of the tillage pertaining to the town should remain to the Christians. Hubert, bishop of Salisbury, and Henry, captain of Judea, together with a numerous band, went up to Jerusalem to worship in the place where the feet of Christ had stood. And there was woful misery to be seen, captive confessors of the Christian name wearing out a hard and constant martyrdom; chained together in gangs, their feet blistered, their shoulders raw, their backsides goaded, their backs wealed; they carried materials to the hands of the masons and stone-layers to make Jerusalem impregnable against the Christians. When the captain and the bishop had returned from the sacred places, they endeavoured to persuade the king to go up; but the worthy indignation of his noble mind could not consent to receive that from the courtesy of the Gentiles, which he could not obtain by the gift of God.

RICHARD OF CIRENCESTER'S

DESCRIPTION OF BRITAIN,

WITH

𝕬 𝕷𝖎𝖋𝖊 𝖔𝖋 𝖙𝖍𝖊 𝕬𝖚𝖙𝖍𝖔𝖗,

TO WHICH IS ADDED,

THE ORIGINAL LATIN TEXT.

by Charles Bertram

NOTICE

OF

THE LIFE AND WORKS

OF

RICHARD OF CIRENCESTER.

RICHARD, surnamed from his birth-place Richard of Cirencester, flourished from the middle to the latter end of the fourteenth century. No traces of his family or connections can be discovered; though they were at least of respectable condition, for he received an education which in his time was far beyond the attainment of the inferior ranks of society. In 1350 he entered into the Benedictine monastery of St. Peter, Westminster, during the abbacy of —— de Lytlington, as appears from the rolls of the abbey; and his name occurs in various documents of that establishment in the years 1387, 1397, and 1399.

He devoted his leisure hours to the study of British and Anglo-Saxon history and antiquities, in which he made such proficiency that he is said to have been honoured with the name of the Historiographer. Pitts informs us, without specifying his authority, that Richard visited different libraries and ecclesiastical establish-

ments in England in order to collect materials. It is
at least certain that he obtained a license to visit Rome,
from his abbot, William of Colchester, in 1391; and
there can be little doubt that a man of so industrious,
observant, and sagacious a character profited by this
journey to extend his historical and antiquarian knowledge, and to augment his collections. This license is
given by Stukeley from the communication of Mr. Wid-
more, librarian of Westminster, and bears honourable
testimony to the morals and piety of our author, and his
regularity in performing the discipline of his order. He
probably performed this journey in the interval between
1391 and 1397, for he appears to have been confined in
the abbey infirmary in 1401, and died in that or the
following year. Doubtless his remains were interred in
the cloisters of the abbey, but we cannot expect to find
any memorial of a simple monk. We have abundant
cause to regret that he was restrained in the pursuit of
his favourite studies, by the authority of his abbot. In
the seventh chapter of his first book he enters into a
spirited justification of himself, but from the preface to
his Chronology he appears to have found it necessary to
submit his better judgment to the will of his superior.

His works are—

Historia ab Hengista ad Ann. 1348, in two parts.
The first contains the period from the coming of the
Saxons to the death of Harold, and is preserved in the
public library of the University of Cambridge, Ff. i. 28.
Whitaker, the historian of Manchester, thus speaks of
it :—" The hope of meeting with discoveries as great in
the Roman, British, and Saxon history as he has given
us concerning the preceding period, induced me to exa-

mine the work. But my expectations were greatly dis-
appointed. The learned scholar and the deep antiquarian, I found sunk into an ignorant novice, sometimes
the copier of Huntingdon, but generally the transcriber
of Geoffrey. Deprived of his Roman guides, Richard
showed himself as ignorant and as injudicious as any of
his illiterate contemporaries about him." (a)

The second part is probably a manuscript contained
in the library of the Royal Society, p. 137, with the
title of *Britonum Anglorum et Saxonum Historia.*

In the library of Bennet Coll. Cambridge is *Epitome
Chronic. Ric. Cor. West. Lib.* I.

Other works of our author are supposed to be preserved in the Lambeth library, and at Oxford.

His theological writings were—

Tractatus super Symbolum Majus et Minus, and
Liber de Officiis Ecclesiasticis.—In the Peterborough
Library.

But the treatise to which Richard owes his celebrity
is that now presented to the reader. Its first discoverer
was Charles Julius Bertram, Professor of the English
Language in the Royal Marine Academy at Copenhagen,
who transmitted to the celebrated antiquary, Doctor
Stukeley, a transcript of the whole in letters, together
with a copy of the map. From this transcript Stukeley
published an Analysis of the work, with the Itinerary,
first in a thin quarto, in 1757, and afterwards in the second volume of his *Itinerarium Curiosum.* In the same
year the original itself was published by Professor Ber-

(a) Hist. of Manchester, vol. i. p. 58, 4to.

tram at Copenhagen, in a small octavo volume, with the remains of Gildas and Nennius, under this title—

Britannicarum Gentium Historiæ Antiquæ Scriptores tres: Ricardus Corinensis, Gildas Badonicus, Nennius Banchorensis, &c.

Of this treatise Bertram thus speaks in his preface: " The work of Richard of Cirencester, which came into my possession in an extraordinary manner with many other curiosities, is not entirely complete, yet its author is not to be classed with the most inconsiderable historians of the middle age. It contains many fragments of a better time, which would now in vain be sought for elsewhere ; and all are useful to the antiquary * * * *. It is considered by Dr. Stukeley, and those who have inspected it, as a jewel, and worthy to be rescued from destruction by the press.   From respect for him I have caused it to be printed."

Of the map he observes: " I have added a very antient map of Roman Britain, skilfully drawn according to the accounts of the ancients, which in rarity and antiquity excels the rest of the Commentary of Richard."

ANCIENT STATE OF BRITAIN.

BOOK I.

CHAPTER I.

1. THE shore of Gaul would be the boundary of the world, did not the Island (a) of Britain claim from its magnitude almost the appellation of another world; for if measured to the Caledonian promontory (b) it extends more than eight hundred miles in length (c).

2. Britain was first called by the ancients Albion (d), from its *white* cliffs; and afterwards in the language of

More correctly 540 miles.

Albion.

(a) The early Greeks and Romans doubted whether Britain was an island, or part of the continent. This uncertainty gave rise to a controversy which was not settled till the time of the propraetor Julius Agricola.—*Tac. Vit. Agric. c.* 38. *Dio Cass. Hist. Rom. lib.* 39.

(b) Dunnet Head.

(c) Richard gives to great an extent to our island, which, according to the most accurate observations, stretches only from lat. 49° 48', the most southern point, to Dunnet Head, which is in lat. 58° 40', or scarcely 540 geographical miles.

(d) Various explanations have been given of the names of Albion and Britain, applied to our island. Some derive Albion from the white rocks which bound the coast; some from Albion, a son of Neptune, who is represented as its first discoverer and cultivator: others have likewise derived the name Britain from the Phœnician or Hebrew *Baratanac,* signifying the land of tin. It was also called

of the natives, Britain. Hence all the islands hereafter described were denominated British (e).

3. Britain is situated between the north and west (f),
opposite to, though at some distance from, Germany,
Gaul, and Spain, the most considerable parts of Europe,
and is bounded by the Atlantic Ocean.

4. On the south of Britain lies Belgic Gaul, from
which coast passengers usually sail to the Rhutupian
Richborough port(g). This place is distant from Gessoriacum(h), a town
Boulogne. of the Morini, the port most frequented by the Britons,
fifty miles, or according to others, four hundred and
fifty stadia. From thence may be seen the country of
the Britons, whom Virgil in his Eclogues describes as
separated from the whole world,—

" — penitus toto divisos orbe Britannos."

5. By Agrippa, an ancient geographer, its breadth is

by the ancients *Hyperborea, Atlantica, Cassiteris, Romana,* and
Thule.

According to the British Triads, " the three names given to the
Isle of Britain, from the beginning, were: before it was inhabited,
the name of *Clas Merddyn* (or the green spot defended by water);
after it was inhabited, *Y Vél Ynys* (the honey island); and, after
it was brought under one government by Prydain, son of Aedd, it
was called *Ynys Prydain* (or the Isle of Britain).

In some old writings it is also termed *Yr Ynys Wen* (or the
white island).

(e) This part is taken from Pliny, who enumerates the British
isles in the following order:—Orcades 40; Acmodæ 7; Hæbudes
30. Between Britain and Ireland, Mona, Menapia, Ricnea, Vectis,
Silimnus, Andros; beneath, Siambis, and Axuntos: on the opposite side, towards the German Sea, the Glessariæ, called Electrides
by the later Greek writers, from the amber found there; and last
of all Thule.

He refers to others mentioned by different authors: *viz.* Mictis,
Scandia, Dumnia, Bergos, and Nerigos.

(f) That is, from Rome. Richard, in copying the Roman writers,
adopted their expressions in regard to the relative positions of
places.

(g) Richborough, Kent.   (h) Boulogne.

estimated at three hundred miles; but with more truth by Bede at two hundred, exclusive of the promontories (i). If their sinuosities be taken into the computation, its circuit will be three thousand six hundred miles. Marcian, a Greek author, agrees with me in stating it at MDIↃↃLXXV (j).

CHAPTER II.

1. ALBION, called by Chrysostom Great Britain, is, according to Cæsar, of a triangular shape, resembling Sicily. One of the sides lies opposite to Celtic Gaul. One angle of this side, which is the Cantian promon- <small>North Foreland.</small> tory (k), is situated to the east; the other, the Ocrinian <small>Lizard Point.</small> promontory (l), in the country of the Damnonii, faces the south, and the province of Tarraconensis in Spain. This side is about five hundred miles in length.

2. Another side stretches towards Ireland, and the west, the length of which, according to the opinion of the ancients, is seven hundred miles.

3. The third side is situated to the north, and is opposite to no land except a few islands (m); but the angle of this side chiefly trends towards Germania Magna (n). The length from the Novantian Chersonesus (o), through <small>Rens of Galloway.</small>

(i) Richard errs in supposing the estimation of Bede more accurate than that of Agrippa.

(j) The numerals are here so incorrect that it is difficult to discover what number was meant by Richard. Marcian observes that the circuit of our island is not more than 28604 stadia, or 3575 miles, nor less than 20526, or 2576 miles. Hence Bertram is led to prefer the greater number.

(k) North Foreland.   (l) Lizard Point.

(m) The Orkney and Shetland isles.

(n) Under this name the ancients comprised not only Germany proper, but Denmark, Norway, &c.

(o) Rens of Galloway.

the country of the Taixali, to the Cantian promontory (*p*) is estimated at eight hundred miles. Thus all erroneously compute the circuit of the island to be two thousand miles; for from the Cantian promontory to Ocrinum (*q*), the distance is four hundred miles; from thence to Novantum, a thousand; and from thence to the Cantian promontory, two thousand two hundred. The circuit of the whole island is therefore three thousand six hundred miles (*r*).

4. Livy and Fabius Rusticus compare the form of Britain to an oblong shield or battle-axe; and as according to Tacitus it bears that figure on the side of Caledonia, the comparison was extended to the whole island, though the bold promontories at its further extremity give it the shape of a wedge. But Cæsar and Pomponius Mela assert that its form is triangular.

5. If credit may be given to the celebrated geographer Ptolemy and his contemporary writers, the island resembles an inverted Z (*s*); but according to the maps the comparison is not exact. The triangular shape, however, seems to belong to England alone (*t*).

(*p*) North Foreland.   (*q*) Lizard Point.

(*r*) Bertram has endeavoured to reconcile the various and discordant calculations given by different ancient authors of the circuit of our island. On such vague principles as these estimations are made, it would be almost impossible, even now, for two persons to produce the same result.

(*s*) Ptolemy's expression is obscure: but he was evidently led to this supposition by the notion that Caledonia or Scotland trended to the east, as appears from his latitudes and longitudes. This form, therefore, he not unaptly compares to the inverted Z. It would be a trespass on the patience of the reader to attempt to reconcile what is irreconcileable.

(*t*) These words are chiefly taken from Tacitus. The obscurity of the expression, and the absurdity of the comparison, will sufficiently show the ignorance of those ancients whose works have reached the present time, in regard to our island.—*Tacit. Vit. Agricolæ, sect.* 10.

CHAPTER III.

1. THE original inhabitants of Britain, whether indi- Original in-
genous or foreign, are, like those of most other countries, habitants.
unknown. The Jews alone, and by their means the
contiguous nations, have the happiness of tracing their
descent since the creation of the world from undoubted
documents.

2. From the difference of personal appearance different conjectures have been drawn. The red hair and
large limbs of the Caledonians proclaim their German
origin ; the painted faces and curled locks of the Silures,
and their situation opposite to Spain, corroborate the
assertion of Tacitus, that the ancient Iberians passed
over, and occupied this country and Ireland. Those
who live nearest the Gauls resemble them, either from
the strength of the original stock, or from the effects
which the same positions of the heavens produce on the
human body.

3. If I were inclined to indulge a conjecture, I might Venetians.
here mention that the Veneti (*u*) in their commercial ex-
peditions first introduced inhabitants and religion into
this country. Writers are not wanting, who assert that
Hercules came hither and established a sovereignty. But
it is needless to dwell on such remote antiquities and
idle tales (*v*).

(*u*) The Veneti, a tribe seated on the coast of Armorica or Bretagne, distinguished for their maritime power, and with whom
Cæsar waged war. Their territory, according to his description,
was part of Celtic Gaul, and the present Vannes was their capital.

(*v*) To these conjectures relative to the original inhabitants, and
subsequent colonists of Britain, it may not be uninteresting to add
the accounts preserved in the Welsh Triads.

The historical Triads record that the first colonists of Britain
were *Cymry*, who originally came from *Defrobani Gwlad Yr Hav*,

Gauls.

4. On the whole, however, it is probable that the Gauls occupied the contiguous regions. According to Tacitus, their sacred rites and superstitions may be traced ; nor is the language very different ; and lastly, the tradition of the druids, with the names of the states which still retain the same appellations as the people sprung from the cities of Gaul, who came hither and began to cultivate the country (*w*).

5. According to Cæsar, the country was extremely populous, and contained numerous buildings, not dissimilar to those of the Gauls. It was rich in cattle.

6. The inhabitants of the southern part were the most civilized, and in their customs differed little from the Gauls. Those of the more distant parts did not raise corn ; but lived on fruits and flesh. They were ignorant of the use of wool and garments, although in severe

---

the summer land, or Tauric Chersonesus. There they have left many traces of their name preserved by ancient authors, among which we may instance the *Cimmerian* Bosphorus.

Subsequent colonists arrived from the neighbouring continent at various times. The *Loegrwys* (Loegrians) from Gascogne ; the *Brython* from *Lydaw* (Britanny), who were descended from the original stock of the *Cymry*. Two descents are also mentioned in Alban, or North Britain ; one called the tribe of *Celyddon*, the other the primitive *Gwyddelians*. Another descent is said to have been made in the south, in *Ynys Wyth*, or the Isle of Wight, by the men of *Galedin* (the Belgæ), when their native country was inundated. Another colony called the *Corani* came from the country of the *Pwyl*, and settled on the sea coast, about the river Humber. A descent in Alban, or North Britain, of a colony of *Gwyddelian Ffçti*, who are described as coming from the sea of *Loçlyn* (the Baltic) ; and a partial settlement of the men of *Loçlyn* (Scandinavians), who were expelled after remaining for three generations.

The arrival of the Romans and Saxons is also mentioned, as well as some partial settlements of the Gwyddelians from Ireland.

(*w*) We discover a few cities in Gaul, bearing nearly the same appellations as those of Britain ; and in both countries we find the Atrebates, the Morini, the Ædui, the Serones, the Menapii, and the Rhemi.

weather they covered themselves with the skins of sheep or deer. They were accustomed to bathe in the rivers.

7. All the Britons formerly stained their bodies of a blue colour, which according to Cæsar gave them a more terrible appearance in battle. They wore their hair long, and shaved all parts of the body except the head and the upper lip.

8. Ten or twelve Britons had their wives in common; and this custom particularly prevailed among brethren, and between fathers and sons; but the children were considered as belonging to him who had first taken the virgin to wife. The mothers suckled their own children, and did not employ maids and nurses.

9. According to Cæsar also they used brass money, and iron rings of a certain weight instead of coin (x).

10. The Britons deemed it unlawful to eat hares (y), fowls, or geese; but they kept those animals for pleasure.

11. They had pearls, bits made of ivory, bracelets, vessels of amber and glass, agates, and, what surpasses all, great abundance of tin.

12. They navigated in barks, the keels and ribs of which were formed of light materials; the other parts were made of wicker and covered with the hides of oxen (z). During their voyages, as Solinus asserts, they abstain from food (a).

(x) The natives of China and Japan follow a similar custom in regard to gold and silver, which are not coined, but pass according to weight.

(y) It seems that they considered the appearance of a hare a fortunate omen; for the Roman historians observe that Boadicea, after haranguing her troops, let loose a hare which she had concealed in her garments.

(z) This species of boat is still used on the Welsh rivers, and is called a coricle in English, and cwm in Welsh. It is so light that a man may carry one on his back.

(a) Richard has mistaken the sense of Solinus, who, in describing the passage from Great Britain to Ireland, observes that from its shortness they abstained from food. " Navigantes escis abstinent, pro freti latitudine." C. 25.

Military af-
fairs.
13. Britain produces people and kings of people, as
Pomponius Mela writes in his third book; but they are
all uncivilized, and in proportion as they are more distant
from the continent, are more ignorant of riches; their
wealth consisting chiefly in cattle and land. They are
addicted to litigation and war, and frequently attack each
other, from a desire of command, and of enlarging their
possessions. It is customary indeed for the Britons to
wage war under the guidance of women, and not to regard the difference of sex in the distribution of power.

14. The Britons not only fought on foot and on horseback, but in chariots drawn by two horses, and armed in
the Gallic manner. Those chariots, to the axle-trees of
which scythes were fixed, were called *covini*, or wains.

15. Cæsar relates that they employed cavalry in their
wars, which before the coming of the Romans were almost perpetual. All were skilled in war; each in proportion to his family and wealth supported a number of
retainers, and this was the only species of honour with
which they were acquainted (*b*).

16. The principal strength of the Britons was in their
infantry, who fought with darts, large swords, and short
targets. According to Tacitus, their swords were blunt
at the point.

17. Cæsar in his fourth book thus describes their mode
of fighting in that species of chariots called *essedæ* (*c*). At
first they drove through the army in all directions, hurling their darts; and, by the terror of the horses, and the

(*b*) In all periods the Britons seem to have been divided into numerous petty communities or states, headed by chiefs, who are here
dignified with the title of kings. From the jealousies and weakness
attending such a state of society, the island first became a prey to
the Romans, and afterwards to the Saxons; and when the Britons
had retired to the mountains of Wales, the same causes hastened
the annexation of their country to England.

(*c*) In the early ages chariots were universally used in war. In
the Scriptures they are frequently mentioned as forming the principal strength of an army; and the mode of fighting in chariots

noise of the wheels, generally threw the ranks of the
enemy into disorder. When they had penetrated between the troops of cavalry, they leaped from their chariots, and waged unequal war on foot. Meanwhile the
chariots were drawn up at a distance from the battle, and
placed in such a position, that if pressed by the enemy,
the warriors could effect a retreat to their own army.
They thus displayed the rapid evolutions of cavalry and
the firmness of infantry, and were so expert by exercise,
as to hold up the horses in steep descents, to check and
turn them suddenly at full speed, to run along the pole,
stand on the yoke, and then spring into the chariot.

18. The mode of fighting on horseback threatened
equal danger to those who gave way, or those who pur-
sued. They never engaged in close lines, but in scat-

among the Greeks and Trojans, according to the description of
Homer, was exactly similar to that of the Britons. The steeds of
his heroes were

> " Practised alike to stop, to turn, to chase,
>   To dare the shock, or urge the rapid race."

His warriors sometimes drive through the ranks of the enemy,
sometimes fight from their chariots, and sometimes alight and maintain the combat on foot, while their chariots retire to the rear.

> " This counsel pleased, the godlike Hector sprung
>   Swift from his seat; his clanging armour rung.
>   The chief's example follow'd by his train,
>   Each quits his car and issues on the plain ;
>   By orders strict the charioteers enjoin'd
>   Compel the coursers to their ranks behind."

The Britons, however, appear to have devised an improvement
in this mode of warfare, which was unknown to the Greeks. Their
chariots seem to have been of two kinds, the *covini* or wains, heavy
and armed with scythes, to break the thickest order of the enemy ;
and the *essedæ*, a lighter kind, adapted probably to situations and
circumstances in which the *covini* could not act, and occasionally
performing the duties of cavalry. The *essedæ*, with the cavalry,
were pushed forward to oppose the first landing of Cæsar ; and
Cassivellaunus afterwards left 4000 *essedæ* as a corps of observation to watch his movements.—*Cæsar. Comment. lib.* 5. § 15.

tered bodies, and with great intervals; they had their appointed stations, and relieved each other by turns; and fresh combatants succeeded those who were fatigued. The cavalry also used darts.

Government.   19. It is not easy to determine the form of government in Britain previous to the coming of the Romans. It is however certain that before their times there was no vestige of a monarchy, but rather of a democracy, unless perhaps it may seem to have resembled an aristocracy (d). The authority of the druids in affairs of the greatest moment was considerable. Some chiefs are commemorated in their ancient records, yet these appear to have possessed no permanent power; but to have been created, like the Roman dictators, in times of imminent danger. Nor are instances wanting among them, as among other brave nations, when they chose even the leader of their adversaries to conduct their armies. He, therefore, who before was their enemy, afterwards fought on their side.

20. The Britons exceeded in stature both the Gauls and the Romans. Strabo affirms that he saw at Rome some British youths, who were considerably taller than the Romans.

Ornaments.   21. The more wealthy inhabitants of South Britain were accustomed to ornament the middle finger of the

---

(d) The government of the ancient Britons may be denominated patriarchal. Each community was governed by its elders; and every individual who could not prove his kindred to some community, through nine descents, and the same number of collateral affinities, was not considered as a freeman. Beyond this degree of kindred, they were formed into new communities. The elders of the different communities were subordinate to the elders of the tribes. But in times of public danger, as is recorded in the Triads, some chief of distinguished abilities was intrusted with the supreme authority over the tribes or communities, who united in common defence.—Such were Caswallon (Cassivellaunus), Caradwg (Caractacus), and Owain, son of Maesen.

left hand with a gold ring; but a gold collar (e) round the neck was the distinguishing mark of eminence. Those of the northern regions, who were the indigenous inhabitants of the island from time immemorial, were almost wholly ignorant of the use of clothes, and surrounded their waists and necks, as Herodian reports, with iron rings, which they considered as ornaments and proofs of wealth. They carried a narrow shield, fitter for use than ornament, and a lance, with a sword pendant from their naked and painted bodies. They rejected or despised the breast-plate and helmet, because such armour impeded their passage through the marshes.

22. Among other particulars, this custom prevailed in Britain. They stopped travellers and merchants, and compelled them to relate what they had heard, or

(e) This *torques,* chain, or rather wreath, is frequently alluded to by the early British bards.

> " Yet in the battle of Arderydd I wore the *golden torques.*"
> *Merddin Avellanaw.*

> " Four and twenty sons I have had
> Wearing the *golden wreath,* leaders of armies."
> *Llywarch Hên.*

> " Of all who went to Cattraeth, wearing the *golden torc or wreath.*"
> *Aneurin.*

The same bard states that in the battle of Cattraeth were three hundred and sixty who wore the *golden torques.*

We give a description of one of these ornaments found near the castle of Harlech, in Merionethshire, in 1692. " It is a wreathed bar of gold, or perhaps three or four rods jointly twisted, about four feet long, but naturally bending only one way, in the form of a hatband. It is hooked at both ends. It is of a round form, about an inch in circumference, and weighs eight ounces."—*Gibson's Camden,* p. 658.

Another mark of dignity was a string of amber beads worn round the head. To this Aneurin alludes—

> " With wreaths of *amber* twined round his temples."

These beads have been frequently found in tumuli, particularly in those on Salisbury Plain.—See *Turner's Vindication of the Welsh Bards.—Owen's Elegies of Llywarch Hên.*

knew, worthy of notice. The common people usually surrounded foreign merchants in the towns, and obliged them to tell from whence they came, and what curious things they had observed. On such vague reports they often rashly acted, and thus were generally deceived; for many answered them agreeably to their desires with fictitious stories (*f*).

Burial.   23. Their interments were magnificent; and all things which they prized during life, even arms and animals, were thrown into the funeral pile. A heap of earth and turf formed the sepulchre (*g*).

(*f*) This is Cæsar's account of a Gallic custom; but it is applied, not without reason, to the Britons, and indeed is equally applicable to all uncivilized people.

(*g*) As the classic authors have left us no description of the modes of interment among the Britons, Richard was induced, by the conformity of their manners and customs to those of the Gauls, to adopt the words used by Cæsar in his account of the Gallic funerals. Unfortunately the remains of the British bards afford little assistance in supplying this deficiency. It appears however that the Britons raised tumuli over their dead, and continued the practice till after the introduction of Christianity; and that their other modes of interment were the *carned*, or heap of stones; the *cistvaen*, or stone chest; and perhaps the *cromleç*, or hanging stone. From a curious fragment commemorating the graves of the British warriors, which is printed in the first volume of the Welch Archæology, we learn further, that they buried their dead on the tops of hills and lofty cliffs, on declivities, in heaths and secluded valleys, on the banks and near the fords of rivers, and on the sea-shore "where the ninth wave breaks." Allusions are also made to corresponding stones raised on these graves; and it is said, "the *long* graves in Gwanas, no one knows to whom they belong nor what is their history."

As the modes of interment among all early nations were in many respects similar, there is perhaps no part of our national antiquities which has given scope to so much conjecture as this. The reader who is desirous of more particular information relative to this subject, may at least find amusement in consulting the works of Stukeley, Douglas's *Nenia Britannica*, the *Archæologia*, and various accounts scattered in different periodical publications.

CHAPTER IV.

1. ALL the Britons, like the Gauls, were much addicted to superstitious ceremonies; and those who
laboured under severe disorders, or were exposed to the
dangers of war, either offered human victims, or made
a vow to perform such a sacrifice.

2. The druids were employed in the performance of
these cruel rites; and they believed that the gods could
not be appeased unless the life of a man was ransomed
with human blood.   Hence arose the public institution
of such sacrifices; and those who had been surprised in
theft, robbery, or any other delinquency, were considered
as the most acceptable victims.   But when criminals
could not be obtained, even the innocent were put to
death, that the gods might be appeased.

3. The sacred ceremonies could not be performed
except in the presence of the druids; and on them de-
volved the office of providing for the public as well as
private rites.   They were the guardians of religion and
the interpreters of mysteries; and being skilled in
medicine, were consulted for the preservation or restoration of health.

4. Among their gods, the principal object of their
worship was Mercury (h).   Next to him they adored Justice (under the name of Astarte), then Apollo, and

(h) This passage has puzzled the British antiquaries, because it
militates against the grand principle of the druidic theology, and
· because, as they assert, no traces of the Greek or Roman deities are
found among the early Britons.   Possibly some of the British
tribes might have brought this mode of worship from Gaul; but
more probably the assertion was derived from the misconception
of the ancient authors themselves, who gave the names of their
own deities to the objects of adoration distinguished by similar
attributes in other countries.   The account is borrowed from
Cæsar's description of the Gauls, lib. vi. § 15.

H

Mars (who was called Vitucadrus), Jupiter, Minerva, Hercules, Victory (called Andate), Diana, Cybele, and Pluto. Of these deities they held the same opinions as other nations.

5. The Britons, like the Gauls, endeavoured to derive their origin from Dis or Pluto, boasting of this ancient tradition of the druids. For this reason they divided time, not by the number of days, but of nights, and thus distinguished the commencement of the month, and the time of their birth. This custom agrees with the ancient mode of computation adopted in Genesis, chapter i. (*i*).

Druids.

6. The druids, being held in high veneration, were greatly followed by the young men for the sake of their instructions. They decided almost all public and private controversies, and determined disputes relative to inheritance or the boundaries of lands. They decreed rewards and punishments, and enforced their decisions by an exclusion from the sacrifices. This exclusion was deemed the severest punishment; because the interdicted, being deemed impious and wicked, were shunned as if contagious; justice was refused to their supplications, and they were allowed no marks of honour (*k*).

· 7. Over the druids presided a chief, vested with supreme authority. At his death he was succeeded by the next in dignity; but if there were several of equal rank, the contest was decided by the suffrages of their body; and sometimes they even contended in arms for this honour (*l*).

(*i*) " And the *evening* and the morning were the first day," &c. ver. 5. We also still say a se'n*night*, a fort*night*.

(*k*) Like the excommunication of the Catholic church.

(*l*) Such a custom would contravene the principles of the druidic or bardic system, which prohibited them from using arms. The remark seems to have been extended to a general application by Richard, from a single instance recorded by Cæsar, of a druidic election in Gaul thus decided.

8. The druids went not to war, paid no tribute like the rest of the people, were exempted from military duties, and enjoyed immunities in all things. From these high privileges many either voluntarily entered into their order, or were placed in it by friends or parents.

9. They learnt a number of verses, which were the only kind of memorials or annals in use among them (*m*). Some persons accordingly remained twenty years under

(*m*) According to the opinion of the Welsh antiquaries, the system of druidical knowledge forms the basis of the Triads. If this be the case, it must be confessed that the bards possessed a profound knowledge of human nature, uncommon critical sagacity, and a perfect acquaintance with the harmony of language and the properties of metre. For example, the subjects of the poetical Triads are,

> The Welsh language.
> Fancy and invention.
> The design of poetry.
> Nature of just thinking.
> Rules of arrangement.
> Rules of description.
> Variety of matter and invention.
> Rules of composition; comprising the laws of verse, rhyme, stanzas, consonancy or alliteration, and accent.

We quote a few of these Triads to show their nature and structure.

The three qualifications of poetry;—endowment of genius, judgment from experience, and happiness of mind.

The three foundations of judgment;—bold design, frequent practice, and frequent mistakes.

The three foundations of learning;—seeing much, suffering much, and studying much.

The three foundations of happiness;—a suffering with contentment, a hope that it will come, and a belief that it will be.

The three foundations of thought;—perspicuity, amplitude, and justness.

The three canons of perspicuity;—the word that is necessary, the quantity that is necessary, and the manner that is necessary.

The three canons of amplitude;—appropriate thought, variety of thought, and requisite thought.

their instruction, which they did not deem it lawful to commit to writing, though on other subjects they employed the Greek alphabet. "This custom," to use the words of Julius Cæsar, "seems to have been adopted for two reasons: first, not to expose their doctrines to the common people; and, secondly, lest their scholars, trusting to letters, should be less anxious to remember their precepts; for such assistance commonly diminishes application, and weakens the memory."

Transmigration of souls. 10. In the first place they circulated the doctrine that souls do not die, but migrate into other bodies (n). By this principle they hoped men would be more powerfully actuated to virtue, and delivered from the fear of death. They likewise instructed students in the knowledge of the heavenly bodies, in geography, the nature of things, and the power of the gods (o).

11. Their admiration of the mistletoe must not be

(n) According to the Triads, the theology of the bards was pure monotheism. They taught also the transmigration of souls; believing that the soul passed by death through all the gradations of animal life, from Anoom, the bottomless abyss, or lowest degree of animation, up to the highest degree of spiritual existence next to the Supreme Being. Human nature was considered as the middle point of this scale. As this was a state of liberty, in which the soul could attach itself to either good or evil; if evil predominated, it was after death obliged to retrace its former transmigrations from a point in the animal creation equal to its turpitude, and it again and again became man till it was attached to good. Above humanity, though it might again animate the body of man, it was incapable of relapse; but continued progressively rising to a degree of goodness and happiness, inferior only to the Deity.

It is remarkable that many singular points of coincidence have been discovered in comparing the religious system of the Hindoos with that of the ancient Britons; and in the languages of these two people some striking similarities occur in those proverbs and forms of expression which are derived from national customs and religious ceremonies.

(o) This account of the druids, like some of the preceding paragraphs, is borrowed from Cæsar's description of the Gauls.

omitted. The druids esteemed nothing more sacred than the mistletoe, and the tree on which it grew, if an oak. They particularly delighted in groves of oaks (*p*), and performed no sacred rite without branches of that tree, and hence seem to have derived their name of druids, Δρυιδες. Whatever grew on an oak was considered as sent from Heaven, and as a sign that the tree was chosen by God himself. The mistletoe was difficult to be found, and when discovered was gathered with religious ceremonies, particularly at the sixth day of the moon (from which period they dated their months and years, and their cycle of thirty years), because the moon was supposed to possess extraordinary powers when she had not completed her second quarter. The mistletoe was called in their language *all heal* (*q*). The sacrifice and the feast being duly prepared under the tree, they led thither two white bulls, whose horns were then bound for the first time (*r*). The priest, clothed in a white vestment, ascending the tree, cut off the mistletoe with a golden bill, and received it in a white cloth. They then slew the victims, invoking the favour of the Deity on their offering. They conceived that the mistletoe cured sterility in animals; and considered it as a specific against all poisons. So great was

(*p*) Gen. ch. xxi. ver. 33.

(*q*) This remark is erroneous. The term *holbiaç, all heal,* is applied to the plant which bears the same name in English. The mistletoe is called in Welsh by the several appellations, Gurgon, Uçelvan, Prenawyn, Uçelwydd.

(*r*) As the plough was fastened to the horns of the beasts, this expression signifies that the animal had never been employed in labour.

It is a singular coincidence of circumstances that bulls perfectly white were sacrificed by the Egyptians to Apis. When such an animal was found unblemished, and without a single black hair, the priest tied a fillet about his horns, and sealed it with the signet of his ring; it being a capital crime to sacrifice one of these animals except it was thus marked.—*Herodotus.*

the superstition generally prevailing among nations with respect to frivolous objects.

12. The doctrine of the druids is said to have been first invented in Britain, and from thence carried into Gaul; on which account Pliny says (in his thirtieth book), " But why should I commemorate these things with regard to an art which has passed over the sea, and reached the bounds of nature? Britain even at this time celebrates it with so many wonderful ceremonies, that she seems to have taught it to the Persians." Julius Cæsar affirms the same in his Commentaries : " And now those persons who wish to acquire a more extensive knowledge of such things, repair to Britain for information."

13. At a certain time of the year the druids retired to a consecrated grove in the island of Mona, whither all persons among whom controversies had arisen, repaired for the decision of their disputes.

Bards. 14. Besides the druids, there were among the Gauls and Britons poets called bards (s), who sung in heroic measures the deeds of the gods and heroes, accompanied with the sweet notes of the lyre.

15. Concerning the druids and bards, I shall conclude this chapter in the words of Lucan :—

> " You too, ye bards! whom sacred raptures fire,
> To chant your heroes to your country's lyre ;
> Who consecrate, in your immortal strain,
> Brave patriot souls, in righteous battle slain,
> Securely now the tuneful task renew,
> And noblest themes in deathless songs pursue.

(s) According to the Welsh antiquaries, these distinctions are erroneous. The druidical, or rather bardic, system consisted of three classes : the bard proper, whose province was philosophy and poetry ; the druid, or minister of religion ; and the ovate, or mechanic and artist. For a curious account of the bardic system and institutions, the reader is referred to the Introduction to Owen's Translations of the Elegies of Llywarch Hên.

The druids now, while arms are heard no more,
Old mysteries and barbarous rites restore,
A tribe who singular religion love,
And haunt the lonely coverts of the grove.
To these, and these of all mankind alone,
The gods are sure revealed or sure unknown.
If dying mortals' doom they sing aright,
No ghosts descend to dwell in dreadful night;
No parting souls to grisly Pluto go,
Nor seek the dreary silent shades below;
But forth they fly immortal in their kind,
And other bodies in new worlds they find:
Thus life for ever runs its endless race,
And like a line death but divides the space,
A stop which can but for a moment last,
A point between the future and the past.
Thrice happy they beneath their northern skies,
Who that worst fear—the fear of death—despise;
Hence they no cares for this frail being feel,
But rush undaunted on the pointed steel;
Provoke approaching fate, and bravely scorn
To spare that life which must so soon return."

Rowe's Lucan, book i.

CHAPTER V.

1. THIS island is rich in corn and wood, is well Productions.
adapted for the maintenance of flocks and cattle, and
in some places produces vines. It also abounds with
marine and land birds, and contains copious springs, and
numerous rivers, stored with fish, and plentifully supplied with salmon and eels.

2. Sea-cows, or seals (*t*), and dolphins are caught, and
whales, of which mention is made by the satirist:

" Quanto delphinis balæna Britannica major."

(*t*) We do not find that Pennant mentions, among the amphibious
animals, the *Vituli Marini*, by which Richard probably meant seals.

3. There are besides several sorts of shellfish, among which are muscles, containing pearls often of the best kind, and of every colour: that is, red, purple, violet, green (*prasini*), but principally white, as we find in the venerable Bede's Ecclesiastical History.

4. Shells (*u*) are still more abundant, from which is prepared a scarlet dye of the most beautiful hue, which never fades from the effect of the sun or rain, but becomes finer as it grows older.

5. In Britain are salt and warm springs, from which are formed hot baths, suited to all ages, with distinct places for the two sexes (*v*).

6. White lead is found in the midland regions, and iron in the maritime, but in small quantities gold and silver are also produced, but brass is imported. Jet of the purest quality abounds; it is of a shining black, and highly inflammable (*w*). When burnt, it drives away serpents, and when warmed by friction attracts bodies like amber.

7. Britain being situated almost under the north pole, the nights are so light in summer, that it is often doubtful whether the evening or morning twilight prevails; because the sun, in returning to the east, does not long remain below the horizon. Hence, also, according to Cleomenes, the longest day in summer, and the longest night in winter, when the sun declines towards the south, is eighteen hours; and the shortest night in summer,

(*u*) Richard calls these shells *Cochleæ*, or snails, though he probably alludes to the species styled by naturalists *Murea*, which contained the famous Tyrian purple, so much valued by the ancients. Yet, whatever our island may have formerly produced, we discern no traces, in later ages, of any testaceous animal yielding a purple or scarlet dye.

(*v*) Richard here doubtless principally alludes to Bath, the Aquæ Solis of the ancients.

(*w*) This substance appears to have been wrought into ornaments for the person. In the barrows, jet heads of a long elliptical form were found, together with others of amber, and a coarse blue glass.

and day in winter, is six hours. In the same manner as in Armenia, Macedon, Italy, and the regions under the same parallel, the longest day is fifteen, and the shortest nine hours.

8. But I have given a sufficient account of Britain and the Britons in general. I shall now descend to particulars; and, in the succeeding pages, shall describe the state and revolutions of the different nations who inhabited this island, the cities which ennobled it, with other particulars, and their condition under the Roman dominion.

CHAPTER VI.

1. BRITAIN, according to the most accurate and authentic accounts of the ancients, was divided into seven parts, six of which were at different times subjected to the Roman empire, and the seventh held by the uncivilized Caledonians. Divisions.

2. These divisions were called Britannia Prima, Secunda, Flavia, Maxima, Valentia, and Vespasiana, which last did not long remain under the power of the Romans. Britannia Prima is separated by the river Thamesis from Flavia, and by the sea (x) from Britannia Secunda. Flavia begins from the German Ocean, is bounded by the Thamesis (y), by the Sabrina (z) on the side of the Silures and Ordovices, and trends toward the north and the region of the Brigantes (a). Maxima, beginning at the extreme boundary of Flavia, reaches

(x) Rather by the æstuary of the Severn.
(y) Thames.   (z) Severn.
(a) Here some word is evidently omitted in the original. We would supply it by comparing this description with that of Britannia Secunda in the second section, and read " *Sabrina et Deva*," &c., " by the Severn and the Dee from the Silures and Ordovices."

to the wall (*b*) which traverses the whole island, and faces the north.   Valentia occupies the whole space between this wall and that built by the emperor Antoninus Pius, from the æstuary of the Bdora (*c*) to that of the Clydda (*d*). Vespasiana stretches from the æstuary of the Bdora to the city of Alcuith (*e*), from whence a line drawn to the mouth of the Varar (*f*) shows the boundary.   Britannia Secunda faces the Irish Sea to the north and west.   But sufficient notice has been taken of the provinces.

3. Before we proceed to a more minute description, let us touch upon the form of government.   In remote times all Britain was divided among petty princes and states, some of whom are said to have existed after the country was occupied by the Romans ; though under the Roman domination they retained scarcely the shadow of regal authority.   A legate being appointed by the emperor over the conquered countries, Britain became a proconsular province.   This form of government continued several ages, although in the mean time the island underwent many divisions, first into the Upper and Lower districts, and then, as we have before shown, into seven parts.   It afterwards became the imperial residence of Carausius and those whom he admitted to a share of his power.   Constantine the Great, the glory and defence of Christianity, is supposed to have raised Maxima and Valentia to consular provinces, and Prima, Secunda, and Flavia, to præsidials.   But over the whole island was appointed a deputy governor, under the authority of the prætorian prefect of Gaul.   Besides whom, an ancient volume, written about that period, mentions a person of great dignity, by the title of *comes* or count of the Britons, another as count of the Saxon coast, and a third as leader or duke of Britain ; with

(*b*) The wall or vallum erected by Severus between the Solway Frith and the mouth of the Tyne.

(*c*) Bodora and Bodotria, Frith of Forth.

(*d*) Clotta. Clyde.   (*e*) Dumbarton.   (*f*) Murray Frith.

many others, who, although possessed of great offices, must be passed over in silence, for want of certain information (g).

4. I now commence my long journey, to examine minutely the whole island and its particular parts, and shall follow the footsteps of the best authors. I begin with the extreme part of the first province, whose coasts are opposite Gaul. This province contains three celebrated and powerful states, namely, Cantium, Belgium, and Damnonium, each of which in particular I shall carefully examine.

First of Cantium.

5. Cantium (h), situated at the eastern extremity of Kent. Britannia Prima, was inhabited by the Cantii, and contains the cities of Durobrobis (i) and Cantiopolis (k), which was the metropolis, and the burial-place of St. Augustin, the apostle of the English; Dubræ (l), Lemanus (m), and Regulbium (n), garrisoned by the Romans; also their primary station Rhutupis (o), which was colonized and became the metropolis, and where a haven was formed capable of containing the Roman fleet which commanded the North Sea. This city was of such celebrity that it gave the name of Rhutupine to the neighbouring shores; of which Lucan,

" Aut vaga cum Thetis Rhutupinaque littora fervent."

From hence oysters of a large size and superior flavour were sent to Rome, as Juvenal observes,

" ——————————— Circæis nata forent, an
Lucrinum ad saxum, Rhutupinove edita fundo
Ostrea, callebat primo deprendere morsu."

(g) These remarks seem to have been drawn from the *Notitia Imperii;* and consequently refer to a late period of the empire.;

(h) Cantium contained the present county of Kent, as far as the Rother, except a small district in which Holwood Hill is situated, and which belonged to the Rhem.

(i) Rochester.　　　　　　(k) Canterbury.
(l) Dover.　　　　　　　(m) Situated on the Lymne.
(n) Reculver.　　　　　　(o) Richborough.

It was the station of the second Augustan legion, under the count of the Saxon coast, a person of high distinction.

6. The kingdom of Cantium is watered by many rivers. The principal are Madus (*p*), Sturius (*q*), Dubris (*r*), and Lemanus (*s*), which last separates the Cantii from the Bibroci.

7. Among the three principal promontories of Britain, that which derives its name from Cantium (*t*) is most distinguished. There the ocean, being confined in an angle, according to the tradition of the ancients, gradually forced its way, and formed the strait which renders Britain an island.

8. The vast forest called by some the Anderidan, and by others the Caledonian, stretches from Cantium an hundred and fifty miles, through the countries of the Bibroci and the Segontiaci, to the confines of the Hedui. It is thus mentioned by the poet Lucan :—

" Unde Caledoniis fallit turbata Britannos."

Bibrocum.   9. The Bibroci (*u*) were situated next to the Cantii, and, as some imagine, were subject to them. They were also called Rhemi, and are not unknown in record. They inhabited Bibrocum (*v*), Regentium (*w*), and Noviomagus (*x*), which was their metropolis. The Romans held Anderida (*y*).

Attrebates.   10. On their confines, and bordering on the Thames, dwelt the Attrebates (*z*), whose primary city was Calleba (*a*).

(*p*) The Medway.
(*q*) The Stour.
(*r*) A rivulet at Dover.
(*s*) The Rother.
(*t*) The North Foreland.
(*u*) The Bibroci, Rhemi, or Regni, inhabited part of Hants, and of Berks, Sussex, Surrey, and a small portion of Kent.
(*v*) Uncertain. Stukeley calls it Bibrox, Bibrax, or the Bibracte of the Itinerary.
(*w*) Chichester.
(*x*) Holwood Hill.
(*y*) Pevensey.
(*z*) Part of Hants, and Berks.
(*a*) Silchester. For the proofs that this place was the site of Calleva, see the Commentary on the Itinerary.

11. Below them, nearer the river Kunetius (*b*), lived _{Segontiaci.} the Segontiaci (*c*), whose chief city was Vindonum (*d*).

12. Below, towards the ocean, and bordering on the _{Belgæ.} Bibroci, lived the Belgæ (*e*), whose chief cities were Clausentum (*f*), now called Southampton ; Portus Magnus (*g*) ; Venta (*h*), a noble city situated upon the river Antona. Sorbiodunum (*i*) was garrisoned by the Romans. All the Belgæ are Allobroges, or foreigners, and derived their origin from the Belgæ and Celts. The latter, not many ages before the arrival of Cæsar, quitted their native country, Gaul, which was conquered by the Romans and Germans, and passed over to this island : the former, after crossing the Rhine, and occupying the conquered country, likewise sent out colonies, of which Cæsar has spoken more at large (*j*).

13. All the regions south of the Thamesis (*k*) were, according to ancient records, occupied by the warlike nation of the Senones. These people, under the guidance _{Senones.} of their renowned king Brennus, penetrated through Gaul, forced a passage over the Alps, hitherto deemed impracticable, and would have razed proud Rome, had not the Fates, which seemed like to carry the Republic in their bosom, till it reached its destined height of glory, averted the threatened calamity. By the cackle of a goose Manlius was warned of the danger, and hurled the barbarians from the Capitol, in their midnight attack. The same protecting influence after-

(*b*) Kennet.   (*c*) Part of Hants, and Berks.
(*d*) Probably Egbury Camp.
(*e*) The Belgæ occupied those parts of Hants and Wilts not held by the Segontiaci.
(*f*) This is an error : the ancient Clausentum was at Bittern, on the Itchin, opposite Northam.   (*g*) Portchester.
(*h*) Winchester.   (*i*) Old Sarum.
(*j*) This passage as printed in the original is very obscure ; but the meaning is supplied by Cæsar, from whom it is taken, and a subsequent page where Richard mentions the same fact.—*Vide the Chronology in b. 2. c. i. sect.* 9.   (*k*) Thames.

wards sent Camillus to his assistance, who, by assailing them in the rear, quenched the conflagration which they had kindled, in Senonic blood, and preserved the city from impending destruction. In consequence of this vast expedition, the land of the Senones (*l*), being left without inhabitants, and full of spoils, was occupied by the above-mentioned Belgæ.

Hedui.

14. Near the Sabrina and below the Thamesis lived the Hedui (*m*), whose principal cities were Ischalis (*n*) and Avalonia (*o*). The Baths (*p*), which were also called Aquæ Solis, were made the seat of a colony, and became the perpetual residence of the Romans who possessed this part of Britain. This was a celebrated city, situated upon the river Abona, remarkable for its hot springs, which were formed into baths at a great expense. Apollo and Minerva (*q*) were the tutelary deities, in whose temples the perpetual fire never fell into ashes, but as it wasted away turned into globes of stone.

Morini.

15. Below the Hedui are situated the Durotriges, who are sometimes called Morini. Their metropolis was Durinum (*r*), and their territory extended to the promontory Vindelia (*s*). In their country the land is gradually contracted, and seems to form an immense arm which repels the waves of the ocean.

16. In this arm was the region of the Cimbri (*t*), whose country was divided from that of the Hedui by the river

---

(*l*) There was a tribe of Celts called Senones seated on the banks of the Seine as late as the time of Cæsar, and this was one of the tribes who marched with Brennus against Rome. But we cannot discover from whence Richard drew his information that these Senones originally emigrated from Britain, leaving their country to be occupied by the Belgæ.

(*m*) Nearly all Somersetshire.   (*n*) Ilchester.

(*o*) Glastonbury.   (*p*) Bath.

(*q*) This is drawn from Solinus, who speaks of Britain in general. We know not on what authority it was applied by Richard to Bath.

(*r*) Maiden Castle, near Dorchester.

(*s*) Isle of Portland.   (*t*) Part of Somerset and Devon.

Uxella (*u*). It is not ascertained whether the Cimbri
gave to Wales its modern name, or whether their origin
is more remote. Their chief cities were Termolus(*v*) and
Artavia(*w*). From hence, according to the ancients, are
seen the pillars of Hercules, and the island Herculea(*x*)
not far distant. From the Uxella a chain of mountains
called Ocrinum extends to the promontory known by the
same name.

17. Beyond the Cimbri the Carnabii inhabited the
extreme angle of the island (*y*), from whom this district
probably obtained its present name of Carnubia (Cornwall). Their chief cities were Musidum (*z*) and Halangium (*a*). But as the Romans never frequented these
almost desert and uncultivated parts of Britain, their
cities seem to have been of little consequence, and were
therefore neglected by historians ; though geographers
mention the promontories Bolerium and Antivestæum (*b*).

18. Near the above-mentioned people on the sea
coast towards the south, and bordering on the Belgæ
Allobroges, lived the Damnonii, the most powerful
people of those parts ; on which account Ptolemy
assigns to them all the country extending into the sea
like an arm(*c*). Their cities were Uxella(*d*), Tamara(*e*),
Voluba (*f*), Cenia (*g*), and Isca (*h*), the mother of
all, situated upon the Isca. Their chief rivers were
the Isca (*i*), Durius (*j*), Tamarus (*k*), and Cenius (*l*).

(*u*) The Parret.   (*v*) Uncertain,—probably in Devonshire.
(*w*) Ibid.   (*x*) Lundy Island.
(*y*) Part of Cornwall.   (*z*) Near Stratton.
(*a*) Carnbre.   (*b*) Land's End, and Lizard Point.
(*c*) Cornwall, Devon, Dorset, and part of Somerset.
(*d*) Probably near Bridgewater.   (*e*) On the Tamar.
(*f*) On the Fowey.   (*g*) On the Fal.
(*h*) Exeter.   (*i*) Ex.
(*j*) The Dart.   (*k*) Tamar.
(*l*) The Fal.

Their coasts are distinguished by three promontories, which will be hereafter mentioned. This region was much frequented by the Phœnicians, Grecians, and Gallic merchants, for the metals with which it abounded, particularly for its tin. Proofs of this may be drawn from the names of the above-mentioned promontories, namely Hellenis (*m*), Ocrinum (*n*), and Κριȣ μέτωπον (*o*), as well as the numerous appellations of cities, which show a Grecian or Phœnician derivation.

Sygdiles.

19. Beyond this arm are the isles called Sygdiles (*p*), which are also denominated Œstromenides and Cassiterides.

20. It is affirmed that the emperor Vespasian fought thirty battles with the united force of the Damnonii and Belgæ. The ten different tribes who inhabited the south banks of the Thames and Severn being gradually subdued, their country was formed into the province of Britannia Prima, so called because it was the first fruit of victory obtained by the Romans.

21. Next in order is Britannia Secunda, which is divided from Britannia Prima by the countries already mentioned, and from the Flavian province by the Sabrina (*q*) and the Deva (*r*) ; and the remaining parts are bounded by the internal sea. This was the renowned region of the Silures (*s*), inhabited by three powerful tribes.

Silures.

(*m*) Probably Berry Head.   (*n*) Lizard Point.
(*o*) Ram Head.   (*p*) Scilly Isles.
(*q*) Severn.   (*r*) Dee.

(*s*) The Silures, with their two dependent tribes, the Dimeciæ and the Ordovices, possessed all the country to the west of the Severn and the Dee, together with the island of Anglesey.

" Of these territories the Dimeciæ had the counties of Pembroke, Cardigan, and Caermarthen ; while the Silures possessed all the rest of South Wales, as well as such parts of England as lay to the west of the Severn and to the South of the Teme : while the Ordovices occupied all North Wales, as well as all the country to the north of the Teme, and to the west of the Severn and the Dee, except a small tract to the West of Bangor and Penmorvay, which

Among these were particularly distinguished the Silures Proper, whom the turbid æstuary of the Severn
divides from the country we have just described. These
people, according to Solinus, still retain their ancient
manners, have neither markets nor money, but barter
their commodities, regarding rather utility than price.
They worship the gods, and both men and women are
supposed to foretell future events.

22. The chief cities of the Silures were, Sariconium (*t*),
Magna (*u*), Gobaneum (*v*), and Venta (*w*) their capital.
A Roman colony possessed the city built on the Isca (*x*),
and called after that name, for many years the station
of the second or Augustan legion, until it was transferred
to the Valentian province, and Rhutupis (*y*). This was
the primary station of the Romans in Britannia Secunda.

23. The country of the Silures was long powerful,
particularly under Caractacus, who during nine years
withstood the Roman arms, and frequently triumphed
over them, until he was defeated by Ostorius, as he
was preparing to attack the Romans. Caractacus, however, escaped from the battle, and in applying for assistance to the neighbouring chieftains was delivered up to
the Romans, by the artifices of a Roman matron, Car-
thismandua, who had married Venutius, chief of Brigantia. After this defeat the Silures bravely defended
their country till it was overrun by Varonius, and being
finally conquered by Frontinus, it was reduced into a
Roman province under the name of Britannia Secunda.

24. Two other tribes were subject to the Silures.
First the Ordovices, who inhabited the north towards Ordovices.

together with the isle of Anglesey belonged to their subordinate
clan the Cangani."

(*t*) Rose or Berry Hill in Weston.   (*u*) Kentchester.
(*v*) Abergavenny.   (*w*) Caerwent.
(*x*) Caerleon, on Usk.   (*y*) Richborough in Kent.

I

Dimetæ.

the isle of Mona (z) ; and secondly the Dimeciæ, who occupied the west, where the promontory Octorupium (a) is situated, and from whence is a passage of thirty miles (b) to Ireland. The cities of the Dimeciæ were Menapia (c) and Muridunum (d) the metropolis. The Romans seized upon Lovantium (e) as their station. Beyond these, and the borders of the Silures, were the Ordovices, whose cities were Mediolanum (f) and Brannogenium (g). The Sabrina, which rises in their mountains, is justly reckoned one of the three largest rivers of Britain, the Thamesis (Thames) and the Tavus (Tay) being the other two. The name of the Ordovices is first distinguished in history on account of the revenge which they took for the captivity of their renowned chief. Hence they continually harassed the Roman army, and would have succeeded in annihilating their power, had not Agricola turned hither his victorious arms, subdued the whole nation, and put the greater part to the sword.

25. The territory situated north of the Ordovices, and washed by the ocean, was formerly under their dominion.

Cangiani.

These parts were certainly inhabited by the Cangiani, whose chief city was Segontium (h), near the Cangian promontory (i), on the Minevian shore, opposite Mona (j), an island long distinguished as the residence of the druids. This island contained many towns, though it was scarcely sixty miles in circuit; and, as Pliny asserts, is distant from the colony Camalodunum two hundred miles. The rivers of the Cangiani were Tosibus (k), called also Canovius, and the Deva (l), which was their boundary. In this region is the stupendous mountain

(z) Anglesey.	(a) St. David's Head.
(b) XXX milliarium.	(c) St. David's.
(d) Caermarthen.	(e) Llanio Issau on the Teivi.
(f) On the bank of the Tanat.	(g) Near Lentwardine.
(h) Caer Segont.	(i) Brach y Pwll Point.
(j) Anglesey.	(k) The Conway. (l) Dee.

Eriri (*m*). Ordovicia, together with the regions of the Cangiani and Carnabii, unless report deceives me, constituted a province called Genania, under the reign of the emperors subsequent to Trajan.

26. I now proceed to the Flavian province ; but for want of authentic documents am unable to ascertain, whether it derived its name from Flavia Julia Helena, mother of Constantine the Great, who was born in these parts, or from the Flavian family.

27. Towards the river Deva were situated in the first place the Carnabii (*n*).   Their principal places were Benonæ (*o*), Etocetum (*p*), and Banchorium (*q*), the last the *Carnabii.* most celebrated monastery in the whole island, which being overthrown in the dispute with Augustin, was never afterwards restored ; and the mother of the rest, Uriconium (*r*), esteemed one of the largest cities in Britain. In the extreme angle of this country, near the Deva, was the Roman colony Deva (*s*), the work of the twentieth legion, which was called Victrix, and was formerly the defence of the region.   This place is supposed to be what is now termed West Chester.

28. Below these people stretched the kingdom, or rather the republic, of the Cassii, called by Ptolemy Catieuchlani, which arose from the union of two nations. *Cassii, or* Those nearest the Sabrina were called the Dobuni, or, *Catieuchlani.* according to the annals of Dio, the Boduni (*t*). In their

(*m*) Snowdon.

(*n*) The territory of the Carnabii was bounded on the north by the Mersey, west by the Severn, east by part of the Watling Street, and to the south by Staffordshire.

(*o*) Benonis ; High Cross.   (*p*) Wall.

(*q*) Banchor.   (*r*) Wroxeter.   (*s*) Chester.

(*t*) The *Dobuni* were bounded on the west by the Severn, on the south by the Thames, on the east by the Charwell, and on the north by the Carnabii.

The *Cassii*, bounded on the south by the Thames, on the west by the Dobuni, on the east by the Trent, and on the north by the Iceni.

country the Thames rises, and, proceeding through the territories of the Hedui, Attrebates, Cassii, Bibroci, Trinobantes, and Cantii, after a long course flows into the German Ocean. The cities of the Dobuni were Salinæ (u), Branogena (v) on the left of the Sabrina (Severn), Alauna (w), and the most venerable of all, Corinium (x), a famous city supposed to have been built by Vespasian. But Glevum (y), situated in the extreme part of the kingdom, towards the territory of the Silures, was occupied by a Roman colony, which, according to the writers of those times, was introduced by Claudius Cæsar. Adjoining to these were the Cassii, whose chief cities were Forum Dianæ (z) and Verulamium (a). But when the last was raised by the Romans to the municipal rank, it obtained the pre-eminence over the other cities. St. Alban the martyr was here born. This city was involved in the ruin of Camalodunum (b), and Londinium (c) in the insurrection of Bonduica, which is related by Tacitus. The Cassii were conspicuous above the other nations of the island; and Cæsar in his second invasion had the severest conflicts with their renowned chief Cassibellinus, to whom many people were tributary; and was repulsed by the Cassii in league with the Silures; to which Lucan alludes :—" *Territa quæsitis ostendit terga Britannis.*" But on the coming of Claudius, they, with the neighbouring people, were subdued, and their country reduced to a Roman province, first called Cæsariensis, and afterwards Flavia.

Trinobantes.   29. Near the Cassii, where the river Thamesis approaches the ocean, was the region of the Trino-

(u) Droitwich.	(v) Near Lentwardine.
(w) Alcester.	(x) Cirencester in Glocestershire.
(y) Glocester.	(z) Dunstable.
(a) Old St. Alban's.	(b) Colchester.
(c) London.	

bantes (*d*), who not only entered into alliance with the Romans, but resigned to them Londinium their metropolis, and Camalodunum situated near the sea, for the purpose of establishing colonies. In this city was supposed to be born Flavia Julia Helena, the pious wife of Constantine Chlorus and mother of Constantine the Great, who was descended from the blood of the British kings. It was the chief colony of the Romans in Britain, and distinguished by a temple of Claudius, an image of Victory, with many ornaments (*e*). But Londinium was and ever will be a city of great eminence. It was first named Trinovantum, then Londinium, afterwards Augusta, and now again Londona. According to the chronicles it is more ancient than Rome. It is situated upon the banks of the Thamesis, and is the great emporium of many nations trading by land or sea. This city was surrounded with a wall by the empress Helena, the discoverer of the Holy Cross; and, if reliance may be placed on tradition, which is not always erroneous, was called Augusta, as Britain was distinguished by the name of the Roman Island.

30. The boundary of this people towards the north was the river Surius (*f*), beyond which lived the Iceni, a Iceni. famous people divided into two tribes. The first of these, the Cenomanni, dwelt to the north towards the Trinobantes and Cassii, and bordered on the ocean towards the east. Their cities were Durnomagus (*g*), and their metropolis Venta (*h*). Camboricum (*i*) was a Roman colony. A tongue of land stretching into the sea towards the east was called Flavia Extrema(*k*). Their most remarkable

(*d*) It stretched from the Thames to the Stour on the north, and on the west to the Brent and the Ouse.

(*e*) This temple with its ornaments is mentioned in Tacitus.

(*f*) Sturius, the Stour.   (*g*) Castor near Chesterton.

(*h*) Castor near Norwich.   (*i*) Cambridge.

(*k*) Part of the Suffolk coast.

rivers are the Garion (*l*), the Surius (*m*), and the Aufona (*n*) which falls into the bay of Metaris (*o*). Beyond the Aufona, bordering on the Carnabii, Brigantes, and the ocean, lived the Coitani (*p*), in a tract of country overspread with woods, which, like all the woods of Britain, was called Caledonia (*q*). This is mentioned by the historian Florus (*r*). The chief city of the Coitani was Ragæ (*s*). Besides this was Lindum (*t*), a Roman colony, on the eastern extremity of the province. The river Trivonia (*u*) divides the whole country into two parts. The nation of the Iceni, being of a warlike character, neglected husbandry as well as the civil arts; they voluntarily joined the Romans; but, revolting, and exciting others to follow their example, were first subdued by Ostorius. A few years afterwards, Præsutagus their king, at his decease, made Cæsar and his descendants his heirs. But the Romans, abusing the friendship of these people and giving themselves up to every species of debauchery, excited their resentment, and the Iceni with their allies, under the warlike Bonduica, widow of Præsutagus, destroyed their colonies, and massacred eighty thousand Roman citizens. They were afterwards reduced by the legate Suetonius, a man highly esteemed for prudence.

31. On the northern part of this region is the river Abus (*v*), which falls into the ocean, and was one of the boundaries of the province Maxima, as Seteja (*w*) was the other. This province was also called the kingdom of Bri-

---

(*l*) The Yar.   (*m*) The Stour.

(*n*) The Nen.   (*o*) Boston Deep.

(*p*) In the map these people are called the Coritani. They seem to have inhabited Lincoln, Leicester, and Nottingham.

(*q*) Calyddon means coverts or thickets.

(*r*) B. iii. ch. 10, where, speaking of Cæsar, he says, "Caledonias sequutus in sylvas."   (*s*) Leicester.

(*t*) Lincoln.   (*u*) Trent.

(*v*) The Humber.   (*w*) The Mersey.

gantia, because it comprehended the region of that name inhabited by three nations. At the eastern point (*x*), where the promontories of Oxellum (*y*) and of the Brigantes (*z*) stretch into the sea, lived the Parisii, whose cities were Petuaria (*a*) and Portus Felix (*b*). Parisii.

32. Above, but on the side of the Parisii, are the proper Brigantes (*c*), a numerous people who once gave law to the whole province. Their towns were Epiacum (*d*), Vinovium (*e*), Cambodunum (*f*), Cataracton (*g*), Galacum (*h*), Olicana (*i*), and the chief city Isurium (*j*). Eboracum (*k*), on the Urus (*l*), was the metropolis, first a colony of the Romans, called Sexta, from being the station of the sixth legion, termed the Victorious, and afterwards distinguished by the presence of many emperors, and raised to the privileges of a municipal city. Brigantes.

33. This province is divided into two equal parts by a chain of mountains called the Pennine Alps, which rising on the confines of the Iceni and Carnabii, near the river Trivona (*m*), extend towards the north in a continued series of fifty miles.

34. The people to the west of this chain (*n*) are the

(*x*) Part of the East Rid. of York.

(*y*) Spurn Head. (*z*) Flamborough Head.

(*a*) Broughton on Humber. (*b*) Near Bridlington Bay.

(*c*) Their territory stretched from the bounds of the Parisii northward to the Tine, and from the Humber and Don to the mountains of Lancashire, Westmoreland and Cumberland.

(*d*) Lanchester. (*e*) Binchester.

(*f*) Slack. (*g*) Catteric.

(*h*) Galgacum, uncertain. (*i*) Ilkley.

(*j*) Aldborough. (*k*) York.

(*l*) Probably from the Ure, which receives the name of Ouse above York, on its junction with the Nid.

(*m*) Trent.

(*n*) To the Voluntii belonged the western part of Lancashire; and to the Sistuntii, the west of Westmoreland and Cumberland as far as the wall.

(*o*) Hence, in § 31, they are called one people.

Voluntii and Sistuntii, who are united in a close confederacy (*o*). Their cities are Rerigonium (*p*), Coccium (*q*), and Lugubalium (*r*). The two last were occupied by Roman garrisons.

35. The northern frontier of this province was protected by a wall (*s*) of stupendous magnitude built by the

---

(*p*) Ribchester.   (*q*) Blackrode.   (*r*) Carlisle.

(*s*) The wall of Severus. The exact site of the barrier erected by Severus against the northern tribes, furnished matter of dispute to many of our antiquaries. The researches of others, particularly Horsley, have, however, set this question at rest. From their information, joined to the scanty evidence of history, it has been proved that three walls or ramparts were erected by the Romans at different times, to secure the northern frontier of their dominions in Britain.

The first was a rampart of earth, from the Solway Frith to the Tine, raised by Hadrian about the year 120; but its form and construction have not been satisfactorily ascertained. It was, however, evidently nothing more than a line intended to obstruct the passage of an enemy between the stations which constituted the real defences of the frontier.

The second was raised by Lollius Urbicus under the reign of Antoninus Pius, about 140, between the Friths of Forth and Clyde. This was likewise of earth, though perhaps faced with stone, and, like that of Hadrian, seems to have been intended as a line connecting the chain of stations, which formed a new barrier on the advance of the Roman arms. In the course of both these was a military road communicating from station to station.

The last and most important is that begun by Severus, after his expedition against the Caledonians, about 208. It runs nearly over the same ground as that of Hadrian; but is a complete and well combined system of fortification. From an examination of its remains it appears to have been built of stone, fifteen feet high and nine thick. It had a parapet and ditch, a military road, and was defended by 18 greater stations placed at intervals of three to six miles; 83 castles at intervals of 6 to 8 furlongs, and, as it is imagined, a considerable number of turrets placed at shorter distances.

Either from superior sagacity or superior information, Richard clearly distinguishes these three walls, which so much puzzled later writers, though it must be confessed that in other places he has suffered himself to be led into some errors in regard to their si-

Romans across the Isthmus, eighty miles in length, twelve feet high and (*nine*) thick, strengthened with towers.

36. We collect from history, that these people were first attacked by the emperor Claudius, then overrun by the legate Ostorius, and finally defeated by Cerealis. By their voluntary submission to Agricola they obtained peace. The actions and unheard-of perfidy of their queen have disgraced their name in history. These people were descended from those powerful nations, who in search of new habitations quitted their country, which was situated between the Danube, the Alps, and the Rhone (*t*). Some of them afterwards emigrated into Ireland, as appears from authentic documents.

37. Further north were situated those powerful nations, who in former times were known under the name of Maeetae, and from whom that fratricide Bassianus (*u*), Maeetae. after the death of his father, basely purchased peace. They possessed Ottadinia towards the east, Gadenia, Selgovia, Novantia, and further north Damnia.

38. Nearest the wall dwelt the Gadeni (*v*), whose Gadeni. metropolis was Curia (*w*). The Ottadini (*x*) were situated nearer the sea. Their chief city was Bremenium (*y*),

---

tuation, and the persons by whom they were erected.—See b. ii. ch. 1, sect. 22, 27, 36, 37; ch. 2, sect. 17, 23. For a detailed account of these works the reader is referred to *Horsley's Britannia Romana; Warburton's Account of the Roman Wall; Hutchinson's Northumberland; Roy's Military Antiquities; Hutton's Account of the Roman Wall.*

(*t*) These were the Helvetii, whose emigration is mentioned in *Cæs. Comm. de Bell. Gall. lib.* i. We have not discovered from what authority Richard draws his account of their emigration to Ireland.

(*u*) Caracalla.

(*v*) The Gadeni appear to have occupied the midland parts from the wall, probably as far as the Forth.

(*w*) Uncertain.

(*x*) The Ottadini stretched along the eastern coast, from the wall as far as the Frith of Forth, and were bounded on the west by the Gadeni.   (*y*) Ribchester.

and their rivers Tueda (*y*), Alauna (*z*), and the two Tinas (*a*), which ran within the wall.

Selgovæ.   39. The Selgovæ (*b*) inhabited the country to the west. Their cities were Corbantorigum (*c*), Uxellum (*d*), and Trimontium (*e*), which, according to ancient documents, was a long time occupied by a Roman garrison. The principal rivers of this region were Novius (*f*), Deva (*g*), and partly the Ituna (*h*).

Novantes.   40. The Novantes (*i*) dwell beyond the Deva, in the extreme part of the island, near the sea, and opposite Ireland. In their country was the famous Novantum Chersonesus (*j*), distant twenty-eight miles from Ireland, and esteemed by the ancients the most northern promontory of Britain (*k*), though without sufficient reason. Their metropolis was Lucophibia, or Casæ Candidæ (*l*); their rivers Abrasuanus (*m*), Jena (*n*), and Deva (*o*), which was the boundary towards the east.

Damnii.   41. The Damnii (*p*) dwelt to the north of the No-

(*y*) Tweed.   (*z*) The Coquet.
(*a*) The North and South Tine.
(*b*) The Selgovæ appear to have occupied all the shire of Dumfries, and part of Kirkudbright.
(*c*) Drumlanrig, or Kirkudbright.
(*d*) Uncertain.   (*e*) Birrenswork Hill.
(*f*) Nith.   (*g*) The Dee.
(*h*) The Eden.
(*i*) The Novantes held the south-western district of Scotland, from the Dee to the Mull of Galloway; that is, the west of Kirkudbright and Wigtown, and part of the Carrick division of Ayr.
(*j*) Rens of Galloway. It is not, however, more than eighteen miles from the nearest part of Ireland.
(*k*) By an error in the geographical or astronomical observations preserved by Ptolemy, the latitudes north of this point appear to have been mistaken for the longitudes, and consequently this part of Britain is thrown to the east.
(*l*) Wigtown, *Horsley*. Whithern, *Stukeley, Roy*.
(*m*) The Luce.   (*n*) Cree, *Roy*.
(*o*) Dee.
(*p*) These people inhabited the principal part of what are called

vantes, the Selgovæ, and the Gadeni, and were separated from them by the chain of the Uxellan mountains (q). They were a very powerful people, but lost a
considerable portion of their territory when the wall
was built, being subdued and spoiled by the Caledonians.
Besides which, a Roman garrison occupied Vanduarium (r) to defend the wall.

42. In this part, Britain, as if again delighted with
the embraces of the sea, becomes narrower than elsewhere, in consequence of the rapid influx of the two
æstuaries, Bodotria and Clotta (s). Agricola first secured
this isthmus with fortifications, and the emperor Antoninus (t) erected another wall celebrated in history, which
extended nearly five-and-thirty miles, in order to check
the incursions of the barbarians. It was repaired, and
strengthened with eleven towers, by the general Ætius.
These regions probably constituted that province, which,
being recovered by the victorious arms of the Romans
under Theodosius, was supposed to have been named
Valentia, in honour of the family from whom the reign-
ing emperor was descended.

43. Beyond the wall lay the province Vespasiana. Vespasi:
This is the Caledonian region so much coveted by the
Romans, and so bravely defended by the natives, facts
which the Roman historians, generally too silent in regard to such things, have amply detailed. In these
districts may be seen the river Tavus (u), which appears
to separate the country into two parts. There are also
found the steep and horrid Grampian hills, which divide
the province. In this region was fought that famous

the Lowlands. Their territories beyond the Isthmus evidently
stretched as far as the Grampians, consisting of great part of Ayr,
all Renfrew and Lanark, a considerable part of Stirling, and perhaps Linlithgow.

(q) The Lothers.   (r) Paisley, or Renfrew, Roy.
(s) Friths of Forth and Clyde.   (t) See page 120.
(u) Tay.

battle between Agricola and Galgacus, which was so decisive in favour of the Romans (v). The magnitude of the works at this day displays the power of the Romans, and the ancient mode of castrametation; for, in the place where the battle was fought, certain persons of our order, who passed that way, affirmed that they saw immense camps, and other proofs which corroborated the relation of Tacitus.

44. The nations which were subject to the Romans shall now follow in their order. Beyond the Isthmus, as far as the Tavus, lived the Horestii (w). Their cities, which before the building of the wall belonged to the Damnii, were Alauna (x), Lindum (y), and Victoria (z), the last not less glorious in reality than in name. It was built by Agricola on the Tavus, twenty miles above its mouth.

Horestii.

45. Above these, beyond the Tavus, which formed the boundary, lived the Vecturones or Venricones (a), whose chief city was Orrea (b), and their rivers Æsica (c) and Tina (d).

46. The Taixali (e) inhabited the coast beyond the boundaries of the Vecturones. Their principal city was

Taixali.

(v) It may perhaps appear superfluous to refer the antiquary to Roy's masterly Commentary on the campaigns of Agricola in this part of Britain; but it will scarcely be deemed so to observe, that we see few instances in which military and local knowledge are so well applied to the elucidation of antiquities.

(w) The Horestii occupied Clackmannan and Kinross, and part of Perth as far the Tay. To them belonged likewise all the country stretching from the Grampians to Loch Lomond.

(x) Uncertain.   (y) Ardoch.

(z) Dealgin Ross.

(a) The Vecturones occupied the eastern part of Perth, Forfar, Kincardin, and part of Aberdeen.

(b) Bertha, or Old Perth.   (c) South Esk.

(d) Tine.

(e) The Taixali held the eastern coast of Aberdeen, apparently as far as Kinnaird Head.

Devana (f), and their rivers the Deva (g) and Ituna (h). A part of the Grampian hills, which extends like a promontory into the sea, as it were to meet Germany, borrows its name from them (i).

47. To the west of these, beyond the Grampian hills, lived the Vacomagi (j), who possessed an extensive tract Vacomagi. of country. Their cities were Tuessis (k), Tamea (l), and Banatia (m). Ptoroton (n), situated at the mouth of the Varar (o), on the coast, was at the same time a Roman station, and the chief city of the province. The most remarkable rivers of this region, after the Varar, which formed the boundary, were the Tuesis (p) and Celnius (q).

48. Within the Vacomagi, and the Tavus, lived the Damnii Albani (r), a people little known, being wholly Damnii Albani. secluded among lakes and mountains.

49. Lower down, to the banks of the Clotta, inhabited the Attacotti (s), a people once formidable to all Attacotti. Britain. In this part is situated the great lake formerly called Lynchalidor (t), at the mouth of which the city of Alcuith (u) was built by the Romans, and not long afterwards received its name from Theodosius, who

(f) Probably Old Aberdeen.   (g) Dee.

(h) Ithan.   (i) Kinnaird Head.

(j) The Vacomagi were spread over an extensive region west of the Taixali and north of the Grampians, comprising a considerable part of Aberdeen, all Banff, Murray, Elgin, and Nairn, with the north-east of Inverness.

(k) On the Spey.   (l) Brae Mar Castle.

(m) Uncertain, but near the Ness; perhaps Inverness or Bonness.

(n) Burgh Head.   (o) Murray Frith.

(p) Spey.   (q) Dovern.

(r) The Damnii Albani may have been a remnant of the Damnii, who, after the erection of the wall, being cut off from the rest of their tribe, were gradually circumscribed by the neighbouring people, to Braidalbane, and a small part of the west of Perth and east of Argyle.

(s) The Attacotti occupied a considerable part of Argyle, as far as Lochfyn.   (t) Loch Lomond.

(u) Dumbarton. It was afterwards called Theodosia.

recovered that province from the barbarians.   These
people deserved high praise for having sustained the
attacks of the enemy after the subjugation of the neighbouring provinces.

50. This province was named Vespasiana, in honour
of the Flavian family, to which the emperor Domitian
owed his origin, and under whom it was conquered.
If I am not mistaken, it was called under the later
emperors Thule, which Claudian mentions in these
lines :

> " ―――――― incaluit Pictorum sanguine Thule,
> Scotorum cumulos flevit glacialis Hierne."

But this country was so short a time under the power
of the Romans, that posterity cannot ascertain its appellations or subjugation.   We have now examined in a
cursory manner the state of Britain under the Romans ;
we shall next as briefly treat of the country of the
Caledonians.

CONCERNING CALEDONIA.

51. Although all the parts of Britain lying beyond
the Isthmus may be termed Caledonia, yet the proper
Caledonians dwelt beyond the Varar, from which a line
drawn accurately points out the boundary of the Roman
empire in Britain.   The hithermost part of the island
was at different times in their possession, and the remainder, as we have related, was occupied by barbarous
Britons.   The ancient documents of history afford some
information thus far ; but beyond the Varar the light is
extinct, and we are enveloped in darkness (v).   Although

(v) It must be confessed that the information preserved by
Richard, in regard to this remote part of our island, is extremely
obscure, and that his descriptions will only assist us in guessing at
the situation of the different tribes.   Perhaps this can scarcely be
deemed extraordinary, when we consider how imperfectly the interior of this country is known even at present.

we know that the Romans erected altars there to mark
the limits of their empire, and that Ulysses, tost by a
violent tempest, here fulfilled his vows; yet the thick
woods and a continued chain of rugged mountains forbid
all further research. We must therefore be satisfied
with the following information, gleaned from the wan-
dering merchants of the Britons, which we leave for the
use of posterity.

52. The Caledonians (*w*), properly so called, inhabited Caledonians.
the country to the westward of the Varar, and part
of their territory was covered by the extensive forest
called the Caledonian wood.

53. Less considerable people dwelt near the coast.
Of these the Cantæ (*x*) were situated beyond the Varar, Cantæ.
and the above-mentioned altars, to the river Loxa (*y*),
and in their territory was the promontory Penoxullum (*z*).

54. Next in order is the river Abona (*a*), and the inhabitants near it, the Logi (*b*). Then the river Ila (*c*), Logi.
near which lived the Carnabii (*d*), the most remote of
the Britons. These people being subdued by the pro-
prætor Ostorius, and impatiently bearing the Roman
yoke, joined the Cantæ, as tradition relates, and, crossing the sea, here fixed their residence. Britain in these
parts branches out into many promontories, the chief of
which, the extremity of Caledonia, was called by the
ancients Vinvedrum, and afterwards Verubium (*e*).

(*w*) The country of the proper Caledonians was the central part
of Inverness and Ross.

(*x*) The Cantæ seem to have held Cromarty and East Ross.

(*y*) Frith of Cromartie, *Stukeley*. Loth R. *Roy*.

(*z*) Tarbet Ness, *Stukeley*. Ord Head, Caithness, *Roy*.

(*a*) Frith of Dornoch, *Stukeley*.

(*b*) The Logi seem to have held the south-east of Strathnavern
and north-east of Sutherland.

(*c*) All, *Stukeley*. Shiel, *Roy*.

(*d*) The Carnabii inhabited part of Caithness, the north of Ross,
and central part of Sutherland.

(*e*) Ness or Noss Head, *Stukeley*.

Catini.
Mertæ.

55. After these people were placed the Catini (*f*), and the Mertæ (*g*) further inland near the Logi. In these regions was the promontory of the Orcades (*h*), contiguous to which are the islands of that name. Beyond this part flowed the Nabæus (*i*), which bounded the territory of the Carnabii.

Carnonacæ.

56. In the lower part of this region were situated the Carnonacæ (*j*), in whose territories was the promontory Ebudum (*k*), beyond which the ocean forms a large bay, formerly called Volsas (*l*). The lower coast of this bay was inhabited by the Cerones (*m*); and beyond the Itys (*n*), the territory of the Creones extended as far as the Longus (*o*). The promontory stretching from thence, and washed by the ocean and the bay Lelanus (*p*), is named after the inhabitants the Epidii (*q*).

57. I cannot repass the Varar without expressing my wonder that the Romans, in other respects so much distinguished for judgment and investigation, should have entertained the absurd notion, that the remainder of Britain exceeded in length and breadth the regions which they had subdued and occupied. There is, however, sufficient evidence that such was their opinion;

(*f*) The Catini held part of Caithness and the east of Sutherland.

(*g*) The Mertæ held the country comprised between the Catini and Carnabii.

(*h*) Dunnet Head, *Stukeley*. Duncansby Head, *Roy*.

(*i*) Navern.

(*j*) The Carnonacæ seem to have held the detached portion of Cromarty, situated near Loch Broom, and a small part on the border of Sutherland.

(*k*) Cape Wrath.   (*l*) Loch Broom.

(*m*) The Cerones held the north-west part of Ross ;—the Creones, south-west of Ross and Inverness, and a part of Argyle.

(*n*) Shiel, *Roy*.

(*o*) Loch Loch, *Stukeley*. Linnhe Loch, *Roy*.

(*p*) Lochfyn.

(*q*) The Epidii probably occupied the western part of Argyle, as far as the Mull of Cantyr, and were bounded on one side by the sea and on the other by Lochfyn.

for whoever attentively considers their insatiable desire of rule, and reflects on the labour employed in the erection of those stupendous works which excite the wonder of the world, in order to exclude an enemy scarcely worthy of their notice or resentment, must in this respect, as in all others, adore the providence of the Divine Being, to whom all kingdoms are subject, and perpetual glory is due, now and for ever. Amen!

CHAPTER VII.

THE different parts of Britain having been cursorily examined according to my original design, it seems necessary, before I proceed to a description of the islands, to attend to a doubt suggested by a certain person (r). " Where," asks he, " are the vestiges of those cities and names which you commemorate ? There are none." This question may be answered by another: Where are now the Assyrians, Parthians, Sarmatians, Celtiberians ? None will be bold enough to deny the existence of those nations. Are there not also at this time many countries and cities bearing the same names as they did two or three thousand years ago ? Judea, Italy, Gaul, Britain, are as clearly known now as in former times; Londinium is still styled in the common language, with a slight change of sound, London. The negligence and inattention of our ancestors in omitting to collect and preserve such documents as might have been serviceable in this particular, are not deserving of heavy censure, for scarcely any but those in holy orders

(r) These remarks prove how much Richard rose superior to the prejudices of his age and his profession. From the tone which he assumes, it is, however, evident that he found it advisable to yield to the remonstrances of his superior.

K

employed themselves in writing books, and such even esteemed it inconsistent with their sacred office to engage in such profane labours. I rather think I may without danger, and without offence, transmit to posterity that information which I have drawn from a careful examination and accurate scrutiny of ancient records, concerning the state of this kingdom in former periods. The good abbot, indeed, had nearly inspired me with other sentiments, by thus seeming to address me: Are you ignorant how short a time is allotted us in this world; that the greatest exertions cannot exempt us from the appellation of unprofitable servants; and that all our studies should be directed to the purpose of being useful to others? Of what service are these things, but to delude the world with unmeaning trifles? To these remarks I answer with propriety: Is then every honest gratification forbidden? Do not such narratives exhibit proofs of Divine Providence? Does it not hence appear, that an evangelical sermon concerning the death and merits of Christ enlightened and subdued a world overrun with Gentile superstitions? To the reply, that such things are properly treated of in systems of chronology, I rejoin: Nor is it too much to know that our ancestors were not, as some assert, Autochthones, sprung from the earth; but that God opened the book of Nature to display his omnipotence, such as it is described in the writings of Moses. When the abbot answered, that works which were intended merely to acquire reputation for their authors from posterity, should be committed to the flames, I confess with gratitude that I repented of this undertaking. The remainder of the work is therefore only a chronological abridgment, which I present to the reader, whom I commend to the goodness and protection of God; and at the same time request, that he will pray for me to our holy Father, who is merciful and inclined to forgiveness.

The following Itinerary is collected from certain fragments left by a Roman general. The order is changed in some instances, according to Ptolemy and others, and, it is hoped, with improvement (r).

AMONG the Britons were formerly ninety-two cities, of which thirty-three were more celebrated and conspicuous. Two municipal (s), Verolamium (t) ; and Eboracum (u). Nine colonial (v); namely, Londinium (w) *Augusta*, Camalodunum (x) *Geminæ Martiæ*, Rhutupis (y), * * * * * Thermæ (z) *Aquæ Solis*, Isca (a) *Secunda*, Deva (b) *Getica*, Glevum (c) *Claudia*, Lindum (d), * * * * Camboricum (e). * * * * Ten cities under the Latian law (f) ; namely, Durnomagus (g), Catarracton (h), Cambodunum (i), Coccium (j), Lugu-

Ninety-two cities.

(r) As the Itinerary is given in the Commentary and in the original Treatise, it is omitted in this place.

(s) Municipia were towns whose inhabitants possessed in general all the rights of Roman citizens, except those which could not be enjoyed without an actual residence at Rome. They followed their own laws and customs, and had the option of adopting or rejecting those of Rome.—*Rosini Antiq. Rom. b. x. c.* 23.

(t) St. Alban's.　　　　　(u) York.

(v) There were different kinds of colonies, each entitled to different rights and privileges; but we have no criterion to ascertain the rank occupied by those in Britain.

(w) London.　　　　　　(x) Colchester.
(y) Richborough in Kent.　(z) Bath.
(a) Caerleon.　　　　　　(b) Chester.
(c) Glocester.　　　　　　(d) Lincoln.
(e) Cambridge.

(f) The Latian law consisted of the privileges granted to the ancient inhabitants of Latium. These are not distinctly known ; but appear principally to have been the right of following their own laws, an exemption from the edicts of the Roman Prætor, and the option of adopting the laws and customs of Rome.—*Rosini.*

(g) Castor on Nen.　　　　(h) Catteric.
(i) Slack.　　　　　　　　(j) Blackrode.

balia (*k*), Ptoroton (*l*), Victoria (*m*), Theodosia (*n*), Corinum (*o*), Sorbiodunum (*p*). Twelve stipendiary (*q*) and of lesser consequence ; Venta Silurum (*r*), Venta Belgarum (*s*), Venta Icenorum (*t*), Segontium (*u*), Muridunum (*v*), Ragæ (*w*), Cantiopolis (*x*), Durinum (*y*), Isca (*z*), Bremenium (*a*), Vindonum (*b*), and Durobrivæ (*c*). But let no one lightly imagine that the Romans had not many others besides those above mentioned. I have only commemorated the more celebrated. For who can doubt that they who, as conquerors of the world, were at liberty to choose, did not select places fitted for their purposes? They for the most part took up their abode in fortresses which they constructed for themselves.

(The Itinerary, which follows here in the original Latin, being a dry list of names, is omitted. See the original Latin, and also the Appendix to the Itinerary.)

CHAPTER VIII.

Ireland.

1. HAVING now finished our survey of Albion, we shall describe the neighbouring country, Hybernia or Ireland, with the same brevity.

2. Hybernia is situated more westerly than any other country except England ; but as it does not extend so

(*k*) Carlisle.

(*l*) Burgh Head, Elgin, Scotland.

(*m*) Dealgin Ross.

(*n*) Dumbarton.

(*o*) Cirencester, Gloc.

(*p*) Old Sarum.

(*q*) The Stipendiary were those who paid their taxes in money, in contradistinction from those who gave a certain portion of the produce of the soil, and were called Vectigales.—*Rosini.*

(*r*) Caerwent, Monmouth.

(*s*) Winchester.

(*t*) Castor, near Norwich.

(*u*) Caer Segont.

(*v*) Caermarthen.

(*w*) Leicester.

(*x*) Canterbury.

(*y*) Dorchester.

(*z*) Exeter.

(*a*) Riechester, Northumberland.

(*b*) Possibly Egbury camp, Hants.

(*c*) Rochester.

far north, so it stretches further than England towards
the south, and the Spanish province of Tarraconensis,
from which it is separated by the ocean (d).

3. The sea which flows between Britain and Hyber- Man.
nia is subject to storms, and, according to Solinus, is
navigable only during a few days in summer. Midway
between the two countries is the island called Mo-
nœda (e), but now Manavia.

4. According to Bede, Hybernia is preferable to Britain, on account of its situation, salubrity and serene
air, insomuch that snow seldom remains more than three
days, nor is it usual to make hay for the winter, or build
stalls for cattle.

5. No reptile is found there, nor does it maintain a
viper or serpent; for serpents frequently carried from
England have died on approaching the shore. Indeed
almost all things in the island are antidotes to poison.
We have seen an infusion of scraped pieces of bark
brought from Hybernia, given to persons bitten by serpents, which immediately deprived the poison of its force,
and abated the swelling.

6. This island, according to the venerable Bede, is rich
in milk and honey; nor is it without vines. It abounds
with fish and birds, and affords deer and goats for the
chase.

7. The inhabitants, says Mela, are more than other
nations uncivilized and without virtue, and those who
have a little knowledge are wholly destitute of piety.
Solinus calls them an inhospitable and warlike people.
The conquerors, after drinking the blood of the slain,
daub their faces with the remainder. They know no
distinction between right and wrong. When a woman
brings forth a son, she places its first food on the point

(d) As we have neither the assistance of an Itinerary to guide us
in our researches, nor a local knowledge of Ireland, we have not
attempted to specify the situation of the ancient states and cities
in that island.   (e) Man.

of her husband's sword, and, introducing it into the mouth of the infant, wishes, according to the custom of the country, that he may die amidst arms and in battle. Those who are fond of ornaments adorn the hilts of their swords with the teeth of marine animals, which they polish to a degree of whiteness equal to ivory; for the principal glory of a man consists in the splendour of his arms.

8. Agrippa states the length of Hybernia to be six hundred miles, and the breadth three hundred. It was formerly inhabited by twenty tribes, of whom (*fourteen* (*f*)) lived on the coast.

9. This is the true country of the Scots, who emigrating from hence added a third nation to the Britons and Picts in Albion. But I cannot agree with Bede, who affirms that the Scots were foreigners. For, according to the testimony of other authors, I conceive they derived their origin from Britain, situated at no considerable distance, passed over from thence, and obtained a settlement in this island. It is certain that the Damnii, Voluntii, Brigantes, Cangi, and other nations, were descended from the Britons, and passed over thither after Divitiacus, or Claudius, or Ostorius, or other victorious generals had invaded their original countries. Lastly, the ancient language, which resembles the old British and Gallic tongues, affords another argument, as is well known to persons skilled in both languages (*g*).

10. The Deucalidonian Ocean washes the northern side of Hybernia; the Vergivian and Internal the eastern, the Cantabric the south, as the great British or Atlantic Ocean does the western. According to this order, we shall give a description of the island and the most remarkable places.

(*f*) In the original is an error in the numerals, the number afterwards specified is fourteen.

(*g*) Nearly one third of the words in the Irish tongue are the same as the modern Welsh, and many idioms and modes of speech are common to both languages.

11. The Rhobogdii occupied the coast of the island Rhobogdii. next to the Deucalidonian Sea. Their metropolis was Rhobogdium. In the eastern part of their territories was situated the promontory of the same name; in the western, the Promontorium Boreum, or Northern Promontory. Their rivers were the Banna, Darabouna, Argitta, and Vidua; and towards the south, mountains separated them from the Scotti.

12. On the coast between the northern and Venicnian Promontory, and as far as the mouth of the Rhebeus, dwelt the Venicnii. To them the contiguous islands owe Venicini. their name. Their capital was Rheba. The Nagnatæ dwelt below the Rhebeus as far as the Libnius, and their celebrated metropolis was called after them. The Auterii lived in a recess of the bay of Ausoba, towards the south, and their chief city was named after them. The Concangii occupied the lower part of the same region, near the southern confines of which flowed the river Senus, a noble river, on which was situated their chief city Macobicum. Hybernia in this part being contracted, terminates in a narrow point. The Velatorii inhabited the country near the southern promontory by the river Senus; their metropolis was Regia, and their river Durius. The Lucani were situated where the river Ibernus flows into the ocean.

13. The southern side of the island stretched from the Promontorium Austriacum, or Southern Promontory, to the Sacred Promontory. Here lived the Ibernii, Ibernii. whose metropolis was Rhufina. Next was the river Dobona, and the people called Vodiæ, whose promontory of the same name lies opposite to the Promontorium Antivestæum in England, at about the distance of one hundred and forty-five miles. Not far from thence is the river Dabrona, the boundary of the Brigantes, who have also the river Briga for their limit, and whose chief city is called Brigantia.

14. The part of this island which reaches from the Sacred Promontory as far as Rhobogdium is called the Eastern. The Menapii, inhabiting the Sacred Promontory, had their chief city upon the river Modona called by the same name. From this part to Menapia (*h*) in Dimetia, the distance, according to Pliny, is thirty miles. One of these countries, but which is uncertain, gave birth to Carausius. Beyond these people the Cauci had their metropolis Dunum; and the river Oboca washed their boundaries. Both these nations were undoubtedly of Teutonic origin; but it is not known at what precise time their ancestors first passed over, though most probably a little while before Cæsar's arrival in Britain.

Menapii.

15. Beyond these were the Eblanæ, whose chief city was Mediolanum, upon the river Lœbius. More to the north was Lebarum, the city of the Voluntii, whose rivers were Vinderus and Buvinda. The Damnii occupied the part of the island lying above these people, and contiguous to the Rhobogdii. Their chief city was Dunum, where St. Patrick, St. Columba, and St. Bridget are supposed to be buried in one tomb.

Voluntii.

16. It remains now to give some account of those people who lived in the interior parts. The Coriondii bordered upon the Cauci and Menapii, above the Brigantes: the Scotti possessed the remaining part of the island, which from them took the name of Scotia. Among many of their cities, the remembrance of two only has reached our times: the one Rheba, on the lake and river Rhebius; the other Ibernia, situated at the east side of the river Senus.

Coriondii.

17. I cannot omit mentioning in this place that the Damnii, Voluntii, Brigantes, and Cangiani were all nations of British origin, who being either molested by

(*h*) St. David's.

neighbouring enemies, or unable to pay the heavy tribute exacted of them, gradually passed over into this country in search of new settlements.   With respect to the Menapii, Cauci, and some other people, it has been before remarked that many things occur which cannot safely be relied on.   Tacitus relates that Hybernia was more frequented by foreigners than Albion.   But in that case, the ancients would undoubtedly have left us a more ample and credible account of this island. While I am writing a description of Hybernia, it seems right to add, that it was reduced under the Roman power, not by arms, but by fear; and moreover, that Ptolemy, in his second map of Europe, and other celebrated geographers, have erred in placing it at too great a distance from Britain, and from the northern part of the province Secunda, as appears from their books and maps.

18. North of Hybernia are the Hebudes, five (i) in Hebudes. number, the inhabitants of which know not the use of corn, but live on fish and milk.   They are all, according to Solinus, subject to one chief, for they are only divided from each other by narrow straits.   The chief possessed no peculiar property, but was maintained by general contribution : he was bound by certain laws; and lest avarice should seduce him from equity, he learned justice from poverty, having no house nor property, and being maintained at the public expense.   He had no wife; but took by turns any woman for whom he felt an inclination, and hence had neither a wish nor hope for children.   Some persons have written concerning these Hebudes, that during winter darkness continues for the space of thirty days; but Cæsar upon diligent

(i) The Hebudes amount to more than five. From hence it may perhaps be inferred that the Roman fleet in their voyage of discovery did not reach these seas, though they coasted the northern part of Scotland, for the Orcades are rightly numbered.

inquiry found this assertion untrue, and only discovered by certain measures of time that the nights were shorter here than in Gaul.

Orcades.

19. The Orcades, according to some accounts, are distant from the Hebudes seven days and nights' sail; but this is erroneous. They are thirty in number, and contiguous to each other. They were uninhabited, without wood, and abounded with reeds: several were formed only of sand and rocks, as may be collected from Solinus and others.

Thule.

20. Thule, the last of the British isles, is placed by Mela opposite to (*j*) the coast of the Belgæ. It has been celebrated in Greek and Roman verse. Thus the Mantuan Homer says,—

" Et tibi serviat ultima Thule."

Here are no nights during the solstice when the sun passes the sign of Cancer; and on the other hand, in winter there are no days, as Pliny asserts. These circumstances are supposed to happen for six whole months. The inhabitants, as Solinus affirms, in the beginning of the spring live among their cattle upon herbs, then upon milk, and lay up fruits against the winter. They have their women in common without marriages. Thule, according to the same author, abounds in fruits. At the distance of a day's sail from Thule the sea is difficult to pass through, and frozen; it is by some called Cronium. From Thule to Caledonia is two days' sail.

Thanatos.

21. The isle of Thanatos (*k*) is bounded by a narrow channel, and separated from the continent of Britain by a small æstuary called the Wantsuam. It is rich in pasture and corn. According to Isiodorus, its soil is

(*j*) Littori apposita, Richard. From the map, and the sense in which this phrase is generally used in geography, it might be rendered *under the same meridian.*   (*k*) Thanet.

not only salubrious to itself, but to others, for no snakes live in it, and the earth being carried to a distance destroys them. It is not far distant from Rhutupis (*l*).

22. The isle of Vecta (*m*), conquered by Vespasian, Vecta. is thirty miles in length, on the side next to the Belgæ, from east to west, and twelve from north to south. In the eastern part it is six miles, in the western three, from the above-mentioned southern shore of Britain.

23. Besides the isles just specified, there were VII Acmodæ (*n*), Ricnea (*o*), Silimnus (*p*), Andros (*q*), Sig- Acmodæ. diles (*r*), XL Vindilios (*s*), Sarna (*t*), Cæsarea (*u*), and Cassiterides (*v*).

24. The island Sena, opposite the Ossismican (*w*) Sena. coast, is according to Mela famous for the oracle of the Gallic deity, of whom the priestesses, sanctified by perpetual virginity, are said to have been nine in number. The Gauls call them Senæ, and suppose them gifted with singular powers; that they raise the winds and the seas with incantations, change themselves into what animals they please, and cure disorders which in other places yield to no remedy; that they have the knowledge of future events, and prophesy. They are not favourable except to mariners, and only to such as go thither for the purpose of consulting them.

25. The rest of the isles of smaller size and consequence which lie round Albion will be better perceived and known by the inspection of the annexed map than from any description. Here, therefore, we stop, and anxiously commend our labours to the favour and judgment of the benevolent reader.

(*l*) Richborough. (*m*) Wight.
(*n*)—(*s*) No geographer has hitherto attempted to ascertain the modern names of these islands. (*t*) Guernsey.
(*u*) Jersey. (*v*) Scilly Isles.
(*w*) From a tribe of the Veneti called Ossismii, who inhabited part of Bretagne.

The first book of the geographical Commentary on the situation of Britain, and those stations which the Romans erected in that island, is happily finished, through the assistance of God, by the hand of Richard, servant of Christ and monk of Westminster. Thanks be to God!

ANCIENT STATE OF BRITAIN.

BOOK II.

PREFACE.

WE have thought proper to add as a supplement to
the description of ancient Britain in the same summary
manner :—I. An epitome of chronology from the creation to the sack of Rome by the Goths: II. A short account of the Roman emperors, and governors, who presided over this country: III. Some persons will perhaps
say that this kind of work is not absolutely necessary
either for divine worship or greater things.   But let
them know that leisure hours may be dedicated to the
study of the antiquities of our country without any de-
rogation from the sacred character.   Yet if censorious
people envy us such pleasures at leisure hours, hastening
to the end and almost arrived at the goal, we here check
our steps.

CHAPTER I.

IV. IN the beginning, the Almighty Creator made this
world, inhabited by us and other creatures, out of nothing, in the space of six days.

Creation.   V. In the year of the world 1656, the Creator, to punish the increasing wickedness of mankind, sent a flood upon the earth, which, overwhelming the whole world, destroyed every living creature except those which had entered the ark, and whose progeny replenished the new world with colonies of living beings.

VI. 3000. About this time some persons affirm that Britain was cultivated and first inhabited, when it was visited by the Greek and Phœnician merchants. Nor are those wanting who believe that London was shortly after built by a king called Bryto.

VII. 3228. The brothers Romulus and Remus laid the foundation of Rome, which in time became the common terror of all nations.

Senones.   VIII. 3600. The Senones, having emigrated from Britain, passed through Gaul, with the intent to invade Italy and attack Rome.

Belgæ.   IX. 3650. The Belgæ entered this country, and the
Celtæ.   Celtæ occupied the region deserted by the Senones. Divitiacus king of the Ædui soon afterwards passed over with an army and subdued great part of this kingdom. About this time the Britons who were expelled by the Belgæ emigrated to Ireland, formed a settlement, and were thenceforward called Scotti.

Cassibelin.   X. 3943. Cassibelinus waged war with the maritime states (a).

Cæsar.   XI. 3946. Cæsar overcame the Germans, Gauls, and also the Britons, to whom, before this time, even the name of the Romans was unknown. The conqueror, having received hostages, rendered the people tributary.

XII. 3947. At length coming a second time into this country, upon the invitation, as he pretended, of the Trinobantes, he waged war with Cassibelinus king of the Cassii. Suetonius, however, asserts, with greater proba-

---

(a) Probably from Cæsar, though the precise date seems to be fixed without authority.—*Cæs. de Bell. Gall. lib.* 5, § 9.

bility, that he was allured by the costly pearls of Britain.

XIII. 4044. The emperor Claudius passed over to Britain, and in the space of six months, almost without effusion of blood, reduced a great part of the island, which he ordered to be called Cæsariensis. *Claudius.*

XIV. 4045. Vespasian, at that time in a private station, being sent by the emperor Claudius with the second legion into this country, attacked the Belgæ and Damnonii, and having fought thirty-two battles and taken twenty cities, reduced them under the Roman power, together with the Isle of Wight. *Vespasian.*

XV. 4047. The Romans occupied Thermæ and Glebon.

XVI. 4050. Ostorius the Roman general, after a war of nine years, overcame Charaticus king of the Silures, great part of Britain was reduced into a province, and the colony of Camalodunum founded. *Ostorius.*

XVII. 4052. Certain cities of the Belgæ were yielded by the Romans to Cogibundus, that he might form a kingdom. About this time the Cangi and Brigantes went over and settled in Ireland.

XVIII. 4061. The emperor Nero, having no courage for military enterprises, nearly lost Britain; for under him its two greatest cities were taken and destroyed. Bonduica, in order to revenge the injury offered to her by the Romans, rose in arms, burnt the Roman colonies of London, Camalodunum, and the municipal town Verulamium, and slew more than eighty thousand Roman citizens. She was at length overcome by Suetonius, who amply avenged the loss, by slaughtering an equal number of her subjects. *Nero.*

XIX. 4073. Cerealis conquered the Brigantes. *Cerealis.*

XX. 4076. Frontinus punished the Ordovices. *Frontinus.*

XXI. 4080. Agricola after a severe engagement subdued Galgacus king of the Caledonians. He ordered all the island to be examined by a fleet, and having sailed round its coasts, added the Orcades to the Roman empire. *Agricola.*

Hadrian.   XXII. 4120. The emperor Hadrian himself came into the island, and separated one part of it from the other by an immense wall.

Urbicus.   XXIII. 4140. Urbicus being sent hither by Antoninus Pius, distinguished himself by his victories.

Aurelius.   XXIV. 4150. Aurelius Antoninus also obtained victories over some of the Britons.

Lucius.   XXV. 4160. Britain was enlightened by the introduction of Christianity, during the reign of Lucius, who first submitted himself to the cross of Christ.

Reuda.   XXVI. 4170. The Romans were driven from the Vespasian province. About this time it is supposed that king Reuda came with his people, the Picts, from the islands into Britain.

Severus.   XXVII. 4207. The emperor Severus, passing over into Britain, repaired the wall built by the Romans which had been ruined, and died not long after, by the visitation of God, at York.

Caracalla.   XXVIII. 4211. Bassianus (Caracalla) obtained a venal peace from the Mæatæ.

XXIX. 4220. During these times the Roman armies confined themselves within the wall, and all the island enjoyed a profound peace.

Carausius.   XXX. 4290. Carausius, having assumed the purple, seized upon Britain; but ten years afterwards it was recovered by Asclepiodorus.

XXXI. 4304. A cruel and inveterate persecution, in which within the space of a month seventeen thousand martyrs suffered in the cause of Christ. This persecution spread over the sea, and the Britons, Alban, Aaron and Julius, with great numbers of men and women, were condemned to a happy death.

Constantius.   XXXII. 4306. Constantius, a man of the greatest humanity, having conquered Alectum, died at Eboracum in the sixteenth year of his reign.

Constantine.   XXXIII. 4307. Constantine, afterwards called the Great, son of Constantius by Helena, a British woman, was created emperor in Britain; and Ireland voluntarily became tributary to him.

XXXIV. 4320. The Scotti entered Britain under the conduct of the king Fergusius, and here fixed their residence. *Scotti.*

XXXV. 4385. Theodosius slew Maximus the tyrant three miles from Aquileia. Maximus, having nearly drained Britain of all its warlike youth, who followed the footsteps of his tyranny over Gaul, the fierce transmarine nations of the Scots from the south, and the Picts from the north, perceiving the island without soldiers and defenceless, oppressed it and laid it waste during a long series of years. *Theodosius.*

XXXVI. 4396. The Britons indignantly submitting to the attacks of the Scots and Picts, sent to Rome, made an offer of submission, and requested assistance against their enemies. A legion being accordingly dispatched to their assistance, slew a great multitude of the barbarians, and drove the remainder beyond the confines of Britain. The legion, upon its departure homewards, advised its allies to construct a wall between the two æstuaries to restrain the enemy. A wall was accordingly made in an unskilful manner, with a greater proportion of turf than stone, which was of no advantage; for on the departure of the Romans the former enemies returned in ships, slew, trampled on, and devoured all things before them like a ripened harvest.

XXXVII. 4400. Assistance being again entreated, the Romans came, and with the aid of the Britons drove the enemy beyond sea, and built a wall from sea to sea, not as before with earth, but with solid stone, between the fortresses erected in that part to curb the enemy. On the southern coast, where an invasion of the Saxons was apprehended, he erected watch towers. This was the work of Stilicho, as appears from Claudian. *Stilicho.*

XXXVIII. 4411. Rome, the seat of the fourth and

L

greatest of the monarchies, was seized by the Goths, as Daniel prophesied, in the year one thousand one hundred and sixty-four after its foundation.

From this time ceased the Roman empire in Britain, four hundred and sixty-five years after the arrival of Julius Cæsar.

XXXIX. 4446. The Roman legion retiring from Britain, and refusing to return, the Scots and Picts ravaged all the island from the north as far as the wall, the guards of which being slain, taken prisoners, or driven away, and the wall itself broken through, the predatory enemy then poured into the country. An epistle was sent filled with tears and sorrows to Fl. Ætius, thrice consul, in the twenty-third year of Theodosius, begging the assistance of the Roman power, but without effect.

CHAPTER II.

1. HAVING followed truth as far as possible, if any thing should occur not strictly consistent with it, I request it may not be imputed to me as a fault. Confining myself closely to the rules and laws of history, I have collected all the accounts of other persons which I found most accurate and deserving of credit. The reader must not expect any thing beyond an enumeration of those emperors and Roman governors who had authority over this island. With an account of these I shall close my book.

2. Julius Cæsar the dictator was the first of the Romans who invaded Britain with an army, during the reign of Cassibelinus; but, although he defeated the inhabitants in one battle, and occupied the coast, as Tacitus observes, he rather seems to have shown the

way. to his successors than to have given them possession.

3. In a short time the civil wars succeeding, the arms
of the chiefs were turned against the republic. Britain
was also long neglected by the advice of Augustus and
the command of Tiberius. It is certain that Caligula
intended to enter Britain; but his quick temper and
proneness to change, or the unsuccessful attempts
against the Germans, prevented him.

4. Claudius, however, carried war into Britain, which Claudius.
no Roman emperor since Julius Cæsar had reached, and,
having transported his legions and allies without danger
or bloodshed, in a few days reduced a part of the island.
He afterwards sent over Vespasian, at that time in a
private station, who fought two and thirty battles with
the enemy, and added to the Roman empire two very
powerful nations, with their kings, twenty cities, and
the isle of Vecta, contiguous to Britain. He overcame
the remainder by means of Cneas Sentius and Aulus
Plautius. For these exploits he obtained a great
triumph.

5. To him succeeded Ostorius Scapula, a man famous Ostorius
in war, who reduced the nearest part of Britain into a Scapula.
province, and added the colony of the veterans, Camalodunum. Certain cities were delivered up to the chief
Cogibundus, who, according to Tacitus, remained faithful till the accession of Trajan to the empire.

6. Avitus Didius Gallus kept possession of what his Avitus Di-
predecessors had acquired, a few posts only being re- dius Gallus.
moved further into the interior, in order to obtain the
credit of extending his dominion.

7. Didius Verannius, who succeeded, died within a Didius Ve-
year. rannius.

8. Suetonius Paulinus continued prosperous for two Suetonius
years. The tribes being reduced and garrisons esta- Paulinus.
blished, he attacked the isle of Mona, because it gave
succour to the rebellious, and afforded opportunities for

invasion. For the absence of the governor removing all fear, the Britons began to recover courage, and rose in arms under the conduct of Bonduica, a woman of royal descent. Having reduced the troops scattered in the garrisons, they attacked the colony (a) itself, as the seat of slavery, and in the height of rage and victory, exercised every species of savage barbarity. Had not Paulinus, on receiving the intelligence, luckily hastened to crush the revolt, Britain must have been lost. But the fortune of one battle restored it to its former submission. Many of the natives, from the consciousness of their defection, and fear of the governor, continued under arms.

Suetonius.   9. Suetonius, in other respects an illustrious man, but arrogant to the vanquished and prompt to avenge his own injuries, being likely to exercise severity, he was replaced by Petronius Turpilianus, who was more merciful, a stranger to the offences of the enemy, and therefore more likely to be softened by their repentance. Having settled the disturbances, he gave up the province to Trebellius Maximus.

Trebellius.   10. Trebellius, being of a slothful disposition and unused to war, retained the province by gentleness. The barbarous Britons' ceasing to be ignorant of luxury, and the termination of civil wars, gave him an excuse for inactivity. But discord called forth his exertions; for the soldiery, when released from military labours, grew wanton from too much rest. Trebellius, having evaded the rage of the army by flight, was shortly allowed to resume the command, the licentiousness of the soldiery becoming as it were a composition for the safety of the general. This sedition ended without bloodshed.

Vectius Bo- 11. Nor did Vectius Bolanus, although the civil wars
lanus.   still continued, harass Britain by restoring discipline.

(a) Camalodunum.

There was the same inactivity towards the enemy, and the same insubordination in the garrisons ; but Bolanus, being a good man and not disliked, acquired affection instead of authority.

12. But when, with the rest of the world, Vespasian had recovered Britain, we see distinguished generals, famous armies, and the enemy dispirited : Petilius Petilius Cerealis immediately excited terror by attacking the state of the Brigantes, which was esteemed the most populous of the province. Many battles were fought, some of which were bloody, and a great part of the Brigantian territory was either conquered or invaded.

13. But although Cerealis had diminished the care and fame of his successor, the burthen was sustained by Julius Frontinus, a man of high courage. Overcoming Julius Frontinus. at once the spirit of the enemy and the difficulties of the country, he subjugated the warlike and powerful nation of the Silures.

14. To him succeeded Agricola, who not only main- Agricola. tained the peace of the province ; but for seven years carried on war against the Caledonians and their warlike king Galgacus. He thus added to the Roman empire nations hitherto unknown.

15. But Domitian, envying the superior glory of Agricola, recalled him, and sent his lieutenant Lucullus Lucullus. into Britain, because he had suffered lances of a new form, *Lucculeas*, to be named after him.

16. His successor was Trebellius, under whom the Trebellius. two provinces, namely, Vespasiana and Mæeta, were wrested from the Roman government ; for the Romans gave themselves up to luxury.

17. About this time the emperor Hadrian visiting Hadrian. this island, erected a wall justly wonderful, and left Julius Severus his deputy in Britain.

18. From this time nothing worthy of attention is related, until Antoninus Pius carried on so many wars by his generals. He conquered the Britons by means

Lollius Ur-
bicus.

of Lollius Urbicus, the propraetor, and Saturninus, prae-
fect of the fleet, and, the barbarians being driven back,
another wall was built.   He recovered the province
afterwards called Valentia.

Aurelius.

19. Pius dying, Aurelius Antoninus gained many
victories over the Britons and Germans.

20. On the death of Antoninus, when the Romans
deemed their acquisitions insufficient, they suffered a

Marcellus.

great defeat under Marcellus.

Pertinax.

21. To him succeeded Pertinax, who conducted himself as an able general.

Clodius Al-
binus.

22. The next was Clodius Albinus, who contended
with Severus for the sceptre and purple.

Virius Lu-
pus.

23. After these, the first who enjoyed the title of
lieutenant was Virius Lupus : he did not perform many
splendid actions; for his glory was intercepted by the
unconquerable Severus, who, having rapidly put the
enemy to flight, repaired the wall of Hadrian, now become ruinous, and restored it to its former perfection.
Had he lived, he intended to extirpate the very name of
the barbarians ; but he died by the visitation of God,
among the Brigantes, in the city of Eboracum.

24. Alexander succeeded, who gained some victories
in the East, and died at Edessa.

25. His successors were the lieutenants Lucilianus,
M. Furius, N. Philippus * * * * * * * * *, who, if we
except the preservation of the boundaries, performed
hardly any thing worthy of notice.

26. Afterwards * * * * *

The rest is wanting.

RICARDI

MONACHI WESTMONASTERIENSIS

COMMENTARIOLI GEOGRAPHICI

DE

SITU BRITANNIÆ

ET

STATIONUM

QUAS ROMANI IPSI IN EA INSULA ÆDIFICAVERUNT

LIBER PRIMUS.

CAPUT I.

1. Finis erat orbis ora Gallici littoris, nisi Brittania insula, non qualibet amplitudine, nomen pene orbis alterius mereretur; octingentis enim et amplius millibus passuum longa porrigitur, ita ut eam in Caledonicum usque promuntorium metiamur. 2. Veteres Britanniam, ab albis rupibus, primum Albionem, postea, vocabulo gentis suæ, Brittaniam cognominaverunt, cum Brittanicæ vocarentur omnes de quibus mox paulo dicemus. 3. Inter septemtriones et occidentem locata est, Germaniæ, Galliæ, Hispaniæ, maximis Europæ partibus magno intervallo adversa, oceano Athlantico clauditur. 4. Habet ipsa Brittania a meridie Galliam Belgicam, cujus proximum littus transmeantibus civitas aperit, quæ Rhutupis portus dicitur : hic abest à Gessoriaco Morinorum, Brit-

tanicæ gentis portu, trajectu millium L. sive, ut quidam
scripsere, stadiorum CCCCL. illinc conspiciuntur Britt-
tones, quos

"—penitus toto divisos orbe—"

canit Virgilius Maro in Eclogis. 5. Agrippa, vetus orbis
descriptor, latitudinem ejus CCC. m. p. credit. Beda
vero rectius CC. exceptis duntaxat prolixioribus diverso-
rum promuntoriorum tractibus, quibus efficitur ut circuitus ejus quadragies octies septuaginta quinque millia
passuum compleat. Marcianus, author Græcus, mecum
MDIƆƆLXXV. milliaria habet.

CAPUT II.

1. ALBION, quæ Brittania Magna a Chrysosthomo authore Græco dicitur, natura, ut refert Cæsar, triquetra
et Siciliæ maxume similis est ; cujus unum latus est contra Galliam Celticam, hujus lateris alter angulus, qui est
ad Cantium, ad orientem solem ; inferior, qui est ad
Ocrinum promuntorium apud Damnonos, ad meridiem
et Hispaniam Tarraconensem spectat. Hoc latus tenet
circiter millia passuum D. 2. Alterum latus vergit ad
Hyberniam et occidentem solem ; hujus est longitudo
lateris, ut fert veterum opinio, DCC. m. p. 3. Tertium
est contra septemtriones, cui parti nulla est objecta terra
præter insulas ; sed ejus angulus lateris maxume ad Germaniam Magnam spectat ; huic a Novanto Chersoneso
per Taixolorum regionis angulum Cantium promuntorium
usque millia passuum DCCC. in longitudinem esse existimatur. Ita omnes insulam computabant in circuitu vicies
centena millia passuum, sed errant, nam a Cantio Ocrinum usque m. p. est distantia CCCC. inde Novantum
M. deinde Cantium MMCC. totius insulæ circuitus, ut
supra, MMMCCCCCC. millia passuum est. 4. Formam

totius Brittaniæ Livius et Fabius Rusticus, veterum doctissimi áuthores, oblongæ scutulæ vel bipenni assimilavere; et, ut annalium conditor Tacitus, est ea facies citra Caledoniam unde et in universam fama est transgressa; sed immensum et enorme spatium procurrentium extremo jam littore terrarum, velut in cuneum tenuatur. Sed Cæsar, inclutissimus dictator, cum Mela Romanorum nobili scriptore, pluribus eam triquetræ dixere similem : de quo supra. 5. Si Ptolemæo, orbis terrarum descriptori egregio, aliisque, coævis illi scriptoribus habenda fides, litteram Z, sed inversam, repræsentat hæc insula, nec tamen ex omni parte exacte quadrare hoc simile sufficienter præbet recentiori ævo descriptarum mapparum inspectio. Triquetra tamen figura soli Angliæ quodammodo videtur conveniens.

CAPUT III.

1. CÆTERUM Brittaniam qui mortales initio coluerint, indigenæ an advecti, ut inter nationes cæteras, parum compertum. Solis quippe Judæis, et per ipsos finitimis quibusdam gentibus, hoc contigit felicitatis, ut a primo inde mundi exordio gentis suæ originem continua serie ex infallibilibus deducere possint monumentis. 2. Habitus corporum varii, atque ex eo argumenta : namque rutulæ Caledoniam habitantium comæ, magni artus, Germanicam originem asseverant; Silurum colorati vultus, et torti plerumque crines, et positu contra Hispaniam, ut author est Tacitus, Iberos veteres trajecisse, easque et in Hybernia sedes occupasse fidem faciunt. Proximi Gallis et similes sunt, seu durante originis vi, seu procurrentibus in diversa terris, positio cœli corporibus habitum dedit. 3. Hic, si luberet indulgere fabulis, notare possem Venetos ope commercii navalis incolas religionesque his terris primum intulisse; imo non desunt

scriptores qui Herculem huc quoque pervenisse, reg-
numque constituisse, referunt: his vero tam alte recon-
ditis antiquitatibus, fabulis hinc inde refertis, immorari
vix operæ pretium videtur.   4. In universum tamen es-
timanti, Gallos vicinum solum occupasse credibile est:
eorum sacra deprehendas, superstitionum, ait Tacitus,
persuasionem; sermo haud multum diversus: pro ulteriori signo inservit Druidum traditio, una cum nominibus
civitatum, quæ vero omnes iis nominibus appellabantur,
quibus gentes, ortæ ex Galliæ civitatibus, quæ eo perve-
nerunt, atque agros colere ceperunt.   5. Hominum est,
inquit Cæsar, infinita multitudo, creberrimaque ædificia,
fere Gallicis consimilia, pecora sine numero.   6. Omnium
tamen humanissimi, qui Brittaniam austrinam incolebant,
neque multum a Gallis differebant consuetudine; ulte-
riores plerique frumenta non ferebant, sed lacte, fructu,
et carne vivebant, lanæ iis usus ac vestium ignotus erat,
et quanquam continuis frigoribus utebantur pellibus, tamen cervinis aut ovinis vestiti erant, et lavabantur in
fluminibus.   7. Omnes vero se Brittones olim vitro infe-
cerunt, quod cœruleum efficit colorem, atque, refert
Cæsar, hoc horribiliore sunt in pugna adspectu: capil-
loque sunt, ut ait Romanorum dux, promisso, atque
omni parte corporis rasa præter caput et labrum supe-
rius.   8. Uxores habebant Brittones deni duodenique
inter se communes, et maxume fratres cum fratribus,
parentes cum liberis; sed, si qui erant ex his nati, eorum
habebantur liberi, a quibus primum virgines quæque
ductæ erant.   Sua quemque mater uberibus alit, nec
ancillis nec nutricibus delectantur.   9. Utebantur aut
nummo æreo, aut annulis ferreis, ad certum pondus exa-
minatis, pro nummis, ut author est Cæsar Dictator.
10. Leporem et gallinam et anserem gustare Brittones
fas non putabant, hæc tamen alebant animi voluptatisque
causa.   11. Erant autem margaritæ, frena heburnea, et
armillæ, et electrina atque vitrea vasa, et gagates lapides,
et, quod cæteris excellit, stannum, magna copia merces.

12. Utebantur et navibus, quarum carinæ primum ac statumina ex levi materia fiebant, reliquum corpus navium ambitus viminibus contextus coriis bubulorum integebatur. Quantocunque tempore cursus tenebant, ut author est Solinus, navigantes, escis abstinent.

De Re Militari Brittonum.

13. Fert ipsa Brittania populos regesque populorum, ut Mela lib. III. scripsit : sed sunt inculti omnes, atque ut longius a continenti absunt, ita aliarum opum ignari, magis tantum pecore ac finibus dites ; causas autem et bella contrahunt, ac se frequenter invicem infestant, maxume imperitandi cupidine studioque ea prolatandi, quæ possident : solitum quidem, Brittones fœminarum ductu bellasse, neque sexum in imperiis discrevisse. 14. Dimicabant Brittones non solum equitatus peditatusque modo, sed etiam bigis et curribus, Gallice armati : covinos, essedas vero, more vulgari, vocabant, quorum falcatis axibus utebantur. 15. Equitum genus est, iis, quum est usus, atque aliquod bellum incidit, ut Cæsar est author, quod ante Romanorum adventum fere quotannis accidere solebat, uti aut ipsi injurias inferrent, aut illatas propulsarent : omnes in bello versantur, atqui eorum, ut quisque est genere copiisque amplissimus, ita plurimos circum se ambactos clientesque habet : hanc unam gratiam potentiamque noverunt. 16. In pedite erat Brittonum robur, prœliantur autem telis et ingentibus gladiis et brevibus cetris. Erant Brittonum gladii, ut ait Tacitus, sine mucrone. 17. Genus hoc erat ex essedis pugnæ, ut Cæsar in IV. narrat. Primo per omnes partes perequitant, et tela conjiciunt ; ac ipso terrore equorum, et strepitu rotarum, ordines plerumque perturbant : et quum se inter equitum turmas insinuavere, ex essedis desiliunt, et pedibus dispari prœlio contendunt. Aurigæ interim paululum e prœlio excedunt, atque ita se collocant, ut, si illi a multitudine hostium premantur, expeditum ad suos receptum habeant : ita mobilitatem equitum,

stabilitatem peditum in prœliis præstant ; ac tantum usu
quotidiano, et exercitatione efficiunt, ut in declivi ac
præcipiti loco incitatos equos sustinere, et brevi mode-
rari, ac flectere, et per temonem percurrere, et in jugo
insistere, et inde se in currus citissime recipere consueve-
rint. 18. Equestris autem prœlii ratio, et cedentibus
et insequentibus par atque idem periculum inferebat.
Accedebat huc, ut nunquam conferti, sed rari, magnis-
que intervallis, prœliarentur, stationesque dispositas haberent, atque alios alii deinceps exciperent ; integrique
et recentes defatigatis succederent. Utebantur et telis.
19. Formam regiminis Brittanici, ante advectos in hanc
insulam Romanos, determinare haud facile : hoc certum,
quod nullum ibi ante hæc tempora Monarchici imperii
vestigium, sed Democraticum fuisse potius videtur, nisi
forte Aristocratiam æmulari·videatur. Druidum in rebus
maxumi momenti authoritas non exigua. Commemorantur quidem in antiquissimis eorum monumentis prin-
cipes nonnulli ; hi vero brevioris plerumque imperii, nec,
nisi ingruente eximio quodam periculo et more dictato-
rum Romanorum ex tempore creati videntur. Nec desunt inter ipsos, apud alias fortes gentes rarissima ex-
empla, electi ab illis in futurum antisignanum ipsius hostium duces, ut pro illis in posterum militaret, quem nuper
hostem habuerant. 20. Proceritate corporis Gallos æque
ac Romanos vincunt Brittones, ita ut visos sibi Romæ
juvenes nondumque adultos Brittones, Strabo philoso-
phus, orbis terræ descriptor antiquissimus, affirmet, qui
solitam Gallorum Romanorumque staturam non levi
momento excedebant. 21. Ditiores australis Brittaniæ
incolæ aureo digitorum sinistræ medium annulo ornare
in more habuerunt, aurea vero e collo suspensa torques
a vilioris conditionis hominibus discernebat optima-
tum eminentiores. Septentrionales vero (hi veteres
erant regni indigenæ) vestium usus sicuti ac a longo
inde tempore avi abavique, tantum non ignari, ventrem
et cervicem ferreo cingunt, ut fert Herodianus, nobilis

Græcorum scriptor, annulo; ornamentum id esse ac divitiarum argumentum existimantes, accedente in usum potius quam ornatum scuto angusto, et lancea, gladioque e nudis et pictis corporibus dependente. Loricam interim galeamque, futura nempe paludes transeuntibus impedimento, rejiciunt atque contemnunt. 22. Inter cætera autem fuit et hoc Brittanicæ consuetudinis, ut viatores et mercatores etiam invitos consistere cogerent, et quod quisque eorum de una alterave re apud exteros memorabile audierit, aut cognoverit, quærerent, et mercatores peregre advenientes in oppidis vulgus circumsisteret ; quibus ex regionibus veniant, quasque ibi res cognoverint, pronunciare cogentes. His rumoribus atque auditionibus permoti, de summis sæpe rebus consilia ineunt, quorum eos e vestigio pœnitere necesse est, quum incertis rumoribus serviant, et plerique ad voluntatem eorum ficta respondeant. 23. Funera eorum sunt magnifica et sumptuosa, omniaque, quæ vivis cordi fuisse arbitrantur, in ignem inferunt, etiam arma et animalia. Sepulchrum tumulus ex cespitibus erigit.

CAPUT IV.

1. Natio Brittonum fuit omnis, ut Gallorum, admodum dedita religionibus; atque ob eam causam qui gravioribus affecti morbis, quique in prœliis periculisque versabantur, aut pro victimis homines immolabant, aut se immolaturos vovebant. 2. Ad peragenda crudelia hæc sacra, druidum utebantur ministerio ; nec credebant placari posse Deos, nisi hominis cædes humano sanguine pensaretur. Hinc instituta publice istiusmodi sacrificia, oblataque, ut gratissima Diis hostia, qui in furto, latrocinio, aliave graviori culpa deprehensi, his vero deficientibus, ad innocentium quoque mactationem descendebant, ut quocunque demum modo Dii placa-

rentur. 3. Nisi adfuerint Druides, res sacra rite cele-
brari non credebatur: hinc publica non minus quam
privata sacra procurandi negotium illis unice incum-
bebat. Erat penes hoc religionis cura, æque ac mys-
teriorum interpretatio, corporis quoque et sanitatis
sive tuendæ, sive restituendæ curam habebant, continuo
medicinæ peritissimi. 4. Inter deos ipsis præcipue co-
lebatur Mercurius, cujus plurima prostabant simulachra,
post hunc Justitiam (qui Brittonibus Adraste dicebatur), hinc Apollinem, Martem (qui etiam Vitucadrus
appellabatur). Jovem, Minervam, Herculem, Victo-
riam (Andatem vocatam), Dianam, Cybelem et Pluto-
nem venerabantur, eandem fere de his numinibus ac
quidem aliæ gentes opinionem amplexi. 5. A Dite
autem, ut et Galli, gentis suæ originem deducere allaborabant Brittones. Antiquissimam hanc venditantes
Druidum traditionem, eam ob causam quælibet temporum spatia, non dierum, sed noctium numero definie-
bant, dieique mensis et anni natalis initia ita numerare
consueverunt, ut capto a nocte initio dies subsequere-
tur; quæ consuetudo omnino convenit cum antiquissima
illa, quæ Gen. I. habetur noctium ac dierum computa-
tione. 6. Ad Druides magnus disciplinæ causa conflue-
bat adolescentium numerus; hi quippe in magno erant
apud ipsos honore, nam fere de omnibus controversiis,
publicis privatisque, constituebant, et si quod admissum
erat facinus, si cædes facta, si de hæreditate, de finibus
controversia erat, iidem decernebant: præmia pœnasque
constituerunt, si quis aut privatus aut publicus eorum
decreto non stetit, sacrificiis interdicebant; hæc exclu-
sionis pœna apud eos erat gravissima. Quibus ita in-
terdictum, ii numero impiorum ac sceleratorum habebantur: iis omnes decedebant, aditum eorum sermonemque
defugientes, ne quid ex contagione incommodi accipe-
rent: neque iis petentibus jus reddebatur, neque honos
habebatur ullus. 7. His autem omnibus Druidibus
præerat unus, qui summam inter eos potestatem habe-

bat et authoritatem. Hoc mortuo, successor dabatur, qui inter reliquos excellebat dignitate; at si plures essent dignitate pares, suffragio Druidum res committebatur; nonnunquam etiam de principatu armis contendebant. 8. Druides à bello abesse solebant, neque tributa una cum reliquis pendebant, militiæ vacationem, omniumque rerum habebant immunitatem; tantis excitati præmiis, et sua sponte, multi in disciplinam conveniebant, et a propinquis parentibusque mittebantur. 9. Magnum ibi numerum versuum ediscere solebant, quod unicum apud eos memoriæ et annalium genus: itaque nonnulli annos vicenos in disciplina permanebant, neque fas esse existimarunt eam litteris mandare, quum tamen in reliquis fere rebus, publicis privatisque rationibus, Græcis litteris uterentur. "Id mihi duabus de causis," inquit D. Julius, "instituisse videntur; quod neque in vulgus disciplinam efferri velint; neque eos, qui discunt, litteris confisos, minus memoriæ studere; quod fere plerisque accidit, ut præsidio litterarum, diligentiam in perdiscendo, ac memoriam remittant." 10. Inprimis hoc persuadere allaborabant, non interire animas, sed ab aliis post mortem transire ad alios; atque hoc maxume ad virtutem excitari putabant, metu mortis neglecto. Multa præterea de sideribus atque eorum motu, de mundi et terrarum magnitudine, de rerum natura, de Deorum vi ac potestate disputabant, et juventuti tradebant sollicite. 11. Non est omittenda de visco admiratio: nihil habebant Druides visco et arbore in qua gignatur (si modo sit robur) sacratius. Jam per se roborum eligebant lucos, nec ulla sacra sine ea fronde conficiebant; ut inde appellati quoque interpretatione Græca possint Δρυιδες (Druides) videri. Enimvero quicquid adnascatur illis, e cœlo missum putabant, signumque esse electæ ab ipso Deo arboris. Est autem id rarum admodum inventu, et repertum magna religione petitur, et ante omnia sexta luna, quæ principium mensium annorumque bis facit, et seculi, post tricesimum

annum; quia jam virium abunde habebat, nec tamen sit
sui dimidia.   Omnia sanantem appellantes suo vocabulo.
Sacrificio epulisque rite sub arbore præparatis, duos
admovebant candidi coloris tauros, quorum cornua tunc
primum vinciantur.   Sacerdos candida veste cultus ar-
borem scandebat, falce aurea dimetiens; candido id
excipiebatur sago: tunc demum victimas immolant,
præcantes, ut suum donum Deus prosperum faceret.
His, quibus dederant, fœcunditatem eo poto dari cui-
cunque animali sterili arbitrabantur, contraque venena
omnia esse remedio: tanta gentium in rebus frivolis
plerumque religio fuerat! 12. Druidarum disciplina in
nostra Brittania reperta, atque inde in Galliam translata
esse existimatur: unde Plinius eleganter declamat lib.
XXX. his verbis: "Sed quid ego hæc commemorem
in arte oceanum quoque transgressa, et ad naturæ inane
pervecta?   Brittania hodieque eam attonite celebrat
tantis ceremoniis, ut dedisse Persis videri possit:" idem
Julius Cæsar affirmat in Ephemeridis: "Et nunc, qui
diligentius eam rem cognoscere volunt, plerumque illo,
discendi caussa, proficiscuntur." 13. Druides certo
anni tempore in finibus Brittaniæ, in insulæ Monæ luco
consecrato, considebant; huc omnes undique, quos inter
controversia, conveniebant, eorumque judiciis decretisque
acquiescebant.   14. Præter Druides apud Gallos atque
Brittones erant bardi poetæ, qui Deûm Heroumque res
gestas, heroicis expositas versibus, cum dulcibus lyræ
modulis cantitabant. 15. De his ambobus ita cecinit
Lucanus vates his versibus, quibus hoc caput finiam:

"Vos quoque, qui fortes animas, belloque peremptas
    Laudibus in longum, vates! dimittitis ævum,
    Plurima securi fudistis carmina bardi.
    Et vos barbaricos ritus, moremque sinistrum
    Sacrorum, druidæ, positis repetistis ab armis.
    Solis nosse Deos, et cœli numina vobis,
    Aut solis nescire datum: nemora alta remotis
    Incolitis lucis.   Vobis authoribus, umbræ
    Non tacitas Erebi sedes, Ditisque profundi

Pallida regna petunt ; regit idem spiritus artus
Orbe alio : longæ, canitis (si cognita) vitæ
Mors media est.   Certe populi, quos despicit Arctos,
Felices errore suo, quos ille timorum
Maxumus, haud urget Lethi metus : inde ruendi
In ferrum mens prona viris, animæque capaces
Mortis ; et ignavum redituræ parcere vitæ."

CAPUT V.

1. Opima frugibus atque arboribus insula, et alendis
apta pecoribus ac jumentis ; vineas etiam quibusdam in
locis germinans. Sed et avium ferax terra marique
generis diversi ; fluviis quoque multum piscosis, ac fontibus præclara copiosis, et quidem præcipue isicio abun-
dat et anguilla.   2. Capiuntur autem sæpissime et vituli
marini, et delphines, nec non et balænæ, de quo apud
Satyricum mentionem inveniamus :

" Quanto delphinis balæna Britannica major ? "

3. Exceptis autem variorum generibus conchyliorum,
in quibus sunt et musculi, quibus inclusam sæpe marga-
ritam omnis quidem coloris optimam inveniunt, id est,
et rubicundi, et purpurei, et hyacinthini, et prasini, sed
maxume candidi, ut scripsit venerabilis Beda in prima
Eccl. Hist. ad Regem Colfulsum.   4. Sunt et cochleæ,
satis superque abundantes, quibus tinctura coccinei coloris conficitur, cujus rubor pulcherrimus, nullo unquam
solis ardore, nulla valet pluviarum injuria pallescere ; sed
quo vetustior est, eo solet esse venustior.   5. Habet
fontes salinarum et fontes calidos, et ex eis fluvios bal-
nearum calidarum, omni ætati et sexui per distincta
loca, juxta suum cuique modum accommodatos.   6.
Nascitur ibi plumbum album in mediterraneis regionibus, in maritimis ferrum ; sed ejus exigua est copia ;
ære utuntur importato ; gignit et aurum, et argentum.

M

Fert et lapidem gagatem plurimum optimumque; est
autem nigrogemmeus et ardens igni admotus, incensus
serpentes fugat, adtritu calefactus adplicita detinet
æque ut succinum. 7. Et quia Britannia prope sub septentrionali vertice mundi jacet, lucidas æstate noctes
habet; ita ut medio sæpe tempore noctis in questionem
veniat intuentibus, utrum crepusculum adhuc permaneat
vespertinum, an jam advenerit matutinum? utpote noc-
turno sole non longe sub terris ad orientem boreales
per plagas redeunte.   Unde etiam plurimæ longitudinis
habet dies æstate, sicut et noctes contra in bruma, sole
nimirum tunc in Lybicas partes secedente, id est, horarum X. et VIII., ut author est Cleomedes: plurimæ
item brevitatis noctes æstate et dies habet in bruma,
hoc est, VI. solummodo æquinoctialium horarum: cum
in Armenia, Macedonia, Italia, cæterisque ejusdem
lineæ regionibus, longissima dies sive nox XV., brevis-
sima VIIII., compleat horas.   8. Sed de Britannia
Britonibusque in genere satis prolixe commemoravi.
Res ipsa requirit ad particularia tandem descendere,
atque, in sequentibus, statum fatumque diversarum, quæ
hanc insulam incoluerunt, nationum, quæ eandem nobi-
litarunt, civitates, *cet.* quales sub ditione Romana erant,
ex ordine depingere mei jam erit propositi.

CAPUT VI.

1. BRITANNIA, secundum accuratissima veterum, quæ
propius fidem sunt, monumenta, erat omnis divisa in partes
septem; quarum sex alio atque alio tempore imperio
Romano adjectæ fuerunt, septima vero sub solis barbaris
Caledoniis. 2. Supra dictæ Britanniæ partes erant Britannia Prima, Secunda, Flavia, Maxima, Valentia, et Vespasiana, quarum ultima non diu stetit in manibus Romanorum.   Ex his Britanniam Primam a Flavia Thamesis
flumen, a Britannia Secunda mare dividit.   Flavia ini-

tium capit a Mari Germanico, continetur Thamesi fluvio,
Sabrina a finibus Silurum Ordovicumque, vergit ad septemtriones et Brigantum regionem. Maxima ab ex-
tremis Flaviæ finibus oritur, pertinet ad inferiorem
partem Muri, qui totam ex transverso percurrit insulam,
spectatque in septemtriones. Spatium inter ambos,
hunc et alium qui ab imperatore Antonino Pio, inter
Bdoram et Clyddam extructus est, Murum, occupat
Valentiana. Vespasiana autem a Bdoræ æstuario ad
civitatem Alcluith, unde linea ad ostium fluminis Vararis ducta terminos ostendit. Secunda ad eam partem
oceani, quæ ad Hyberniam pertinet, spectat inter occasum et septemtriones. Sed de provinciis satis. 3.
Necessarium vero ducimus, antequam ad accuratiorem
nos conferamus descriptionem, regiminis in hisce provinciis constitutionem paucis attingere. Deprehendimus
adeoque totam, antiquissimis temporibus, plurium regu-
lorum statuumque arbitrio divisim paruisse Britanniam,
·quorum nonnulli, etiam post occupatam a Romanis provinciam, superfuisse commemorantur ; sed vix umbra
regiæ dignitatis istis principibus relicta, contrarium
nempe dissuadente politica illa, qua Romani olim, præ
cultissimis etiam quibusque gentibus, inclaruerunt pru-
dentia. Victricibus Romanorum armis subjugatæ imperatoria authoritate constitutus præerat Legatus, ipsa
Brittannia vero provincia erat proconsularis. Per plures
hæc imperii constitutio duravit ætates ; licet in plures
interim ipsa insula divisa fuerit partes ; primum nempe
in Superiorem et Inferiorem, deinceps vero, uti antea
demonstravimus, in septem dispertita provincias, mutata
regiminis forma : deinde diu paruit, ut imperatoria
sedes, hæc insula Carausio, eisque quos in societatem
adsciverat tyrannis. Gloria et præsidium Christianismi,
Constantinus Magnus, creditur Maximam et Valentiam
Consulares, Primam, Secundam, et Flaviam Præsidiales,
fecisse. Toti vero insulæ præpositus est Vicarius, vir
perspicabilis, sub dispositione viri illustris Domini

Præfecti Prætorii Galliæ ; præter quem in vetusto quodam volumine circa eadem tempora commemoratur
aliquis eximiæ dignitatis vir, titulo Comitis Britanniarum
insignis, alius itidem, Comes littoris Saxonici, tertius
præterea Dux Britanniæ dictus, aliique plures, magnis
præfecti muneribus, quæ, cum distincta eorum notitia,
injuria temporis, impetrari non potuerit, cogimur taciti
præterire.   4. Prolixum nunc tandem iter ingredior,
totam non minus insulam, quam singulas ejus partes
curiosa lustraturus indagine, pressurusque optimorum in
hoc negotio authorum vestigia.   Fiat vero ab extrema
Primæ provinciæ ora initium, cujus littora Galliæ obji-
ciuntur.   Tres vero laudatissimos validissimosque status,
Cantianum nempe, Belgicum, et Damnonicum, complectitur hæc provincia, de quibus ea, qua fieri poterit,
cura nobis sigillatim agendum.   Cantium primo lustremus.   5. Ad extremam Britanniæ Primæ orientalem
oram remotam Cantium, Cantiis quondam habitatum,
civitatibus Durobrobi et Cantiopoli, quæ eorum metropolis ; hic sepultus est D. Augustinus Anglorum apos-
tolus : Dubræ, Lemanus, et Regulbium, præsidio a
Romanis munita, eorumque primarium Rhutupi, deducta
eo colonia, metropolis factum, portusque classi Romanorum, quæ oceano septentrionali dominabatur, reci-
piendæ factus idoneus.   Tanti nominis fuit hæc civitas,
ut littora vicina ex ea dicta sint Rhutupina, de quibus
Lucanus poeta :

> " Aut vaga cum Thetis Rhutupinaque littora fervent."

Inde quoque ingentia et grati saporis ostrea Romam
translata, ut author est Juvenalis Satyricus his verbis :

> " —————————— Circæis nata forent, an
> Lucrinum ad saxum, Rhutupinove edita fundo
> Ostrea, callebat primo deprendere morsu."

Statio etiam fuit, sub dispositione viri spectabilis Comitis
littoris Saxonici, legionis secundæ Augustæ.   6. Quam
plurimis hoc Cantiorum regnum fluminibus rigatur,

quorum celebriora, Madus, Sturius, Dubris, et Lemanus,
qui Cantios a Bibrocis discernebat. 7. Inter tria ista
præcipua Britanniæ promontoria, eminet illud, quod a
Cantio nomen habet: ibi oceanus in angulum quasi
redactus, cursum ita promovet fluxionemque suam,
donec, ut veteres tradunt, fretum istud oceani, quod
jam Britanniæ format insulam, effecerit. 8. A Cantio,
vasta illa quæ Anterida nonnullis, aliis Caledonia dicta
sylva, late extenditur ad CL. milliaria per Bibrocorum
ac Segontiacorum terras, ad Heduorum usque fines
excurrens. De hac sylva ita cecinit Lucanus:

    " Unde Caledoniis fallit turbata Britannos."

9. Cantiis proximi, et, ut putant nonnulli, subjecti,
Bibroci, qui et aliis Rhemi dicuntur; natio in monu-
mentis non penitus ignota, quibus habitatum Bibroicum,
Regentium, Noviomagumque metropolis. Anderidam
vero occupatam tenuerunt Romani. 10. Confines illis
apud ripam Thamesis habitabant Attrebates, quorum
urbs primaria Caleba. 11. Infra hos, propius flumen
Cunetium, habitabant Segontiaci, quorum caput fuit
Vindonum. 12. Ad oceanum, Bibrocis affines, inferius
habitabant, sic dicti, Belgæ, quorum urbes primariæ
Clausentum, quod nunc Sotheamptona dicitur, Portus
Magnus, omniumque præcipua Venta, nobilissima civitas
ad flumen Antonam sita. Sorbiodunum vero tenebat
præsidium Romanorum. Omnes enim Belgæ Allobroges
sunt, et suam a Celtis Belgisque originem traxere: hi,
non multis ante Cæsaris adventum in hanc insulam
seculis, relicta patria, Gallia, a Germanorum Romanorumque populis infestata, atque devicta; illi, qui, trajecto
flumine Rheni, eorum expugnatas occupavere regiones,
de quo autem prolixius M. Dictator Cæsar, sedem hic
sibi elegerunt. 13. Omnes regiones quæ Thamesi,
versus meridiem, adjacent, olim, uti vetera monumenta
declarant, a bellicosa Senonum gente fuerunt occupatæ;
qui, sub ductu et auspicio decantatissimi regis Brenni,

peragrata Gallia, Alpibusque, adhuc inviis, sibi pate-
factis, Romam fastu elatam ista incursione vastam solo
facile æquassent, nisi Rempublicam Romanam, quam
more nutricis in sinu quasi gestare (dum infra destina-
tum ab illis fastigium agebat) videbantur Fata, cladem
aversura Manlium clangore anseris excitassent, qui,
circa montem unum pendentes, et nocte subeuntes, barbaros a summo Capitolio dejecit. Huic eadem Numi-
num cura Camillum postea auxilio misit, qui abeuntes a
tergo aggressus ita cecidit, ut Senonici sanguinis inun-
datione omnia incendiorum vestigia deleret, urbemque
ita ruinæ proximam ab interitu vindicaret. Senones
autem ob valentissimam hanc expeditionem natale
solum, ut cultoribus vacuum, ita præda refertissimum,
alienæ genti, quam Belgas supra nominatos fuisse satis
liquet, concesserunt. 14. Ad Sabrinam, Thamesi inferius, habitabant Hedui, urbes eorum Ischalis et Avalonia. Thermæ, quæ et Aquæ Solis nuncupabantur,
Romanorum, qui hanc Britanniæ oram tenebant, factæ
colonia et perpetua sedes; urbs nominatissima hæc
erat, ad flumen Abonam sita, ibique fontes calidi, opi-
paro exsculpti apparatu, ad usus mortalium; quibus
fontibus præsules erant Apollinis ét Minervæ Numina,
in quorum ædibus perpetui ignes nunquam labascunt in
favillas, sed ubi ignis tabuit vertitur in globos saxeos.
15. Infra Heduorum terras siti erant Durotriges, qui et
Morini alias vocantur. Metropolin habebant Durinum
et promontorium Vindeliam. In horum finibus sensim
coarctatur Britannia, et immensum efformare videtur
brachium, quod irruptionem minitantem commode re-
pellit oceanum. 16. In hoc brachio, quæ, intermis-
sione Uxellæ amnis, Heduorum regioni protenditur, sita
erat regio Cimbrorum. Utrumne vero modernum
Walliæ nomen dederint, an vero antiquior sit Cimbrorum origo, non æque constat. Urbes illis præcipuæ
Termolus et Artavia. Visuntur hic, antiquis sic dictæ,
Herculis columnæ, et non procul hinc insula Herculea.

Sed a fluminis Uxellæ finibus continuum procurrit montium jugum, cui nomen Ocrinum, extremumque ejus ad promontorium ejusdem nominis extenditur. 17. Ultra Cimbros extremum insulæ angulum incolebant Carnabii, unde forsitan, quod hodieque retinet nomen, obtinuit Carnubia. Urbes habebant Musidum et Halangium : cum vero has olim desertas propemodum et incultas Britanniæ partes Romani nunquam salutaverint, minoris omnino momenti urbes eorum fuisse videntur, et historicis propterea neglectæ ; geographis tamen memorantur promontoria Bolerium et Antivestæum. 18? Memoratis modo populis in littore oceani austrum versus affines ad Belgas-Allobroges sedem habebant Damnonii, gens omnium validissima, quæ ratio movisse videtur Ptolemæum, ut totum hunc terræ tractum, qui in mare brachii instar prætenditur, illis adscripserit. Urbes habebant Uxellam, Tamaram, Volubam, Ceniam, omniumque matrem Iscam, fluvio cognomini imminentem. Fluvii apud ipsos præcipui memorati modo Isca, Durius, Tamarus, atque Cenius. Ora eorum maritima promontoria exhibet tria, de quibus mox paulo dicemus. Hanc regionem, utpote metallis abundantem, Phœnicibus, Græcis, et Gallis mercatoribus probe notam fuisse constat : hi enim ob magnam quam terra ferebat stanni copiam eo sua frequenter extendebant negotia ; cujus rei præcipua sunt documenta supra nominata tria promontoria, Helenis scilicet, Ocrinum, et Κριȣ μέτωπον, ut et nomina civitatum, Græcam Phœniciamque originem redolentia. 19. Ultra brachium in oceano sitæ sunt insulæ Sygdiles, quæ etiam Œstrominides et Cassiterides vocabantur, dictæ. 20. Cum prænominatis Damnoniis Belgisque conjunctis XXX. prœlia commisisse narratur valentissimus ille imperator Vespasianus. Decem hi ad australes Thamesis et Sabrinæ ripas habitantes populi, a Romanis sensim subacti, eorumque regiones in provinciæ formam redactæ, quæ Britannia Prima fuit appellata, cum hic fuerit in istis terris pri-

mus Romanorum victoriæ fructus.   21. Succedit ordine
Britannia Secunda, quæ a prioribus, interfluente Sabrina
amne, discernitur : a provincia autem Flavia, tum me-
moratus amnis, tum Deva fluvius eandem sejungit, reliquum cingitur a mari interno.   Hæc erat celebrata illa
regio Silurum, tribus validissimis habitata populis, quos
inter præ reliquis celebres Silures, proprie sic dicti,
quam ab ora relicta turbidum Sabrinæ fretum distin-
guit : cujus homines, ut eruditissimus Solinus est
author, etiam nunc custodiunt morem vetustum, nun-
dinas ac nummum refutant, dant res et accipiunt ; mu-
tationibus necessaria potius quam pretiis parant.   Deos
percolunt, scientiam futurorum pariter viri ac fœminæ
ostendunt.   22. Civitates Silurum, Sariconium, Magna,
Gobaneum, et Venta eorum caput, fuerunt.   Iscæ vero,
flumini imminentem urbem cognominem, tenebat Romanorum colonia, ibique per annos plures secunda legio,
quæ Augusta alias vocabatur, stationem habebat, donec
Valentiam et Rhutupin transferebatur.   Hæc erat provinciæ Secundæ primaria Romana.   23. Olim ac diu
potens erat hæc Silurum regio, sed, cum eam regno
Charaticus tenuit, longe potentissima: hic continuis
novem annis, omnia Romanorum arma pro ludibrio ha-
bita, sæpe evertit, donec de illo, conjunctis viribus
Romanos aggressuro, triumphavit Legatus Ostorius.
Charaticus enim, prælio evadens, auxiliumque a vicinis
regibus petens, per astutiam matronæ Romanæ Carthis-
manduæ cum rege Brigantiæ Venutio nuptæ, Romanis
deditus est.   Post id temporis mascule tantum suam
ipsius ditionem idem ille populus defendit, usque dum a
Varionio spoliatus, ac tandem a Frontino devictus, in
formam Romanæ, cui Britannia Secunda, ut supra meminimus, nomen erat, provinciæ suum redigi pateretur
imperium.   24. Duæ aliæ sub Siluribus gentes fuere,
primum Ordovices, qui in septentrionali versus insulam Monam ; et deinde Dimeciæ, qui in extrema
versus occidentem parte degebant, ubi promonto-

rium quod Octorupium nuncupatur, unde in Hyberniam transitus XXX. milliarium. Dimeciarum urbes Menapia, et primaria Muridunum. Lovantium vero sibi habitandum vendicaverant Romani. Ultra hos et Silurum terminos siti Ordovices, quorum urbes Mediolanum et Brannogenium. Sabrina in montibus illorum oriunda, majoribus tribus Britanniæ fluviis merito accensetur, addito nempe Thamesi et Tavo. Elucet imprimis in historia nomen Ordovicum ob sumtam de inclutissimi ipsorum regis captivitate vindictam. Hinc enim toties redactum in angustias exercitum Romanorum tam misere vexarunt, ut de illorum fere imperio in hac regione actum fuisset, ni in tantæ cladis vindictam postea surrexisset dux Agricola, qui, victricia circumferens arma, totam quoque hanc gentem subjugavit, maximamque partem ferro delevit. 25. Huc quoque referendum illud, quod a septentrione Ordovicum situm, ab oceano alluitur, territorium, cum illorum regimini aliquandiu fuerit subjectum; hoc certo constat, quod illum Cangiani quondam inhabitaverint tractum, quorum urbs unica Segontium, promontorio Cangano vicina. Incluta hæc erat civitas, freto Meneviaco, contra Monam, religiosissimam insulam, ubi olim druides habitare, adjacet. In hac insula plurima sita erant oppida, tota autem insula in circuitu LX. m. p. fere complectitur, atque, ut refert Plinius, a Camaloduno colonia CC. m. p. abest. Fluvii apud ipsos Tosibus, qui et Canovius; pro terminis vero erat utraque Deva. In hac vero regione mons Eriri celsissimus maxumusque invenitur. Ordovicia una cum Cangiorum Carnabiorumque regionibus, ni fama me fallit, nomine Genaniæ, sub imperatoribus post Trajani principatum inclarescebat. 26. Ordo jam ad illam nos deducit provinciam, quæ Flavia Romanis vocata : unde vero hoc nomen acceperit, utrum a matre Constantini Magni Flavia Julia Helena, ex his terris oriunda? an vero a Romanorum familia Flavia? — quominus determinari possit, obstat injuria temporum, quæ nobis invidet ge-

nuina quæ huc facerent antiquitatis monumenta. 27. Ad
fluvium Devam primo siti erant Carnabii, quibus habi-
tatæ fuerunt Benonæ, Etocetum, Banchorium (monaste-
rium totius insulæ celeberrimum, quod, in contentione
Augustini eversum, non postea resurrexit), et reliquarum
mater Uriconium, quæ, inter Britanniæ civitates maxu-
mas, nomen possidebat. In extremo hujus terræ angulo
flumini Devæ imminebat cognominis Romanorum colonia
Deva, opus vicesimæ legionis, quæ Victrix dicebatur, et
olim illius erat regionis tutela. Hæc eadem esse existimatur quæ jam *West-Chester* vocatur. 28. Infra nominatos regnum Cassium, a rege Ptolemæo Catieuchlani
appellatum, extendebatur, aut respublica potius, quæ ex
binis gentibus coaluerat. Harum, quæ Sabrinæ proxima
vocabatur Dobuni, vel, ut Dio celeberrimus scriptor annalibus inseruit, Boduni. Apud hos oritur flumen
Thamesis, et deinde longo spatio per fines Heduorum,
Attrebatum, Cassiorum, Bibrocorum, Trinobantum, et
Cantiorum citatus fertur, et oceanum Germanicum influit.
Urbes Dobunorum erant Salinæ, Branogena, ad sinis-
tram Sabrinæ ripam, Alauna, et, cui reliquiæ nomen
laudemque debent, Corinum, urbs perspicabilis, opus, ut
tradunt, Vespasiani ducis. Glevum vero, in extremo
regni contra regionem Silurum situm, Romana tenebat
colonia, quam deduxit Claudius Cæsar, ut scriptores de
istis temporibus affirmant. Finitimi illis Cassii, quorum
urbes Forum Dianæ et Verulamium : cum vero hæc ad
municipiam dignitatem a Romanis evecta, ejus præ aliis
urbibus eminentia illis omnino adscribenda. Hic natus
erat D. Albanus Martyr. Hæc civitas ruina Camalo-
duni, Londiniique, in seditione a Bonduica excitata,
cujus in annalibus mentionem facit eruditissimus Tacitus,
involuta erat. Hi Cassii olim, præ ceteris insulæ gentibus, caput extulere, atque cum inclutissimo eorum rege
Cassibellino (cui non paucæ nationes fuere tributariæ)
dictator Cæsar multos eosdemque gravissimos, sub read-
ventum ipsius in hanc insulam, habuit conflictus ; sed ab

eadem ille gente cum Siluribus conjuncta fugatus, unde
et emendatissimus Lucanus :

"Territa quæsitis ostendit terga Britannis."

Adventante autem ipso imperatore Claudio, omnes cum
vicinis fracti sunt, eorumque regio in formam Romanæ
provinciæ redacta, nomineque, Cæsariensis, et postea
Flavia, nuncupata. 29. Juxta Cassios, ubi se oceano
Thamesis propinquavit, regio Trinobantum sita erat ;
natio quæ non modo sponte in Romanorum concessit
amicitiam, sed illis quoque, ut colonias ibi ponerent, me-
tropolim suam Lundinum et Camalodunum ad mare sita
obtulerunt. In hac urbe Flavia Julia Helena, piissima
conjux Constantini Chlori, materque Constantini Magni,
e sanguine regum Britannicorum nasci memoriæ proditum dicunt. Prima autem hæc Romanorum in Britannia
coloniarum erat, templo Claudii, imagine Victoriæ, cum
aliis diversis ornamentis insignis. Lundinum enim mundo
cognita civitas erat et erit. Primum Trinovantum,
postea Londinium, dein Augusta, et nunc Londona rur-
sum. Urbe Roma, secundum chronicorum fidem, sane
antiquior est ; super ripam Thamesis fluminis posita, et
ipsa multorum emporium populorum terra marique veni-
entium. Hæc a piissima illa imperatrice Helena, S. S.
Crucis inventrice, circumvallata, atque, si fides sit penes
traditiones, quæ non semper erroneæ sunt, nominata est
Augusta ; tota autem Britannia Romana Insula. 30.
Limes huic populo ad septentrionem flumen Surius, ultra
quem habitabant Iceni, celeberrima natio, in duas gentes
divisa, quarum prior, Cenomanni habitans, ad septentrionem Trinobantes et Cassios, ad orientem oceanum
spectabat. Horum urbes Durnomagus et caput regionis
Venta. Romanorum colonia erat Camboricum ; in mare
orientem versus procurrens lingula dicitur Flavia Extrema. Fluminum notissima sunt Garion, Surius, et
Aufona, in sinum Metorin sese exonerans. Ex altera
parte ad Aufonam incolebant, Carnabiis Brigantibus, et

oceano vicini, Coitanni, in tractu sylvis obsito, qui, ut
aliæ Britonum sylvæ, Caledonia fuit appellata. De hac
autem III. mentionem facit historicus ille Florus. Civitas primaria Coitannorum erat Ragæ; et præter hanc
Romanorum colonia Lindum, in extrema ad orientem
provinciæ ora. Totam vero regionem bifariam secat
fluvius Trivona. Hæc Icenorum gens, quæ, utpote fero-
cissima bellique post hominum memoriam studiosissima,
omissis tam rusticis quam civilibus artibus, sua sponte
in Romanorum societatem accesserat, non tantum mox
defecerat, sed ad sui quoque imitationem alios quam plurimos excitaverat, ab Ostorio duce primum sub jugum
missa est. Aliquot post annos, quum rex ipsorum, et
animo et opibus valentissimus, Præsutagus moriens Cæsarem ejusdemque posteros heredes fecerat. Romani
autem Icenorum sic abutentes amicitia, ut nulli non se
luxuriæ dederint, ab iisdem postea sociisque, sub ductu
bellicosissimæ Bonduicæ, viduæ regis supra nominati,
ita infesti ipsis sunt redditi, ut combustis deletisque ipsorum coloniis ac municipio, civium denique Romanorum LXXX. M. ferro misere sint trucidati; sed postea
ad officium redegit Suetonius legatus, multis prudentiæ
nominibus suspiciendus. 31. Ad septentrionalem hujus
regionis plagam oceano occurrit fluvius Abus, quondam
terminorum provinciæ Maximæ unus, uti alter Seteja.
Dicta quoque hæc provincia fuit Brigantiæ Regnum,
scilicet ejusdem nominis regionem complexa, tribusque
habitata nationibus. In extrema orientali plaga, ubi
promontoria Oxellum et Brigantum extrema in mare
procurrunt, habitabant Parisii, quorum urbes Petuaria
et Portus Felix. 32. Supra hos, uti et ad latus, siti
erant proprie sic dicti Brigantes, gens numerosissima,
toti olim provinciæ leges præscribens. His cultæ civitates, Epiacum, Vinovium, Cambodunum, Cataracton,
Galacum, Olicana, et primaria Isurium. Eboracum vero,
ad Urum fluvium, caput provinciæ; primum colonia
nomine Sextæ a Romanis factum, sextæque deinde le-

gionis, quæ Victrix dicebatur, sedes ; deinceps vero plurium imperatorum præsentia illustrior factum, municipii
quoque auctum prærogativis. 33. Totam in æquales fere
partes provinciam dividunt montes Alpes Penini dicti ;
hi, ad Icenorum Carnabiorumque fines, ad fluvium Trivonam surgentes, continua serie per CL. milliaria septentrionem versus decurrunt. 34. Populi, ad occidentalem
hujus jugi partem habitantes, sunt Volantii Sistuntiique,
arctiori ut videtur fœdere conjuncti. Urbes habebant
Rerigonum, Coccium et Lugubalium, quarum tamen pos-
teriores binas Romanorum tenebant præsidia. 35. Septentrionales hujus terræ limites tegebat murus iste
stupendæ molis, a Romanis per isthmum ad longitudinem
LXXX. milliarium extensus, cujus altitudo XII. cras-
sities vero IIX. pedes æquabat, turribusque ornatus,
murus erat. 36. Gentem hanc, ab imperatore Claudio
primum infestatam, deinde ab Ostorio legato devictam,
postea a Cereali fractam, et magnam partem debellatam,
ex historia colligitur : cum vero sponte se Agricolæ de-
disset, pacem illi datam esse percepimus. Famam hujus
gentis in historiis præcipue delerunt turpia Reginæ ipsorum gesta inauditaque perfidia. Ipsa harum potentium
nationum progenies erat, quæ novas electura sedes, ulti-
mum ultro, patriæ, inter Alpes, Danubium, et Rhoda-
num jacenti, valedicebat. Ex his in Hyberniam postea
nonnulli, sedem ibi fixuri, transierunt, ut ex documentis
constat. 37. His borealiores erant nationes istæ vali-
dissimæ olim sub nomine Maætarum venientes, a quibus,
mortuo patre, fratricida iste Bassianus suam turpiter
pacem emit. Regiones, quas tenuere, sequentes erant,
in orientem Ottadinia, inde Gadenia, post hanc Selgovia,
deinde Novantia, supra hos etiam Damnia. 38. Muro
proximi habitabant Gadeni, quorum metropolis Curia.
Ad oceanum vero propius siti Ottadini, eorumque caput
Bremenium, ac apud hos fluvii Tueda, Alauna, et utraque
Tina, infra murum decurrentes. 39. His occidentaliores
ad Oceanum siti erant Selgovæ, eorumque urbes Corban-

torigum, Uxellum et Trimontium, quam tamen sat diu
tenuit præsidium Romanorum, quod antiqua memorant
monumenta.   Hujus regionis fluvii præcipui fuerunt
Novius, Deva, et, ex parte, Ituna.   40. Ultra Devam,
nuper dictam, ad oceani quoque oram in extrema insulæ
parte, Hyberniam versus, Novantes siti erant.   Apud
quos celebris illa Novantum Chersonesus, Hybernia distans milliaria XXVIII., hæc inter cuncta Britanniæ
promontoria maxume borea antiquis credebantur, juxta
vero, æque ac illi, causam non video.   Metropolis horum
Lucophibia, alias Casæ candidæ; fluvii vero Abrasuanus,
Jena, et, ad orientem regionis terminus, Deva.   41. Supra Novantes, Selgovas, et Gadenos, interveniente montium Uxellorum serie, habitabant Damnii, prævalens
quidem natio; sed quæ condito muro non parvum regionis suæ tractum amisit, a Caledoniis subjugatum et
spoliatum.   Præter illud, quod murum tuebatur præsidium Vanduarium tenebat Romanus miles.   42. Hic
Britannia, rursus quasi amplexu oceani delectata, angus-
tior evadit, quam alibi, idque ob duo ista rapidissima
quæ infunduntur æstuaria, Bodotriam scilicet et Clottam.
Contractus hic isthmus ab Agricola legato primum præsidio munitus erat; alium murum, in historiis nobilis-
simum, erexit imperator Antoninus, ad XXXV. circiter
milliaria protensum; ut hoc medio barbarorum sisteret
incursiones, qui et ab Ætio duce demum reparatus est,
undecimque firmatus turribus.   Has vero regiones pro
illa habeo provincia, quæ per victoriosam Romanorum
aciem sub imperatore Theodosio revocata, atque in honorem imperatoris, tunc ad clavum imperii sedentis, Valentiana dicta putatur.   43. Extra murum sita provincia
Vespasiana.   Hæc est illa Caledonia regio, a Romanis
nimium quantum et desiderata militibus, et incolis valde
defensa; negotium, cujus amplam historiæ Romanæ,
alias nimis de istiusmodi rebus silentes, mentionem
faciunt.   Hic fluvium Tavum conspicere licet, qui longo
cursu regionem in duas quasi partes dissecare videtur.

Hic quoque arduum atque horrendum jugum Grampium offendimus, quod provinciam istam bifariam secabat. Atque hæc eadem erat regio, quæ, a commisso inter Agricolam et Galgacum prœlio, Romanis utilissimo, famam in annalibus habet insignem. Hic vires eorum veteresque castrametationes hodieque magnitudo ostendit mœnium; nam in loco ubi ingens supradictum prœlium habitum erat, quidam ordinis nostri, hanc viam emensi, affirmant se immania vidisse castra, aliaque argumenta Taciti relationem confirmantia. 44. Nationes vero, Romanis hic subjectæ, ordine jam sequentur. Ultra isthmum, usque ad Tavum, gens erant Horestii, quorum urbes, post prætenturam quidem extructam, prius enim Damniis accensebantur, fuerunt Alauna, Lindum, et, re non minus quam nomine reliquis gloriosior, Victoria, ab Agricola ad flumen Tavum XX. milliaria ab ejusdem in mare exitu, ædificata, memoriæ proditum dicunt. 45. Supra hos ultra Tavum, qui limites constituit, erant Vecturones, sive Venricones, quorum urbs primaria Orrea, fluvii vero Æsica et Tina. 46. Oceani littus, ultra horum fines, accolebant Taixali, his urbium princeps Divana, fluvii autem Deva et Ituna. Pars Grampii montis, quæ, ut promontorium, late se in oceanum, quasi in Germaniæ occursum, extendit, ab illis nomen mutuatur. 47. His contermini ad occidentem, interveniente montium Grampiorum serie, exstitere Vacomagi, qui amplissimam regionem tenebant, quorum urbes Tuessis, Tamea, et Banatia. Romanorum autem statio, simulque provinciæ urbs primaria, erat, ad ostium fluvii Varar in littore situm, Ptoroton. Notiores hujus regionis fluvii præter Vararem, qui provinciam terminabat, fuerunt Tuesis et Celnius. 48. Infra Vacomagos Tavumque habitabant Damnii-Albani; gentes parum notæ, et intra lacuum montiumque claustra plane reconditæ. 49. Inferius adhuc Clottæ ripas accolebant Attacoti, gens toti aliquando olim Britanniæ formidanda. Maximus hic visitur lacus, cui nomen olim Lyncalidor, ad cujus ostium

condita a Romanis urbs Alcluith, brevi tempore a duce
Theodosio nomen sortita, qui occupatam a barbaris provinciam recuperaverat : cum hac comparari potuit nulla,
utpote quæ, post fractas cæteras circumjacentes provincias, impetum hostium ultimo sustinuit. 50. Hæc provincia dicta est, in honorem familiæ Flaviæ, cui suam
Domitianus imperator originem debuit, et sub quo ex-
pugnata, Vespasiana. Et, ni fallor, sub ultimis imperatoribus nominata erat Thule, de qua Claudianus vates his
versibus facit mentionem :

> " ———— incaluit Pictorum sanguine Thule,
> Scotorum cumulos flevit glacialis Hierne."

Sed non tam diu sub aquila suopte tenuerunt Romani, ut
posteritati innotescerent ejusdem et nomina et subjectio.
Cursorio hucusque oculo, qualis sub Romanorum imperio
erat, Britanniam lustravimus ; restat ut parili compendio
Caledoniorum terras lustremus.

De Caledonia.

51. Licet tota ultra isthmum prædictum Britannia non
improprie dici posset Caledonia, ipsi tamen Caledonii
ultra Vararem sedem habuere, unde ducta linea termi-
num Romani in Britanniam imperii accurate satis ostendit. Citerior vero insulæ pars alio atque alio tempore
ab illis possessa fuit, reliqua, ut supra meminimus, a Britonibus barbaris occupata. Hucusque et proficiscentibus
lumen aliquod fœnerant antiqua historiarum monumenta ;
trajicientes autem Varar flumen, extincto lumine, in ob-
scuro quasi versamur ; et quamvis non nobis ignotum sit,
extructas ibi pro limitibus imperii Romani fuisse aras,
Ulyssemque, tempestate fluctibusque jactatum, hic vota
persolvisse, siquidem condensæ arboribus sylvæ, cum
perpetuis montium saxetis, ab ulteriori nos scruta-
tione prohibent. Relationem sequentem a mercatoribus
Britonibus fugitivis acceptam posterisque relictam, ut
sufficientem æstimemus, necesse est. 52. Ad occidentem igitur Vararis habitabant Caledonii, proprie sic

dicti, quorum regionis partem tegebat immensa illa Caledonia sylva. 53. Littus incolebant minores quidam
populi, ex quorum numero, ultra Vararem et erectas
supradictas aras, ad Loxam fluvium habitabant Cantæ, in
quorum finibus promontorium Penoxullum. 54. Huic
ordine proximus est fluvius Abona ejusdemque accolæ
Logi. Hinc Ila fluvius, et ad illum siti Carnabii Britonum extremi, qui ab Ostorio proprætore subjugati, jugum
Romanum indigne ferentes, adscitis in societatem Cantiis, ut referunt traditiones, trajectoque mari ibi sedem
eligunt. In varia hic promontoria sese extendit Britannia, quorum primum antiquis dictum Vinvedrum, tum
Verubrium, aut extremitas Caledoniæ. 55. Post illos
Catini; deinde, interiores Logisque proximi, Mertæ siti
sunt. In his oris promontorium Orcadum positum, cui
adjacebant Orcades insulæ. Ulterius manabat Nabæus
fluvius, qui terminus erat Carnabicæ jurisdictionis. 56.
Ad inferiorem hujus regionis partem habitabant Carnonacæ, in quorum finibus promontorium Ebudum, ad
cujus extrema eximium oceanus sinum efformat, qui olim
Volsas appellatus. Ad inferiorem istius sinus ripam
tendebant Cerones, et infra Ityn Creones ad Longum
usque procurrit. Inde oceanum inter et sinum Lelanum
dictum ab incolis Epidiis promontorium. 57. Provectus
jam ultra flumen Vararis, idem illud remetiri non possum, quin in transgressu admirer Romanos, alias satis
expertos judicio atque experientia, hic quasi destitutos
tam perabsurda opinione laborasse, ut istam Britanniæ
partem, quæ jam armis ipsorum intacta quiescebat,
reliquam jam subactam atque possessam, longe ma-
jori et longitudine et latitudine metirentur, (quam
tamen eos fovisse opinionem satis superque constat).
Qui enim ea, qua par est, mente insignem Romanorum
ambitionem atque insatiabilem regnandi cupidinem con-
sideraverit, et quo hostem vix ira ipsorum et notitia,
nedum timore dignum excluderent, stupenda ista, quæ
totum orbem in admirationem sui facile trahunt, opera

N

erexisse, in hoc ut in cæteris quam plurimis magnam summi Numinis merito providentiam veneremur, cui ut omnia subjecta sunt regna, ita et sempiterna ab incolis gloria debetur et erit. Amen !

CAPUT VII.

Lustratis ita pro instituti ratione cursim terris Britannicis, necessarium videtur, antequam ad Insularum descriptionem aggrediar, dubio a non nemine moto occurrere ; ubinam, inquit ille, earum quas tu nobis commemoras urbium nominumque vestigia? Habentur nulla ! Licet vicissim quærere, ubinam hodie sint Assyrii, Parthi, Sarmatæ, Celtiberi? At qui has celeberrimas gentes exstitisse neget, impudentem satis spero futurum neminem. Nonne inveniuntur hodiernum regiones urbesque permultæ eisdem, quæ ante duo vel plura annorum millia habuerunt, quæ compellantur, nominibus? Judæa, Italia, Gallia, Britannia, non hodie minus quam priscis illis temporibus nota! Londinum hodieque lingua vernacula, sono non adeo discrepante, *London* appellatur. Incuria majorum et in colligendis ac conservandis illis, quæ huc facere et tunc temporis non difficulter haberi poterant, monumentis negligentia si attendatur, non adeo quidem graviter illa videtur increpanda, vel ut hujus defectus unica et primaria causa censenda, vix enim præter illos, qui ordini sacrorum se dederant, operam libris scribendis commodabant. Hi vero a sacro alienum censuerunt munere profanis istiusmodi, ut vocabant, negotiis operam suam impendere. Crediderim potius nos sine periculo scire, et sine piaculo ad posteros transmittere posse, illa quæ de prisco regnorum statu sedula veterum monumentorum perlustratio et accuratius scrutinium poterit investigare. Ad aliud vero sentiendum me fere compulisset bonus ille Antistes, ita me compellare visus ; Tune solus ignoras quam breve, nobis in hoc orbe, temporis spatium sit exigendum, omnesque nostros etiam laboriosissimos conatus ab inutilium servorum nomine nos non posse reddere immunes? omniaque nostra studia proximi usum pro scopo debent habere? Hæc! cui unquam sunt usui? Bullatis istiusmodi nugis mundum deludi! His merito reponimus: An ergo prohibita nobis simul omnis honesta delectatio? Nonne eximia divinæ providentiæ documenta produnt istiusmodi narrationes? Indene patet, quomodo evangelia de morte et merito Christi concio universum collustraverit et vicerit orbem gentilibus antea superstitionibus obnoxium? Obvertenti porro, non incongrue forte Chronologiæ istiusmodi res in compendio tractari, denuo repono: Nec ergo nimium quidquam est novisse, majores nostros non, ut nonnulli fabulantur, Autochthones fuisse, e terra prosilientes. Deum potius naturæ librum aperuisse, ut in illo constaret magni opificis omnipotentia, qualis in Mosis voluminibus eadem descripta proponitur. Denique forte respondenti, operibus, authori apud cæteros nomen laudemque parituris, exploratorium ignem esse subeundum, hæc inquam dicenti, et in his subsistendi gratus profiteor tantum his verbis efficaciæ fuisse, ut etiam suborta mihi nonnunquam fuerit cœpti hujus laboris pœnitentia. Ex altera proinde hujus opusculi parte præter Chronologicam rerum commemorationem amplius quidquam exspectare nolit Benevolus Lector, quem adeo benevolentiæ tutelæque Divinæ, paria ab ipso mihi promittens, devotus commendo, sperans, ut me simul cœlesti Patri, qui misericors et condonationis plenus, commendet.

Ex fragmentis quibusdam a duce quodam Romano consignatis et posteritati relictis, sequens collectum est Itinerarium, ex Ptolemæo et aliunde nonnullis, ordinem quoque, sed quod spero in melius mutatum, hinc inde deprehendes.

FUERUNT olim apud Britones XCII. urbes, earum

vero celebriores et præ reliquis conspicuæ XXXIII.;
municipia scilicet II., Verolamium et Eboracum. VIIII.
coloniæ, sc. Londinium *Augusta*, Camalodunum *Geminæ
Martiæ*, Rhutupis, ... Thermæ *Aquæ Solis*, Isca
Secunda, Deva *Getica*, Glevum *Claudia*, Lindum, . . .
. . . . Camboricum . . . . . . Et civitates Latio jure
donatæ X., sc. Durnomagus, Catarracton, Cambodunum,
Coccium, Lugubalia, Ptoroton, Victoria, Theodosia, Corinum, Sorbiodunum.   Deinde XII. stipendiariæ mino-
risque momenti, scilicet Venta Silurum, Venta Belgarum, Venta Icenorum, Segontium, Muridunum, Ragæ,
Cantiopolis, Durinum, Isca, Bremenium, Vindonum, et
Durobrovæ.   At præter allatas modo urbes, plures in
Britanniis non habuisse Romanos ne quis temere credat;
celebriores enim tantum commemoravi; quis enim du-
bitet, illos, ut orbis terrarum dominatores, pro lubitu
elegisse sibique vindicasse, quæ suis usibus commoda
intelligebant loca? plerumque alias in castris, quæ con-
diderant ipsi, degebant.

Diaphragmata.

ITER I. Rhutupis prima in Britannia insula civitas
versus Galliam apud Cantios sita a Gessoriago Bonnoniæ
portu, unde commodissimus in supradictam insulam
transitus obtingit, CCCCL. stadia, vel ut alii volunt
XLVI. mille passuum remota: ab eadem civitate ducta
est via Guethelinga dicta, usque in Segontium per m. p.
CCCXXIIII. plus minus sic:—Cantiopoli, quæ et Du-
roverno, m. p. X.   Durosevo XII.   Duroprovis XXV.
deinde m. p. XXVII. transis Thamesin intrasque provinciam Flaviam et civitatem Londinium (Augustam),
Sulo Mago m. p. VIIII. Verolamio municipio XII. unde
fuit Amphibalus et Albanus Martyres. Foro Dianæ
XII. Magio Vinio XII. Lactorodo XII. Isanta Varia XII. Tripontio XII. Benonis VIIII. Hic bise-
catur via, alterutrumque ejus brachium Lindum usque,

altérum versus Viriconium protenditur, sic :—Manduessuedo m. p. XII. Etoceto XIII. Pennocrucio XII. Uxaconia XII. Virioconio XI. Banchorio XXVI. Deva Colonia X. Fines Flaviæ et Secundæ, Varis m. p. XXX. Conovio XX. Seguntio XXIIII.

ITER II. A Seguntio Virioconium usque, m. p. LXXIII. sic :—Heriri monte m. p. XXV. Mediolano XXV. Rutunio XII. Virioconio XI.

ITER III. A Londinio Lindum coloniam usque, sic :— Durosito m. p. XII. Cæsaro Mago XVI. Canonio XV. Camaloduno colonia VIIII. ibi erat templum Claudii, arx triumphalis, et imago Victoriæ deæ. Ad Sturium amnem m. p. VI. et finibus Trinobantum Cenimannos advenis, Cambretonio m. p. XV. Sito Mago XXII. Venta Cenom. XXIII. . . . . Camborico colonia XX. Durali ponte XX. Durno Mago XX. Isinnis XX. Lindo XX.

ITER IV. A Lindo ad Vallum usque, sic :—Argolico m. p. XIIII. Dano XX. Ibi intras Maximam Cæsariensem, Legotio m. p. XVI. Eboraco municip. olim colonia sexta m. p. XXI. Isurio XVI. Cattaractoni XXIIII. ad Tisam X. Vinovio XII. Epiaco XVIIII. ad Murum VIIII. trans Murum intras Valentiam. Alauna amne m. p. XXV. Tueda flumine XXX. ad Vallum. . . . .

ITER V. A limite Præturiam usque, sic:—Curia m. p. . . . ad Fines m. p. . . . Bremenio m. p. . . . Corstoplio XX. Vindomora VIIII. Vindovio XVIIII. Cattaractoni XXII. Eboraco XL. Derventione VII. Delgovicia XIII. Præturio XXV.

ITER VI. Ab Eboraco Devam usque, sic :—Calcaria m. p. VIIII. Camboduno XXII. Mancunio XVIII. Finibus Maximæ et Flaviæ m. p. XVIII. Condate XVIII. Deva XVIII.

ITER VII. A Portu Sistuntiorum Eboracum usque, sic :—Rerigonio m. p. XXIII. ad Alpes Peninos VIII. Alicana X. Isurio XVIII. Eboraco XVI.

Iter VIII. Ab Eboraco Luguvalium usque, sic:—
Cattaractoni m. p. XL. Lataris XVI. Vataris XVI.
Brocavonacis XVIII. Vorreda XVIII. Lugubalia
XVIII.

Iter VIIII. A Luguballio Ptorotonim usque, sic:—
Trimontio m. p. . . . . Gadanica m. p. . . . . Corio
m. p. . . . ad Vallum m. p. . . . Incipit Vespasiana.
Alauna m. p. XII. Lindo VIIII. Victoria VIIII. ad
Hiernam VIIII. Orrea XIIII. ad Tavum XVIIII. ad
Æsicam XXIII. ad Tinam VIII. Devana XXIII. ad
Itunam XXIIII. ad Montem Grampium m. p. . . . .
ad Selinam m. p. . . . . Tuessis XVIIII. Ptorotone
m. p. . . . . . .

Iter X. Ab ultima Ptorotone per mediam insulæ
Isca Damnonorum usque, sic:—Varis m. p. VIII. ad
Tuessim XVIII. Tamea XXVIIII. . . . .
. . . . m. p. XXI. in Medio VIIII.
Orrea VIIII. Victoria XVIII. ad Vallum XXXII.
Luguballia LXXX. Brocavonacis XXII. ad Alaunam
m. p. . . . . Coccio m. p. . . . . Mancunio XVIII.
Condate XXIII. Mediolano XVIII. Etoceto m. p. . . . .
. . . . Salinis m. p. . . . .
. . . . . . Glebon colonia m. p. . . . Corino XIIII.
Aquas Solis m. p. . . . ad Aquas XVIII. ad Uxellam
amnem m. p. . . . . Isca m. p.
. . . . .

Iter XI. Ab Aquis per Viam Juliam Menapiam
usque, sic:—ad Abonam m. p. VI. ad Sabrinam VI.
unde trajectu intras in Britanniam Secundam et stationem Trajectum m. p. III. Venta Silurum VIII.
Isca colonia VIIII. unde fuit Aaron Martyr. Tibia
amne m. p. VIII. Bovio XX. Nido XV. Leucaro XV.
ad Vigesimum XX. ad Menapiam XVIIII. Ab hac
urbe per XXX. m. p. navigas in Hyberniam.

Iter XII. Ab Aquis Londinium usque, sic:—Ver-
lucione m. p. XV. Cunetione XX. Spinis XV. Calleba Attrebatum XV. Bibracte XX. Londinio XX.

Iter XIII. Ab Isca Uriconium usque, sic :—Bultro m. p. VIII. Gobannio XII. Magna XXIII. Brano-genio XXIII. Urioconio XXVII.

Iter XIIII. Ab Isca per Glebon Lindum usque, sic : —Ballio m. p. VIII. Blestio XII. Sariconio XI. Gle-bon colonia XV. ad Antonam XV. Alauna XV. . . . . Vennonis XII. Ratis-corion XII. Venromento XII. Margiduno XII. ad Pontem XII. Croco colana Lindum XII.

Iter XV. A Londinio per Clausentum in Londinium, sic :—Caleba m. p. XLIIII. Vindomi XV. Venta Bel-garum XXI. ad Lapidem VI. Clausento IIII. Portu Magno X. Regno X. ad Decimum X. Anderida portu m. p. . . . . ad Lemanum m. p. XXV. Lemaniano portu X. Dubris X. Rhutupis colonia X. Regulbio X. Contiopoli X. Durelevo XVIII. Mado XII. Vagnaca XVIII. Novio Mago XVIII. Londi-nio XV.

Iter XVI. A Londinio Ceniam usque, sic :—Venta Belgarum m. p. XC. Brige XI. Sorbioduno VIII. Ven-tageladia XII. Durnovaria VIIII. Moriduno XXXIII. Isca Damnon. XV. . . . . Durio amne m. p. . . . . Tamara m. p. . . . . Vo-luba m. p. . . . . Cenia m. p. . . . . . .

Iter XVII. Ab Anderida [Eboracum] usque, sic :— Sylva Anderida m. p. . . . . Noviomago m. p. . . . . Londinio m. p. XV. ad Fines m. p. . . . . . . Durolisponte m. p. . . . . Durnomago m. p. XXX. Corisennis XXX. Lindo XXX. in Medio XV. ad Abum XV. unde transis in Maximam, ad Petuariam m. p. VI. deinde Eboraco, ut supra, m. p. XLVI.

Iter XVIII. Ab Eboraco per medium insulæ Clau-sentum usque, sic :—Legiolio m. p. XXI. ad Fines XVIII. . . . m. p. XVI. . . . . . . m. p. XVI. . . . .

. . . . Derventione m. p. XVI. ad Trivonam
XII. Etoceto XII. Manduessuedo XVI. Benonnis
XII. Tripontio XI. Isannavaria XII. Brinavis XII.
Ælia castra XVI. Dorocina XV. Tamesi VI. Vindo-
mi XV. Clausento XLVI.

Plurima insuper habebant Romani in Britanniis castella, suis quæque muris, turribus, portis, et repagulis
munita.

Finis Itinerariorum.

Quod hactenus auribus, in hoc capite percipitur pene
oculis intuentibus : nam huic adjuncta est mappa Britanniæ artificialiter depicta, quæ omnia loca cet. evidenter
exprimit, ut ex ea cunctarum regionum incolas dignos-
cere detur.

CAPUT VIII.

1. Lustravimus jam Albionem, dissitæ non procul inde
Hyberniæ, eadem, qua hactenus usi fuimus brevitate,
descriptionem daturi. 2. Hybernia omnium, post Albionem dictam nuper, maxume est ad occidentem quidem sita, sed, sicut contra septemtriones ea brevior, ita
in meridiem sese trans illius fines plurimum protendens,
usque contra Hispaniæ Tarraconensis septentrionalia,
quamvis magno æquore interjacente, pervenit. 3. Mare,
quod Britanniam et Hyberniam interfluit, undosum et
inquietum est, toto, ut author est Solinus, anno, non nisi
æstivis pauculis diebus, navigabile.   In medio inter
ambas insula est, quæ olim appellabatur Moncœda, nunc
autem Manavia. 4. Hybernia autem, et sui status con-
ditione, et salubritate ac serenitate aëris, multum Britanniæ præstat, ut opinatur Beda, ita, ut raro ibi nix plus
quam triduaria remaneat, nemo propter hiemem aut
fœna secet, aut stabula fabricet jumentis. 5. Nullum
ibi reptile videri solet, nullæ viperæ aut serpentes valent ;
nam sæpe illo de Britannia allati serpentes mox, ut

proximante terris navigio odore aëris illius adtacti
fuerint, intereunt. Quin potius omnia pene, quæ de
eadem insula sunt, contra venenum valent. Denique
vidimus, quibusdam a serpente percussis, rasa folia codi-
cum, qui de Hybernia fuerunt, et ipsam rasuram aquæ
immissam ac potui datam talibus protinus totam vim
veneni grassantis totum inflati corporis absumsisse, ac
sedasse tumorem. 6. Dives lactis et mellis insula, nec
vinearum expers, piscium volucrumque, sed et cervorum
caprearumque venatu insignis, ut author est venerabilis
Beda. 7. Cultores ejus, inquit Mela, inconditi sunt et
omnium virtutum ignari, magis quam aliæ gentes, ali-
quatenus tamen gnari pietatis ad modum expertes.
Gens inhospita et bellicosa a Solino Polyhistore dicti
sunt. Sanguine interemptorum hausto prius victores
vultus suos oblinunt. Fas ac nefas eodem animo ducunt.
Puerpera, si quando marem edidit, primos cibos gladio
imponit mariti, inque os parvuli summo mucrone, auspi-
cium alimentorum leviter infert, et gentilibus votis optat,
non aliter quam in bello et inter arma mortem'oppetat.
Qui student cultui, dentibus mari nantium belluarum
insigniunt ensium capulos, candicant enim ob eburneam
claritatem. Nam præcipua viris gloria est in armorum
splendore. 8. Agrippa, geographus Romanus, longitudinem Hyberniæ DC. millia passuum esse, latitudinem
vero CCC. statuit. XX. olim gentibus habitata, quarum
XIIX. littus tenebant. 9. Hæc autem propria Scottorum patria erat ; ab hac egressi, tertiam in Albione
Britonibus et Pictis gentem addiderunt. Sed non
idem cum magno authore Beda sentio, qui Scottos pere-
grinos esse affirmat : nam, ut existimo, suam ex Britannia non procul sita originem duxerunt, inde trajecisse,
atque in .hac insula sedes occupasse, fidem faciunt au-
thores. Certissimum vero est Damnios, Voluntios,
Brigantes, Cangos, aliasque nationes origine fuisse Britannica, quæ eo postea trajecerunt, postquam, vel Divitiacus, vel Claudius, vel Ostorius, vel duces alii victores,

illis domi tumultum fecerant.   Pro ulteriori argumento
inservit lingua antiqua, quæ cum antiqua illa Britannica
et Gallica non parum consonat, id quod omnibus utri-
usque linguæ gnaris satis planum videtur.   10. Septentrionali Hyberniæ lateri obtenditur oceanus Deucaledo-
nicus ; orientale tegunt Vergivus et Internus, Canta-
bricus vero australe, uti occidentale magnus ille Bri-
tannicus, qui et Atlanticus oceanus ; quem nos quoque
ordinem secuti dabimus insulæ et præcipuorum in illa
locorum descriptionem.   11. Illud, quod ab oceano
Deucaledonico alluitur, hujus insulæ latus habitabant
Rhobogdii, cujus metropolis Rhobogdium erat ; in quorum orientali regione situm erat ejusdem nominis promontorium, in occidentali, Boreum promontorium. Fluvii vero Banna, Darabouna, Argitta, et Vidua, austrum
versus a Scottis ipsos separabant montes.   12. Infra
promontorium Boreum littus Britannici maris ad Venic-
nium usque caput incolebant gentes Venicniæ, quibus
nomen debent ab illis dictæ vicinæ insulæ Venicniæ,
inferius ad ostium usque Rhebii fluminis, quarum metropolis Rheba.   Infra Rhebeum Nagnatæ habitabant
ad Libnium usque, quorum celebris erat ejusdem nominis metropolis.   Austrum versus, in recessu sinus Au-
sobæ siti erant Auterii, quibus urbium caput erat ejusdem nominis.   Inferiorem ejusdem regionis partem
occupabant Concangii, ad quorum fines austrum versus
manabat Senus, amplus omnino fluvius, cui adjacebat
urbium primaria Macobicum.   In angustum hic apicem
coarctata desinit Hybernia.   Prope Austrinum promontorium, ad flumen Senum, sedes habebant Velatorii,
quorum metropolis Regia, fluviusque Durius.   Lucani
vero habitabant, ubi oceano miscetur fluvius Ibernus.
13. Ultra Austrinum meridionale insulæ latus ab eodem
promontorio ad Sacrum usque extremum tendebat.
Ibernii ad illud habitabant, quibus metropolis Rhufina.
Hinc fluvius Dobona, ac deinde Vodiæ, cum promontorio ejusdem nominis, quod promontorio Albionis Anti-

vestæo obvertitur, distans inde milliaribus CXXXXV.
Non procul inde Dabrona fluvius Brigantum regionis terminus, qui fines regionis fluvium Brigas et urbem habebant Brigantiam. 14. Pars hujus insulæ, a Sacro promontorio ad Rhobogdium usque extensa, Orientalis cen-
setur. Habitantes supra promontorium Sacrum Menapii,
primariam habebant ejusdem nominis urbem ad fluvium
Modonam. Hinc ad Menapiam, in Dimetia sitam,
XXX. milliaria numerantur, ut Plinius refert. Harum
unam, quamnam vero incertum, patriam habebat Carausius. _Ultra horum terminos metropolin Dunum habebant Cauci, quorum fines alluebat fluvius Oboca. Teuto-
nicæ binas has nationes originis esse extra dubium est :
incertum vero quo tempore primum in has terras eorum
majores trajecerint. Brevi ante Cæsaris in Britanniam
transitum id contigisse maxume videtur probabile. 15.
Eblanæ ulterius habitabant, primariam vero ad Lœbium
flumen habentes Mediolanum. Septentrionali viciniores
Voluntii civitatem habebant Lebarum, fluvios autem
Vinderum et Buvindam. Superiorem his insulæ partem, Rhobogdiis affinem, tenebant Damnii, his urbium
caput Dunum, ubi sepulti creduntur D. Patricius, D.
Columba, et D. Brigitta, eodem tumulo reconditi. 16.
Restat jam, ut eorum qui interiorem hujus insulæ
partem habitabant populorum mentio injiciatur. Contermini Caucis et Menapiis, supra Brigantes autem, incolebant Coriondii, reliquam insulæ partem Scotti habebant,
quibus Scotiæ nomen tota exinde debet. Plures inter,
quas illi habebant, civitates præ cæteris innotuerunt
tantum duæ, quarum ad nos pervenit memoria. Altera
Rheba ad flumen et lacum Rhebium, Ibernia altera, sita
ad orientale Seni fluminis latus. 17. Non possum non
hoc loco monere Damnios, Voluntios, Brigantes, et Can-
gianos omnes fuisse Britannicæ originis nationes, quæ,
eum vel ab hoste finitimo non daretur quies, vel tot
tantaque exigerentur tributa, quibus solvendis se im-
pares intelligerent, sensim, novas quæsituræ sedes, in

hanc terram trajecerant.   Dictum jam antea de Menapiis, Chaucis, nec de iis, quæ offeruntur ulterius, plura
occurrunt, quibus tuto fides potest haberi.   Refert quidem, Augustæ Historiæ scriptor, Tacitus, quod pluribus
quam Albion peregrinis Hybernia fuerit frequentata.
At, si res ita revera se habuisset, vix dubitandum videtur,
plura nobis de statu Hyberniæ, et fide digniora veteres
fuisse relicturos.   Relicturoque jam mihi descriptionem
Hyberniæ non abs re fore videtur docere, hanc, non armis,
sed metu tantum sub Romanorum redactam fuisse imperium.   Quin potius regem Ptolemæum in secunda
Europæ tabula, aliosque veterum inclutissimorum geo-
graphorum, in situ illius delineando errasse, utpote qui
hanc non solum justo longius a Britannia, sed etiam
prorsus a parte boreali provinciæ Secundæ, statuerunt;
id quod ex ipsorum libris et tabulis huc spectantibus
patet abunde.   18. Super Hyberniam sitæ erant Hebudes, V. numero, quarum incolæ nesciunt fruges, pisci-
bus tantum et lacte viventes.   Rex unus est, ut scribit
Solinus, universis, nam quotquot sunt, omnes angusto
interluvio dividuntur.   Ille rex nihil suum habebat,
omnia universorum.   Ad æquitatem certis legibus ad-
stringitur, ac, ne avaritia a vero rectoque eum seduceret,
discebat ex paupertate justitiam, utpote cui nihil esset
rei familiaris, verum alitur e publico.   Nulla illi dabatur
fœmina propria, sed per vicissitudines, in quamcunque
commotus fuisset, sibi vendicat usurariam, unde ei nec
votum nec spes conceditur liberorum.   De Hebudibus
hisce nonnulli scripserunt dies continuos XXX. sub
bruma esse noctem, sed dictator Cæsar nihil de eo,
studiose licet inquirens, reperiebat, nisi, quod certis ex
aqua mensuris breviores fuisse noctes quam in Gallia
intellexerit.   19. Secundam a continenti stationem
Orcades præbent, quæ ab Hebudibus porro, sed erroneè,
sunt VII. dierum totidemque noctium cursu, ut scripserunt nonnulli; numero XXX., angustis inter sese deductæ spatiis, vacabant homine, non habebant sylvas,

tantum junceis herbis horrescentes. Cætera earum nil
nisi arenæ et rupes tenent, ut ego, ex Solino cum aliis
colligi posse, habeo persuasum. 20. Thule ultima omnium, quæ Britannicæ vocantur, Belgarum littori apposita statuitur a Mela. Græcis Romanisque celebrata
carminibus, de quo Homerus Mantuanus :

" ———— Et tibi serviat ultima Thule."

In ea solstitio nullas esse noctes indicavimus, cancri
signum sole transeunte, ut author est Plinius, nullosque
contra per brumam dies ; hæc quidem senis mensibus
continuis fieri arbitrantur. Qui hic habitant, ut refert
Solinus, principio veris inter pecudes pabulis vivunt,
deinde lacte, in hyemem conferunt arborum fructus.
Utuntur fœminis vulgo, certum matrimonium nullis.
Thule autem larga et diutina pomona copiosa est,
ut tradit idem author. Ultra Thulen unius diei na-
vigatione accepimus pigrum esse et concretum mare, a
nonnullis Cronium appellatur. A Thule in Caledoniam
bidui navigatio est. 21. Thanatos insula alluitur freto
oceani, a Britanniæ continente æstuario tenui, Wantsuam dicto, separata ; frumentariis campis felix, et
gleba uberi ; nec tantum sibi soli, verum et aliis salu-
bribus locis, ut author est Isidorus, cum ipsa nullo
serpatur angue, asportata inde terra, quoquo gentium
invecta sit, angues necat. Hæc non longe abest a
Rhutupi sita. 22. Vecta, a Vespasiano devicta
olim, insula est, proximum Belgis habet ab oriente in
occasum XXX. circiter millia passuum, ab austro in
boream XII. in orientalibus suis partibus mari VI.
millium, in occidentalibus III., a meridionali supra
scripto littore distans. 23. Præter supradictas insulas
fuerunt etiam VII. Acmodæ, Ricnea, Silimnus, Andros,
Sigdiles XL., Vindilios, Sarna, Cæsarea, et Cassiterides.
24. Sena, Ossismicis adversa littoribus, Gallici Numinis
oraculo insignis est, ut author est Mela ; cujus antistites,
perpetua virginitate sanctæ, numero IX. esse traduntur ;
Senas Galli vocant, putantque ingeniis singularibus præ-

ditas, maria ac ventos concitare carminibus, seque in
quæ velint animalia vertere, sanare quæ apud alios in-
sanabilia sunt.　Scire ventura et prædicere, sed non nisi
deditæ navigantibus, et ob id tantum ut se consulerent
eo profectis.　25. Reliquæ Albioni circumfusæ minoris
peripheriæ et momenti insulæ, ex depictæ adjectæque
mappæ inspectione melius, quam ex nudo quodam re-
censu, censeri ac dignosci possunt.　Hic itaque sub-
sisto meumque his rebus locatum studium Benevolo
Lectori, ejusque favori et judicio studiose commendo.

Explicit feliciter, Deo juvante, Liber primus Commen-
　　tarioli Geographici de situ Brittaniæ, et stationum
　　quas Romani ipsi in ea Insula ædificaverunt, per
　　manum meam Ricardi, famuli Christi et monachi
　　Westmonasteriensis.　Deo gratias.

LIBER SECUNDUS.

PRÆFATIO.

In supplementum datæ hucusque Britanniæ antiquæ
descriptionis deductum parili compendio subjungere
consultum duxi :—

I. Chronologiæ, a prima inde orbis origine ad vastatam a Gothis Romam deductæ, epitomen, et

II. Imperatorum Legatorumque Romanorum qui huic
regioni cum imperio præfuerant brevem recensum.

Dicant forte nonnulli potuisse istiusmodi operam,
utpote non absolute necessariam, vel cultui divino, vel
majoris momenti rebus impendi.　At sciant illi et sub-
secivas horas antiquitatibus patriis pristinique terrarum
status investigationi posse vindicari, ut tamen nihil
propterea sacro cultui decedat.　Sin vero Momus istius-

modi captatam ex otio licito voluptatem nobis invideat, ad finem properans metæque jam adstitutus, hic pedem figo.

CAPUT I.

In principio mundum, nobis hodiernum reliquisque creaturis habitatum, VI. dierum spatio ex nihilo condidit omnipotens Creator.

Anno Mundi MDCLVI. Crescentem continuo usu humani generis malitiam vindicaturus, Creator diluvium orbi immisit, quod totum obruens mundum, omnem delevit viventium ordinem, solis, quæ arcam intraverant, exceptis et servatis, quorum deinceps propago novis animalium colonis novum orbem replevit.

A. M. MMM. Circa hæc tempora cultam et habitatam primum Britanniam arbitrantur nonnulli, cum illam salutarent Græci Phœnicesque mercatores. Nec desunt, qui a rege quodam Brytone non diu postea conditum credunt Londinium.

A. M. MMMCCXXVIII. Prima urbis Romæ, quæ gentium exinde communis terror, fundamenta posuerunt fratres Romulus et Remus.

A. M. MMMDC. Egressi e Britannia per Galliam Senones Italiam invasere, Romam oppugnaturi.

A. M. MMMDCL. Has terras intrarunt Belgæ, Celtæque desertam a Senonibus regionem occuparunt. Non diu postea cum exercitu in hoc regnum transiit rex Æduorum Divitiacus, magnamque ejus partem subegit. Circa hæc tempora in Hyberniam commigrarunt, ejecti a Belgis Britones, ibique sedes posuerunt, ex illo tempore Scotti appellati.

A. M. MMMDCCCCXLIII. Gestum est Cassibelini cum civitatibus maritimis bellum.

A. M. MMMDCCCCXLVI. Cæsar Germanos et Gallos capit, et Britones quoque, quibus ante eum ne nomen quidem Romanorum cognitum fuerat, victor, obsidibus acceptis, stipendarios facit.

A. M. MMMDCCCCXLVII. Denuo in has terras profectus, bellum gessit cum rege Cassiorum Cassibellino, invitatus, ut ipse quidem prætendit, a Trinobantibus. Sed, quod majore veri specie tradit Suetonius, potius avaritiem ipsius sollicitantibus prætiosis Britanniæ margaritis.

A. M. MMMMXLIV. Ipse in Britanniam profectus imperator Claudius, semestri spatio, absque ulla vi aut sanguinis effusione, magnam insulæ partem in suam redegit potestatem, quam exinde Cæsariensem jussit vocari.

A. M. MMMMXLV. Missus ab imperatore Claudio cum II. legione in has terras Vespasianus, adhuc in privata vita, Belgas Damnoniosque oppugnavit, tandemque, commissis præliis XXXII. urbibus XX. expugnatis, sub obsequium Romani imperii redegit, una cum insula Vecta.

A. M. MMMMXLVII. Thermas et Glebon occupaverunt Romani.

A. M. MMMML. Post novennale bellum regem Silurum Charaticum vicit dux Romanorum Ostorius, magna Britanniæ pars in formam provinciæ redacta, et Camalodunensis coloniæ posita fundamenta.

A. M. MMMMLII. Cogibundo urbes quædam apud Belgas a Romanis concessæ, ut inde sibi conderet Regnum. Circa hæc tempora, relicta Britannia, Cangi et Brigantes in Hyberniam commigrarunt sedesque ibi posuerunt.

A. M. MMMMLXI. Nero imperator, in re militari nihil omnino ausus, Britanniam pene amisit. Nam duo sub illo nobilissima oppida illic capta atque eversa sunt. Nam insurrexit contra Romanos Bondvica, illatam sibi a Romanis injuriam vindicatura, colonias illas Romanorum, Londinium, Camalodunum, et municipium Verulamium igne delevit, occisis ultra octoginta millibus civium Romanorum. Superata illa tandem a Suetonio, qui acerrime illatum Romanis damnum vindicavit, occiso subditorum ejus æquali numero.

A. M. MMMMLXXIII. Brigantes vicit Cerealis.

A. M. MMMMLXXVI. Ordovices plectit Frontinus.

A. M. MMMMLXXX. Magnum cum rege Caledoniorum Galgaco prælium committit Agricola, eoque devicto, totam insulam cum classe lustrari jubet, maritimamque ipsius oram totus obiens, Orcades submittit imperio Romano.

A. M. MMMMCXX. Ipse in Britanniam transit Hadrianus imperator, immensoque muro unam insulæ partem ab altera sejungit.

A. M. MMMMCXL. Missus ab Antonino Pio Urbicus victoriis inclarescit.

A. M. MMMMCL. Nonnullas quoque a Britannis victorias reportat Aurelius Antoninus.

A. M. MMMMCLX. Luce Christianismi, regnante Lucio rege, collustratur Britannia ; rege Cruci Christi se primum submittente.

A. M. MMMMCLXX. Provincia Vespasiana ejiciuntur Romani. Hoc circiter tempore, ex insulis in Britanniam cum Pictis suis advenisse creditur Reuda rex.

A. M. MMMMCCVII. Destructum, a Romanis conditum, murum restituit transiens in Britanniam Severus imperator, et non diu post Eboraci, manu Dei, moritur.

A. M. MMMMCCXI. Venalem a Mæatis pacem obtinuit Bassianus.

A. M. MMMMCCXX. Per hæc tempora intra mœnia se continent Romani milites, altaque pace tota perfruitur insula.

A. M. MMMMCCXC. Carausius, sumpta purpura, Britannias occupavit ; post X. annos per Asclepiodorum Britannia recepta.

A. M. MMMMCCCIIII. Persecutio crudelis et crebra flagrabat, ut intra unum mensem XVII. millia marty-

o

rum pro Christo passa inveniantur; quæ et oceani limbum transgressa Albanum, Aaron, et Julium Britones, cum aliis pluribus viris et fœminis, felici cruore damnavit.

A. M. MMMMCCCVI. Constantius, XVI. imperii anno, summæ mansuetudinis et civilitatis vir, victo Alecto, in Britannia diem obiit Eboraci.

A. M. MMMMCCCVII. Constantinus, qui Magnus postea dicitur, Constantii ex Britannica Helena filius, in Britanniis creatus imperator, cui se sponte tributariam offert Hybernia.

A. M. MMMMCCCXX. Ductu regis Fergusii in Britanniam transeunt Scotti, ibique sedem figunt.

A. M. MMMMCCCLXXXV. Theodosius Maximum tyrannum III. ab Aquileia lapide interfecit. Qui, quoniam Britanniam omni pene armata juventute copiisque spoliaverat militaribus, quæ, tyrannidis ejus vestigia secutæ in Gallias, nunquam ultra domum rediere, videntes, transmarinæ gentes sævissimæ, Scottorum a circio, Pictorum ab aquilone, destitutam milite ac defensore insulam, adveniunt, et vastatam direptamque eam multos per annos opprimunt.

A. M. MMMMCCCXCVI. Britones Scottorum Pictorumque infestationem non ferentes, Romam mittunt, et, sui subjectione promissa, contra hostem auxilia flagitant, quibus statim missa legio magnam barbarorum multitudinem sternit, cæteros Britanniæ finibus pellit, ac, domum reversura, præcepit sociis, ad arcendos hostes, murum trans insulam inter duo æstuaria statuere. Qui, absque artifice magistro magis cespite quam lapide factus, nil operantibus profuit : nam mox, ut discessere Romani, advectus navibus prior hostis, quasi maturam segetem, obvia quæque sibi cædit, calcat, devorat.

A. M. MMMMCCCC. Iterum petiti auxilia Romani advolant, et cæsum hostem trans maria fugant conjunctis sibi Britonibus, murum non terra, ut ante pulvereum, sed saxo solidum, inter civitates, quæ ibidem ob metum hostium fuerunt factæ, a mari usque ad mare collocant.

Sed et in littore meridiano maris, quia et inde hostis Saxonicus timebatur, turres per intervalla ad prospectum maris statuunt. Id Stilichontis erat opus, ut ex his Claudiani versibus constat :

" —————— Caledonio velata Britannia monstro,
Ferro Picta genas, cujus vestigia verrit
Cærulus, oceanique æstum mentitur, amictus :
Me quoque vicinia pereuntem gentibus, inquit,
Munivit Stilicho, totam cum Scottus Hybernam
Movit, et infesto spumavit remige Thetys.
Illius effectum curis, ne bella timerem
Scotica, ne Pictum tremerem, ne littore toto
Prospicerem dubiis venturum Saxona ventis."

A. M. MMMMCCCCXI. Occupata a Gothis est Roma, sedes quartæ et maxumæ monarchiarum, de quibus Daniel fuerat vaticinatus, anno millesimo centesimo sexagesimo quarto suæ conditionis. Ex quo autem tempore Romani in Britannia regnare cessarunt, post annos ferme CCCCLXV. ex quo C. Julius Cæsar eandem insulam adiit.

A. M. MMMMCCCCXLVI. Recedente a Britanniis legione Romana, cognita Scotti et Picti reditus denegatione, redeunt ipsi, et totam ab aquilone insulam pro indigenis muro tenus capescunt, nec mora, cæsis, captis, fugatisque custodibus muri et ipso interrupto, etiam intra illum crudelis prædo grassatur. Mittitur epistola lachrymis ærumnisque referta ad Romanæ potestatis virum Fl. Ætium, ter consulem, vicesimo tertio Theodosii principis anno petens auxilium, nec impetrat.

CAPUT II.

VERITATEM, quoad fieri licuit, sectatus fui, si quid occurrat forte, illi non exacte congruum, illud mihi ne imputetur vitiove vertatur rogo. Me enim ad regulas legesque historiæ sollicite componens, ea bona fide collegi

aliorum verba et relationes, quæ sincera maxume depre-
hendi et fide dignissima.   Ad cætera præter elenchum
imperatorum legatorumque Romanorum, qui huic insulæ
cum imperio præfuerunt, amplius quidquam expectare
nolit lector, quocumque meum opus finiam.

Igitur, primus omnium Romanorum dictator Julius
cum exercitu, principatu Cassibellini, Britanniam in-
gressus, quamquam prospera pugna terruerit incolas, ut
Tacitus refert, ac littore potitus sit, potest videri osten-
disse posteris, non tradidisse.

Mox bella civilia, et in rempublicam versa principum
arma, ac longa oblivio Britanniæ etiam in pace.   Consi-
lium id Augustus vocabat, Tiberius præceptum. Agitasse
Caligulam de intranda Britannia satis constat, ni velox
ingenio, mobilisque pœnitentia, et ingentes adversus
Germaniam conatus frustra fuissent.

Claudius vero Britanniæ intulit bellum, quam nullus
Romanorum post Julium Cæsarem attigerat, transvectis
legionibus auxiliisque, sine ullo prœlio ac sanguine, intra
paucissimos dies partem insulæ in ditionem recepit.
Deinde misit Vespasianum, adhuc in privata vita, qui
tricies et bis cum hoste conflixit, duas validissimas gentes
cum regibus eorum, XX. oppida et insulam Vectem,
Britanniæ proximam, imperio Romano adjecit. Reliquas
devicit per Cnæum Sentium et Aulum Plautium, illus-
tres et nobiles viros, et triumphum celebrem egit.

Subinde Ostorius Scapula, vir bello egregius, qui in
formam provinciæ proximam partem Britanniæ redegit.
Addita insuper veteranorum colonia Camalodunum.
Quædam civitates Cogiduno regi donatæ; is ad Trajani
usque principatum fidelissimus mansit, ut Tacitus scribit.

Mox Avitus Didius Gallus parta a prioribus continuit,
paucis admodum castellis in ulteriora promotis, per quæ
fama aucti officii quæreretur.

Didium Verannius excepit, isque intra annum exstinc-
tus est.

Suetonius hinc Paulinus biennio prosperas res habuit,

subactis nationibus, firmatisque præsidiis, quorum fiducia Monam insulam, ut vires rebellibus ministrantem, aggressus terga occasioni patefecit. Namque legati absentia remoto metu Britones accendere, atque Bonduica, generis regii fœmina, duce, sumpsere universi bellum; ac sparsos per castella milites consectati, expugnatis præsidiis, ipsam coloniam invasere, ut sedem servitutis, nec ullum in barbaris sævitiæ genus omisit ira et victoria. Quod, nisi Paulinus, eo cognito provinciæ motu prospere subvenisset, amissa Britannia foret, quam unius prœlii fortuna veteri patientiæ restituit; tenentibus arma plerisque, quos conscientia defectionis, et proprius ex legato timor, agitabat.

Hic cum egregius cætera, arrogantes in deditos et ut suæ quoque injuriæ ultor, durius consuleret; missus Petronius Turpilianus tanquam exorabilior et delictis hostium novus, eoque pœnitentiæ mitior: compositis prioribus, nihil ultra ausus, Trebellio Maximo provinciam tradidit.

Trebellius segnior et nullis castrorum experimentis, comitate quadam curandi, provinciam tenuit. Didicere jam barbari quoque Britones ignoscere vitiis blandientibus; et interventus civilium armorum præbuit justam segnitiæ excusationem. Sed discordia laboratum, cum assuetus expeditionibus miles otio lasciviret. Trebellius fuga ac latebris vitata exercitus ira, indecorus atque humilis, præcario mox præfuit, ac velut pacti, exercitus licentiam, dux salutem. Hæc seditio sine sanguine stetit.

Nec Vectius Bolanus manentibus adhuc civilibus bellis, agitavit Britanniam disciplina. Eadem inertia erga hostes, similis petulantia castrorum: nisi quod innocens Bolanus et nullis delictis invisus caritatem paraverat loco authoritatis.

Sed ubi, cum cætero orbe, Vespasianus et Britanniam recuperavit, magni duces, egregii exercitus, minuta hostium spes: et terrorem statim intulit Petilius Cerealis, Brigantum civitatem, quæ numerosissima provinciæ totius perhibetur, aggressus. Multa prœlia et aliquando non incruenta : magnamque Brigantum partem aut victoria amplexus, aut bello.

Sed cum Cerealis quidem alterius successoris curam famamque obruisset, sustinuit quoque molem Julius Frontinus, vir magnus quantum licebat ; validamque et pugnacem Silurum gentem armis subegit, super virtutem hostium locorum quoque difficultates eluctatus.

Successit huic Agricola, qui non solum acquisitam provinciæ pacem constituit, sed etiam annis septem plus minus continuis Caledonios, cum bellicosissimo rege ipsorum Galgaco, debellavit. Quo facto Romanorum ditioni gentes non antea cognitas adjunxit.

Majorem vero Agricolæ gloriam invidens Domitianus, domum eum revocavit, legatumque suum Lucullum in Britannias misit, quod lanceas novæ formæ appellari Luculeas passus esset.

Successor ejus Trebellius erat, sub quo duæ provinciæ, Vespasiana scilicet et Maæta, fractæ sunt. Romani se ipsos autem luxuriæ dederunt.

Circa idem tempus insulam hancce visitans Hadrianus imperator murum, opus sane mirandum et maxume memorabile, erexit, Juliumque Severum legatum in Britanniis reliquit.

Postea nihil unquam notatu dignum audivimus esse perpetratum, donec Antoninus Pius per legatos suos plurima bella gessit, nam et Britones, per Lollium Urbicum proprætorem et Saturninum præfectum classis, vicit, alio muro, submotis barbaris, ducto. Provinciam postea Valentiæ nomine notam revocavit.

Pio mortuo, varias de Britonibus Germanisque victorias reportavit Aurelius Antoninus.

Mortuo autem Antonino, cum ea quæ Romanis ademerant satis non haberent, magnam a legato Marcello passi sunt cladem.

Hic Pertinacem habuit successorem, qui fortem quoque se gessit ducem.

Hunc excepit Clodius Albinus, qui de sceptro et purpura cum Severo contendit.

Post hos primus erat Virius Lupus, qui legati nomine gaudebat. Non huic multa præclara gesta adscribuntur, quippe cujus gloriam intercepit invictissimus Severus, qui, fugatis celeriter hostibus, murum Hadrianeum, nunc ruinosum, ad summam ejus perfectionem reparavit; et, si vixerat, proposuerat exstirpare barbaros, quibus erat infestus, cum eorum nomine, ex hacce insula. Sed obiit, manu Dei, apud Brigantes in municipio Eboraco.

Ejusque in locum subiit Alexander, qui orientis quasdam victorias reportavit, in Edissa (*Sicilia*) mortuus.

Successores habuit legatos Lucilianum, M. Furium, N. Philippum. . . . . qui si defensionem terminorum ab ipsis observatam exceperimus, nil fere egerunt.

Post. . . . .

Desunt reliqua.

APPENDIX,

CONTAINING THE

ANCIENT AND MODERN NAMES OF THE STATIONS IN
THE ITINERARY.—From the London Edit., 8vo, 1809.

Iter I.	Corrected numbers.	Sites of the Stations.
(1) A Rhutupi ducta est "*Via Guethelinga*" dicta, usque in Segontium, per m. p. CCCXXIIII plus minus, sic :—		From Richborough to Caer Segont, by the Watling Street.
(2) Cantiopoli quæ et Duroverno X	XI	Canterbury.
(3) Durosevo XII	XII	Stone Chaple, in Ospringe.
(4) Duroprovis XXV	XVI	Rochester.
Deinde m. p. XXVII transis Thamesin intrasque provinciam et civitatem	XXVII	
(5) Londinium Augustam		London.
(6) Sulo Mago VIIII	XII	On the site of Mr. Napier's house at Brockley Hill.
(7) Verolamio Municipio XII	VIIII	Verulam.
Unde fuit Amphibalus et Albanus, martyres.		
(8) Foro Dianæ XII	XII	Dunstable.
(9) Magio Vinio XII	XII	Old Fields, S. of Fenny Stratford.
(10) Lactorodo XII	XVI	Berry Mount, in Towcester.
(11) Isanta Varia XII	XII	Burnt walls near Daventry.
(12) Tripontio XII	XII	Near Lilbourn.
(13) Benonis VIIII	VIIII	High Cross.
Hic bisecatur Via; alterutrumque ejus brachium Lindum usque, alterum versus Viriconium protenditur, sic :—		
(14) Manduessuedo XII	XII	Manceter.
(15) Etoceto XIII	XVI	Wall.
(16) Pennocrucio XII	XII	On the Penk.
(17) Uxaconia XII	XII	Red Hill, near Okenyate.
(18) Virioconio XI	XI	Wroxeter.
(19) Banchorio XXVI	XXVI	Probably Banchor.
(20) Deva Colonia X	XV	Chester.
Fines Flaviæ et Secundæ		
(21) Varis XXX	XXVII	Banks of the Clwydd, near Bodfari.
(22) Conovio XX	XX	Caer Hûn.
(23) Segontio XXIIII	XXIIII	Caer Segont, near Caernarvon.

The first Iter having run uniformly on the traces of the British Watling Street before described (except the small distance from Southfleet to London), and the road remaining tolerably perfect, there can be little difficulty in fixing the several stations, or indeed in correcting the sometimes corrupted numbers of the Itinerary.   It begins at Richborough, and, although at present obscure from the improved cultivation of the country, may be easily traced to Canterbury, from whence it went in the direction of the present turnpike to Rochester, leaving the intermediate station at Stone Chaple, in Ospringe, a little to the left hand.   At Rochester it passed the Medway, considerably above the present bridge, and instead of running to the right with the modern turnpike, it went as straight as the nature of the ground would permit, by Cobham Park, and Shinglewell, to Barkfields, in Southfleet (the station *Vagniacis* in Antonine), then to Swanscombe Parkwood, through which it passed, and rejoined the Dover road between the fifteenth and sixteenth milestone, near Dartford Brent.   Hence it went by Shooter's Hill over the Thames to London; and then, as before mentioned, by the site of Mr. Napier's house at Brockley Hill, Verulam, Dunstable, Fenny Stratford, Towcester, Burnt Walls,* near Lilbourne, High Cross, Manceter, Wall, Okenyate, to Wroxeter.   Here, quitting the south-west branch of the Watling Street, it bore to the right by Uffington, Broughton, Overley, Hammer, and Sarn Bridge to Banchor; and from thence ran clearly by Stockach and Aldford, over the Dee to Chester.

The Roman road here joining the North-east Watling Street, before mentioned, continued with it to Bodfari, and crossing Denbighshire, went over the Conway to Caer Hûn; and is supposed to have run as straight as the country would permit, to Caer Segont, about half a mile south of Caernarvon.

ITER II.			SITES OF THE STATIONS.
(23) A Segontio Virioconium usque, m. p. LXXIII. sic :—			From Caer Segont to Wroxeter.
		Corrected numbers.	
(24) Heriri Monte	XXV	XXV	Tommen y Mur, in Maentrwg.
(25) Mediolano	XXV	XXVII	On the bank of the Tanad.
(26) Rutunio	XII	XVI	Rowton.
(18) Virioconio	XI	XI	Wroxeter.

* Burnt Walls was the Roman post of *Isannavaria* ; Borough Hill, on the hill above it, was the great British fortification, *Bennavenna.*

This Iter runs on a branch of the South-east Watling Street, from Caer Segont, nearly in the direction of the present road to Tommen y Mur, an undoubted station in the parish of Maentrwg, by the common name of Sarn Helen, or the " paved way of the Legion." From hence it is continued to Bala; and on the banks of the Tanad, not far from the point where it is intersected by the Roman road from Caersws to Chester, was probably the lost town of *Mediolanum*. From *Mediolanum* the road runs under the north end of the Brythen, straight, although obscurely, to Rowton, and from thence over the Severn to Wroxeter.

ITER III.			Corrected numbers.	SITES OF THE STATIONS.
(5) A Londinio Lindum coloniam usque, sic :—				From London to Lincoln.
(27) Durosito	XII		XII	Near Rumford.
(28) Cæsaro Mago	XVI		XVI	Near Chelmsford.
(29) Canonio	XV		XV	On the east of Kelvedon.
(30) Camaloduno	Colonia VIIII		VIIII	Colchester.
Ibi erat templum Claudii, arx triumphalis, et imago Victoriæ deæ.				
(31) Ad Sturium amnem	VI		VI	Banks of the Stour.
Et finibus Trinobantum Cenimannos advenis				
(32) Cambretonio	XV			
(33) Sito Mago	XXII			
(34) Venta Cenom.	XXIII			Castor, near Norwich.
. . . . . . *				
(35) Camborico Colonia	XX			North side of the Cam, Cambridge.
(36) Duraliponte †	XX		XV	Godmanchester.
(37) Durno Mago ‡	XX		XX	Castor.
				Durobrivis was Chesterton on the Nen, near it.
(38) Isinis §	XX		XXV	Ancaster.
(39) Lindo ‖	XX		XXI	Lincoln.

As it is fifty-one measured miles from London to Colchester, and as it is probable that the stone from whence the Roman miles were measured was at least one mile west of Whitechapel church, we cannot allow any material deviation from the course of the present road, except in the neighbourhood of the capital, where the Roman

* Icianis XXVIII. *Stukeley.*   † Durolisponte, Iter 17.   ‡ Iter 17, XXX.
§ Corisennis XXX. Iter 17.   ‖ Iter 17, XXX.

road, instead of passing through Mile End, went much straighter
over the Lee at Old Ford, and fell again into the course of the present turnpike at Stratford, The Itinerary allowing only fifty-two
miles between London and Colchester, and the fifth Iter of Antonine agreeing with this of Richard, by stating twenty-eight as the
distance between London and *Cæsaromagus*, we may implicitly
adopt the distances here given, and fix the intermediate stations
near Rumford, Chelmsford, and Kelvedon. From Colchester the
road ran to the Stour, where probably stood the Mansio *ad Ansam*.
From hence to Castor, near Norwich, (the *Venta Icenorum*), the
stations and course of the road are unknown. Some commentators
have supposed it ran westerly, by Brettenham and Thetford;
others by Ipswich, Stowmarket, and Scole Inn; and others have
carried it more easterly, by Ipswich and Blythburgh, or Dunwich, to
the capital of the Iceni. In favour of the first, there is merely the
supposed resemblance of the name of Brettenham to *Cambretonium :*
of the second, traces of a Roman way, called the Pye Road ; and of
the third, a British track-way, and another Roman road, called the
Stone Street. But the distances suit none of these sites, and no
Roman remains have any where been found, between the Stour
and Castor, sufficient to justify an alteration of the numerals.

Icianis may have been Icklingham; and *Camboricum* was most
probably at Cambridge, from whence there is a Roman road dis-
coverable to Lincoln. To the first station, Godmanchester, this
Iter goes on the great communication between Colchester and
Chester, which for the sake of distinction may be called the *Via
Devana ;* and from Godmanchester to Lincoln, on the eastern
branch of the Ermyn Street, which was adopted by the Romans.
Twenty miles from Godmanchester, we find the great station of
Chesterton, on one side of the Nen, and Castor on the other;
which probably gave rise to the two names of *Durobrivæ*, and *Durnomagus*, the Roman and British towns severally noticed by Antonine and Richard. About twenty-five miles further, in the course
of the road, which cannot be mistaken, we find Ancaster, the
Isinnis, Corisennis, or *Causennis* of the Itineraries, from whence
twenty-one additional miles bring us to Lincoln.

ITER IV.			SITES OF THE STATIONS.
(39) A Lindo ad Vallum usque, sic :—			From Lincoln to the Wall.
		Corrected numbers.	
(40) Argolico	XIIII	XIIII	Littleborough.
(41) Dano	XX	XXI	Doncaster.
Ibi intras Maximam Cæsariensem			
(42) Legotio * m. p. XVI		XVI	Castleford.
(43) Eburaco Municip. olim Colonia Sexta†	XXI	XXI	York.
(44) Isurio	XVI	XVII	Aldborough.
(45) Cattaractoni‡	XXIIII	XXIIII	Catterick.
(46) Ad Tisam	X	XII	Pierce Bridge.
(47) Vinovio	XII	X	Binchester.
(48) Epiaco	XVIII ⎫	XIIII	Lanchester.
(49) Ad Murum	VIIII ⎬	VIIII	Halton Chester on the Wall.
trans Murum intras Valentiam			
(50) Alauna amne	XXV	XXV	Banks of the Coquet.
(51) Tueda flumine	XXX	XXXV	Banks of the Tweed.
(52) Ad Vallum			The Wall.

The fourth Iter left Lincoln with the Eastern Ermyn Street, which ran to the Humber; and, after continuing on it about five miles, turned suddenly to the left, pursuing its course in a straight line to the Trent, which it passed immediately opposite to the station of Littleborough. The Roman road may be traced from hence to Austerfield and Doncaster, where it fell in with the Western Ermyn Street, and is visible all the way by Castleford, Aberford, and Tadcaster, to York. In this Iter, the station of Tadcaster is passed unnoticed, as in the former the station of Brig Casterton, near Stamford.

From York the Iter is continued along the left bank of the Ouse, till it crossed the river to Aldborough. From hence rejoining the Western Ermyn Street, it passed the Eure, and ran straight through Catterick to the Tees, which it crossed at Piercebridge. It continued by the Royal Oak, St. Andrew Aukland, and the Bishop's Park, to Binchester, where, after fording the Were, it went with the North Watling Street to Lanchester; and, without noticing either Ebchester or Corbridge, over the Tyne to Halton Chester on the Wall. Here separating from the North Watling Street, it ran with the Ermyn Street, now known in Northumberland by the name of the Devil's Causeway, to the bank of the Coquet, and the Tweed, and entering Scotland on the East, was continued to the wall of Antonine.

* Legiolio, Iter 18.   † Iter 5 and 8, Eburaco.   ‡ Cataractone XL.

Iter V.			Sites of the Stations.
(52) A Limite Præturiam usque, sic :—			To Flamborough Head.
		Corrected numbers.	
(53) Curia *			
(54) Ad fines			Chew Green.
(55) Bremenio		VII	Riechester.
(56) Corstoplio	XX	XXV	Corbridge.
(57) Vindomora	VIIII	VIIII	Ebchester.
(47) Vindovio †	XVIIII	XVIIII	Binchester.
(45) Cattaractoni	XXII	XXII	Catterick.
(43) Eboraco	XL	XL	York.
(58) Derventione	VII	VII	On the Derwent, near Stamford Bridge.
(59) Delgovicia	‡ XIII		. . . . . .
(60) Præturio	‡ XXV	XXXVIII	Near Flamborough Head.

In regard to part of the country traversed by this Iter, there appears to have been so little connection between the work of our author and the map which accompanies it, that we can rely little on the latter either to assist or correct us. This Iter is made to begin from *Curia*, a town probably on the confines of some petty kingdom, and to pass to the first certain post of *Bremenium*, or Riechester. Now, on referring to the map, *Curia*, the principal town of the Gadeni, so far from lying on the road which leads to *Bremenium*, the capital of the Ottadini, is considerably to the westward of its course. From this disagreement, commentators have suspected a mistake of the transcriber, and imagine that *Curia* is intended for *Corium*. It is certain, at least, that this Iter, running on the east side of the island, on the track of the Northern Watling Street, enters Northumberland at Chew Green, goes from thence to Riechester (leaving unnoticed the station at Risingham), and runs with it to Corbridge, Ebchester, Binchester, Catterick, and York.

From York to Flamborough Head, a Roman road may still be traced; and as the distance agrees with the Itinerary, and there must have been a Roman post on or near that headland, we should think it more probable that this was the site of *Præturium*, § although we have not yet discovered the remains of any post on the Derwent, or the intermediate station of *Delgovicia*. So many Roman roads from different quarters point towards Stamford bridge, that there is no doubt the station of *Derventio* was near it.

* Probably Corium, *Stukeley.* † Vinovio, Iter 4. ‡ XXXVIII.
§ This *Præturium* and the *Prætorium* of Antonine must be carefully distinguished from the *Petuaria*, mentioned by our author in the 17th Iter, for *Petuaria* was certainly at Brough on the Humber.

Iter VI.			Sites of the Stations.
(43) Ab Eboraco Devam usque, sic :—			From York to Chester.
		Corrected numbers.	
(61) Calcaria m. p. VIIII		VIIII	Tadcaster.
(62) Camboduno	XXII	XXXII	Slack.
(63) Mancunio*	XVIII	XXIII	Manchester.
(64) Finibus Maximæ et Flaviæ	XVIII	VI	Stretford on Mersey.
(65) Condate*	XVIII	XXIII	Kinderton.
(20) Deva	XVIII	XVIII	Chester.

Such appears to be the incorrectness of the numerals attached to this Iter, as well as to the corresponding Iter of Antonine, that, although four of the six stations are well known, and a fifth can scarcely be mistaken, yet we can no other way obviate the difficulty than by supposing a station omitted, or by altering the numerals, none of which, except the first, agree with the distances between the vestiges of the different stations and their supposed sites; for example, in the first part between York and Manchester, where the Itinerary gives only 49 miles, the nearest road through Heathersfield amounts to 65.

As the only great and undoubted Roman station between Tadcaster and Manchester is at Slack (for the camps at Kirklees, and Castleshaw, are only temporary posts), it will perhaps be justifiable to fix this point as the site of *Cambodunum ;* to suppose ten miles omitted in this stage; and in the next to conjecture that, by a common error in copying the Roman numerals, XVIII. has been substituted for XXIII. the exact distance from Slack to Manchester.

As the Mersey was undoubtedly the boundary on the West between the Roman provinces of Maxima and Flavia, and as the Roman road still existing crossed it at Stretford, we fix the next point there, and change the number XVII. to VI. The two next stations of *Condate* and *Deva,* the numerals (with a slight alteration) permit us to fix at Kinderton and Chester. It is worthy of remark, that with these alterations the sum total of the numerals remains nearly the same.

* Iter 10, Mancunio—Condate XXIII.

Iter VII.			Sites of the Stations.
(66) A Portu Sistuntiorum Eboracum usque, sic :—			From Freckleton to York.
		Corrected numbers.	
(67) Rerigonio	XXIII	XIII	Ribchester.
(68) Ad Alpes Peninos	VIII	XXIII	Burrens in Broughton.
(69) Alicana	X	X	Ilkley.
(44) Isurio *	XVIII	XVIII	Aldborough.
(43) Eboraco	XVI	XVII	York.

This Iter runs from Freckleton on the Ribble to Ribchester, and then over the mountains to Broughton, Ilkley, Aldborough, and York. As the Roman road is tolerably perfect all the way to Aldborough, and the vestiges of the stations are undoubted, we are justified in the alteration of the two first numbers, as by this alteration they will correspond with the present distances and the situations of the posts.

Iter VIII.			Sites of the Stations.
(43) Ab Eboraco Luguvalium usque, sic :—			From York to Carlisle.
		Corrected numbers.	
(45) Cattaractoni	XL	XL	Catterick.
(70) Lataris	† XVI	XVIII	Bowes.
(71) Vataris	‡ XVI	XIIII	Brough.
(72) Brocavonacis	§ XVIII	XIII	Kirby Thur.
(Brovonacis)			
(73) Vorreda	XVIII	XIIII	Plumpton Wall.
(74) Lugubalia	‖ XVIII	XIII	Carlisle.

The road from York to Catterick has been traced before, and the Roman way from thence to Carlisle ran nearly in the direction of the present turnpike. The only doubt which occurs, therefore, in this Iter, is whether, from a similarity of sound, the transcriber of Richard has not erroneously written Brocavonacis for Brovonacis, which are two neighbouring posts in this direction, the first Brougham, and the second Kirby Thur. As the conjecture is not improbable, the corrected distance is given from the latter.

It is worthy of observation that in this Iter four successive V's have been added by mistake of the transcriber, as is the case in regard to the X's omitted in the third Iter.

* *Stukeley*, XVIIII.   † Lataris XVII. *Stuk.*
‡ XVI. *Stuk.*   § XX. *Stuk.*
‖ Iter 10 inverted, Brocavonacis—Luguvallia, XXII.

ITER IX.			SITES OF THE STATIONS.
(74) A Luguballio Ptorotonim usque, sic :—			From Carlisle to Burgh Head.
		Corrected numbers.	
(75) Trimontio m. p.			Birrenswork Hill.
(76) Gadanica			
(77) Corio			
(52) Ad Vallum			Camelon.
Incipit Vespasiana			
(78) Alauna	XII	XIII	Kier.
(79) Lindo	VIIII	VIIII	Ardoch.
(80) Victoria	VIIII	VIIII	Dealgin Ross.
(81) Ad Hiernam	VIIII	VIIII	Strageth.
(82) Orrea	XIIII	XIIII	On the Tay above Perth.
(83) Ad Tavum	XVIIII	XVIIII	Near Invergowrie.
(84) Ad Æsicam	XXIII	XXIII	Brechin on South Esk.
(85) Ad Tinam	VIII	VIII	Fordun.
(86) Devana	XXIII	XXIII	Norman Dikes near Peter Culter.
(87) Ad Itunam	XXIIII	XXVI	Glenmailin on the Ithan.
(88) Ad Montem Grampium		XIII	Near Knock Hill.
(89) Ad Selinam		X	On the Cullen near Deskford.
(90) Tuessis	XVIIII	XVII	On the Spey near Bellie.
(91) Ptorotone		XVII	Burgh Head.

Innumerable difficulties occur on every side in endeavouring to explain this Iter. There is great reason to believe that the *Trimontium* of this Iter was Birrenswork Hill, and that the road ran from thence along the western side of the island as it is traced in the map of Richard. Camelon is allowed by all antiquaries to be the *Ad Vallum:* but it is impossible to draw the line between these two points; for although General Roy has mentioned a road from Carlisle on the eastern side of the Eildon Hills, and another on the western beyond Cleghorn to Castle Cary, there is little authority for the existence of either. Lynekirk has every appearance of a station, lay within the territories of the Gadeni, and would suit the situation assigned to *Gadanica,* but no road has hitherto been discovered leading to or from it. If the western trended at Biggar as much to the east, as that part which remains in the direction of Glasgow does to the West, it would have passed Borthwich Castle or the Gore, which Roy supposes was the *Corium.* Admitting the identity of this station would clear up the whole of this Iter to the Wall. There is no doubt that the sites of *Lindum, Victoria,* and *Ad Hiernam* were at Ardoch, Dealgin Ross, and Strageth.

Notwithstanding the difficulties which occur in tracing this Iter from Carlisle to the Wall, yet from thence to the Tay the direction of the road, and the situation of the stations as fixed by General Roy agree so perfectly with the Itinerary, as to leave no doubt that he has ascertained their real position. But although he discovered a road north of the Tay, yet, as he found no vestiges of stations, Mr. Chalmers seems to have been more successful in fixing the posts between that river and *Ptoroton*.

It does not appear that the road was ever completed: however, from *Orrea* on the Tay, a little above Perth, he observes, that the communication ran through the passage of the Sidlaw Hills, and along the Carse of Gowrie to the north end of the æstuary of the Tay near Dundee; two miles west of which place, and half a mile north of Invergowrie, are the remains of a Roman camp about two hundred yards square, fortified with a high rampart and spacious ditch. Here he places *Ad Tavum*. Proceeding hence north-easterly through the natural opening of the country, and passing in the way the camp at Harefaulds, at the distance of twenty-three miles is Brechin on the South Esk, the station *Ad Æsicam*, exactly in the line laid down in Richard's map, and at the distance given in the Itinerary. Continuing from the South Esk in a north-north-easterly direction, at the distance of five miles and a half, we reach the North Esk, the supposed *Ad Tinam*. We pass that river at King's Ford, and proceeding up the valley of Lutherwater, at the distance of eight miles and a half find Fordun, where there are the remains of two Roman camps. From thence proceeding seventeen miles, to the well known camp at Raedikes, and continuing in a northerly direction six miles beyond, is the rectangular camp on the Dee at Peter Culter, called Norman Dikes, the *Devana* of the Iter. This point is exactly thirty-one miles from Brechin on the South Esk, agrees with the aggregate distances in the Itinerary *Ad Tinam* VIII, and *Ad Devanam* XXIII, and corresponds with the track delineated on Richard's map.

The obvious openings through this rugged country point out the way by which the Romans must have penetrated northerly by the right of Achlea Fiddy and Kinmundy, to Kintore on the Don. They followed the Strath to the ford where the high road has always passed to Inverurie, and proceeded north-north-west through the moorlands, to the sources of the Ithan, and the camp at Glenmailin, the *Ituna* of Richard, a distance of twenty-six miles. From thence proceeding northward, across the Doverna at Achengoul, where are still considerable remains of military works; and at the distance of thirteen miles, we reach the high ground north of Foggy lone, at the east side of Knock Hill, the *Mons Grampius* of the Iter.

Hence the road runs to *Ad Selinam*, which is supposed to be on the Cullen, near the old Tower of Deskford, at the distance of ten miles. Following the course of the river, and the coast of the

Murray Frith, seventeen miles, we arrive at the Roman post of *Tuessis*, on the high bank of the Spey, below the church of Bellie. Seventeen miles further is Burgh Head, the *Ptorotone* of Richard.

ITER X.			SITES OF THE STATIONS.
(91) Ab ultima Ptorotone per mediam insulæ Isca Damnonorum usque, sic :—			From Burgh Head, through the middle of the island to Exeter.
		Corrected numbers.	
(92) Varis * m. p. VIII			Fores VIIII
(93) Ad Tuessim XVIII			Cromdall on Spey XX
(94) Tamea XXVVIII			Braemar Castle XXX
(95) —————— XXI	Names and Numerals from Gen. Roy.		Barra Castle on Ila XXX
(96) In Medio VIIII			Inchstuthill XII
(82) Orrea VIIII			Bertha on Tay VIIII
(80) Victoria XVIII			Dealgin Ross XXIIII
(52) Ad Vallum † XXXII			Camelon XXXII
(74) Luguballia LXXX			Carlisle CXVIIII
(97) Brocavonacis XXII		XXII	Brougham.
(98) Ad Alaunam		XXXXVII	Lancaster.
(99) Coccio		XXXVI	Blackrode.
(63) Mancunio XVIII		XVIII	Manchester.
(65) Condate XXIII		XXIII	Kinderton.
(100) Mediolano XVIII		XVI	Chesterton.
(15) Etoceto		XXXV	Wall.
(101) Salinis m. p.		XXII	Droitwich.
(102) Glebon Colon. m. p.		XXXIIII	Gloucester.
(103) Corino XIIII		XVIII	Cirencester.
(104) Aquas Solis m. p. ..		XXX	Bath.
(105) Ad Aquas XVIII		XX	Probably Wells.
(106) Ad Uxellam amnem m. p.		XXI	Probably Bridgewater.
(107) Isca m. p.		XXXXV	Exeter.

The first part of this Iter is taken from General Roy; and as we have none of the intermediate stations between Carlisle and the Wall, every commentator may choose what route he pleases, although none will coincide with the distances of the Itinerary. From Carlisle, if we place any reliance on the numbers, the next station, *Brocavonacis*, can only be fixed at Brougham. Thence the road to the banks of the Lune, as well as the station on it, is uncertain; for, whether we choose Overborough or Lancaster, we

---

* VIIII. *Stukeley.* † XXX. Iter 9.

know of no road to direct us; and the only reason for preferring
the latter is the supposed site of the next station, *Coccium*, at
Blackrode, and the course of the road through Lancaster, tending
more immediately to that point, than the road through Overborough.   The two next stations, *Mancunium* and *Condate*, as well
as the connecting line of road, are well known.   From Kinderton,
although there is a Roman way pointing to Chesterton in Staffordshire, the *Mediolanum* of this Iter, and the site of *Etocetum* is undoubtedly Wall, yet we speak with hesitation of the line of communication betwixt them; though we presume it ran through
Newcastle, Stone, and Ridgeley.   From Wall, which is on the
Watling Street, the Iter continues along the Ryknield Street,
through Sutton Colfield Park, to Birmingham.   There falling in
with the first Salt-Way, it proceeds to Droitwich, and is continued
by the Western Road, through Worcester to Gloucester.   Here,
turning nearly at a right angle, it passes by the well known Roman
road over Birdlip Hill to Cirencester; and trending to the right,
proceeds by the Foss to *Aquæ Solis* or Bath.   Quitting the Foss,
and still bearing to the right, it continues along the lower road to
Wells, and from thence to *Uxella*, which was probably at Bridgewater.   From the banks of the Parret it ran in the track of the
British Way, and the present turnpike by Taunton, Wellington,
and Collumpton, to Exeter.

ITER XI.			SITES OF THE STATIONS.
(104) Ab Aquis, per Viam Juliam, Mena- piam usque, sic :—			From Bath by the Julian Way to St. David's.
		Corrected numbers.	
(108) Ad Abonam m. p. VI		VI ⎫	Bitton.
(109) Ad Sabrinam VI		VIIII ⎭	
Unde Trajectu * in- tras in Britanniam Secundam			Sea Mills.
(110) Et Stationem Trajec- tum † III		III	Severn Side.
(111) Venta Silurum ‡ VIII		VIIII	Caerwent.
(112) Isca Colonia VIIII		VIIII	Caerleon.
Unde fuit Aaron Martyr.			
(113) Tibia Amne § VIII		XV	Banks of the Taaf, possibly Caireu or Caerdiff.

* Statio Trajectus. *Comm.*   † Ad Sabrinam. *Comm.*
‡ VIIII. *Stuk.*   § Tibia VII. *Stuk.*

ITER XI.—*continued.*

(114)	Bovio	XX	XX	In Evenny Park.	
(115)	Nido	XV	XX	Near Neath.	
(116)	Leucaro	XV	X	Perhaps Lwghor.	
	(Muridunum	omitt.			
		XX)	XX	Caermarthen.	
(117)	Ad Vigesimum	XX	XX	Castel Flemish.*	
(118)	Ad Menapiam	XVIIII	XVIII	Near St. David's.	
	Ab hac urbe per m. p.				
		XXX			
	Navigas in Hyberniam.				

As the course of the Roman road connecting the stations of this Iter is still discernible, we do not hesitate in correcting the imperfections of Richard by the corresponding Iter of Antonine. At Bitton, six miles from Bath, we find marks of a post attended with *tumuli,* which whether called *Abone* or *Trajectus*† is of little importance, because, like the next, Sea Mills, it will suit either appellation, from its position on the Avon, and commanding a passage over that river. From Bitton the Roman way ran nearly in the direction of the present turnpike, north of the river as far as St. George's church; thence it proceeded straight near St. Paul's; ascended the Downs behind Mr. Daubeney's house to the direction-post, from whence it crossed Durdham Down, and skirted Mrs. Jackson's park wall to Sea Mills, a great maritime post at the confluence of the Trim and the Avon. It continued by Lord De Clifford's house straight to the Severn, crossed that river, and passed by Caldecot Castle through Caerwent and Caerleon to the bank of the Taaf and Eweny Park, which last place Roman remains lead us to conjecture was the site of *Bovium.* At Neath we have also little hesitation in fixing the site of *Nidus,* because a road from the *Gaer* near *Brecon* evidently leads to the same spot.

The remainder of this Iter is obscure. *Leucaro* has been fixed at Lwghor, principally from the resemblance of the name. From thence the road may have run to Caermarthen (*Maridunum*), which appears to have been omitted; and was probably continued as straight as the country would permit to Castel Flemish and St.

---

* This station has been recently discovered by Mr. Fenton during his researches for his History of Pembrokeshire, which is shortly to be published. It lies in the parish of Ambleston.

† We prefer the name of *Abone* for Sea Mills, because it bears that name in old deeds; on the other hand, there appears to be no instance in which the name of *Trajectus* is applied to a town unless at the passage of a river.

David's, where we would place the stations *Vigesimum* and *Menapia.*[*]

Iter XII.				Sites of the Stations.
(104) Ab Aquis Londinium usque, sic :—				
		Corrected numbers.		
(119) Verlucione m. p. XV		XV		Highfield, near Sandy Lane.
(120) Cunetione	XX	XV		Folly Farm, E. of Marlborough.
(121) Spinis	XV	XX		Spene.
(122) Calleba Attrebatum				
	XV			Silchester.
(123) Bibracte	XX }		XXXXIIII	London.
(5) Londinio	XX }			

As the traces of a Roman road from Bath towards Marlborough are still visible, we have only to examine in what points of its course remains have been found sufficient to justify us in determining the sites of the different stations. Accordingly, at fifteen miles from Bath we have Highfield, in Sandy Lane, near Heddington; and at fifteen more Folly Farm, near Marlborough. From hence twenty miles bring us to Spene; and although at this place few remains have been discovered, yet the direction of another Roman road, from Cirencester to the same point, sufficiently proves the existence of a station. Of the site of *Calleva* at Silchester † there can be little doubt; although the course of the road

---

* The bishops of St. David's being called in Latin *Menapienses* by the earliest of our ecclesiastical writers, is an argument that the station is near the present town. The site of the station itself was probably at a short distance from the modern city, at a place called the Burrows, and just above a fine harbour called the Porth Mawr.

† Few of the Roman stations have been fixed at so many different places as that of *Calleva Attrebatum*. It has been placed at Silchester, Henley, Wallingford, and Reading, by different antiquaries; yet in no doubtful case do more testimonies concur to ascertain the site. It was evidently a station of importance, because it appears as a central point, to which the roads traversed by three different Iters of Antonine (the 13th, 14th, and 15th,) converge. It was the capital of the Attrebates; situated at known distances from London, Winchester, Bath, Spene, and Caerleon; and at a doubtful one, though easily supplied, from Cirencester and Old Sarum. These circumstances cannot by any expedient be brought to coincide, either with Henley, Wallingford, or Reading; but all agree in regard to Silchester. Its distance nearly accords with the Itinerary distance of *Calleva* from London, Bath, Spene, Winchester,

from Spene is uncertain. The road from Silchester, still known
by the name of the Devil's Causeway, as it runs over Bagshot
Heath, as well as evident traces of it between Staines and London,
still exist; but the intermediate station of *Bibracte* is doubtful.
If the numbers in this Iter be correct, we cannot deviate from the
straight line, and this post must be placed near the hill at Egham,
or the head of the Virginia Water.

ITER XIII.				SITES OF THE STATIONS.
(112) Ab Isca Uriconium usque, sic :—				From Caerleon to Wroxeter.
			Corrected numbers.	
(124) Bultro m. p.	VIII		VIII	Usk.
(125) Gobannio	XII		XII	Abergavenny.
(126) Magna	XXIII		XXIII	Kentchester.
(127) Branogenio	XXIII		XXIII	Lentwardine.
(18) Urioconio	XXVII		XXVII	Wroxeter.

The beginning of this Iter cannot be traced, notwithstanding
two out of the three stations are well known; and we have little
doubt that *Bultrum* or *Burrium* was at Usk (though no Roman
remains have been found there), because the distance given from
Caerleon to *Gobannium* or Abergavenny will not admit of any
deviation from the straight line. From Abergavenny, after passing
the Munnow, the Roman road still exists, particularly near Mad-
ley, pointing to Kentchester, and from thence may be traced by
the next post of Lentwardine on the Teme, to Wroxeter.

and Caerleon, and, if a station (which is evidently lost) in the Iter of Antonine
be supplied, with that from Cirencester. The present remains are those of a
great Roman town; it is situated in the district formerly inhabited by the
Attrebates; and in every direction traces of Roman roads converging to this
point still plainly exist, from London, Spene, Winchester, Old Sarum, Bath,
and Cirencester.

ITER XIV.			SITES OF THE STATIONS.
(112) Ab Isca, per Glebon, Lindum usque, sic :—			From Caerleon, by Gloucester, to Lincoln.
		Corrected numbers.	
(124) Ballio* m. p. VIII			Usk.
(128) Blestio	XII	XIII	Monmouth.
(129) Sariconio	XI	XII	Rose or Berry Hill in Weston.
(102) Glebon Colonia	XV	XV	Gloucester.
(130) Ad Antonam	XV	XX	On the Avon.
(131) Alauna	XV	XV	Alcester on the Aln.
(121) ———	. . .	XVIIII	Camp at Chesterton on the Foss, near Harwood's house.
(13) Vennonis	XII	XXI	High Cross.
(133) Ratiscorion	XII	XII	Leicester.
(134) Venromento	XII	XII	Willoughby.
(135) Margiduno	XII	XII	East Bridgeford.
(136) Ad Pontem	XII	VII	Near Thorpe turnpike.
(137) Crococolana		VII	Brugh.
(39) Lindum	XII	XII	Lincoln.

This Iter ran, like the former, from Caerleon to Usk, where bending to the right it traversed the country to Monmouth. From hence, although we cannot trace the exact line of the road, yet we have no doubt that it crossed the Wye to the next station at Berry Hill, in Weston, under Penyard; and continued nearly in a direct line to Gloucester. As the author has only left the name of a river for the next station, it must be placed in such a situation on the Avon as to admit the distance of fifteen miles from the next station of Alcester, which was the site of *Alauna.* This would carry it to the westward of Evesham. From Alcester likewise, till we reach the Foss, we have neither a road nor distance, nor even the name of a station. For this reason we deem ourselves justified in considering the undoubted Roman camp at Chesterton on the Foss, as the post omitted by our author, and from thence we proceed on that known military way to the certain stations of High Cross, Leicester, Willoughby, Bridgeford, Brough, and Lincoln.

* Bultro, It. 13.

ITER XV.			SITES OF THE STATIONS.
(5) A Londinio, per Clausentum, in Londinium usque, sic:—			From London, through Bittern, again to London.
		Corrected numbers.	
(122) Caleba m. p. XLIIII		XLIIII	Silchester.
(138) Vindomi	XV	XV	Near St. Mary Bourne.
(139) Venta Belgarum	XXI	XXI	Winchester.
(140) Ad Lapidem	VI	VI	Stoneham.
(141) Clausento	IIII	IIII	Bittern, near Southampton.
(142) Portu Magno	X	XV	Portchester.
(143) Regno	X	XV	Chichester.
(144) Ad Decimum	X	X	On the Arun.
(145) Anderida Portu . . .		*XLV	Pevensey.
(146) Ad Lemanum	XXV	XXV	On the Rother.
(147) Lemaniano Portu	X	XX	Lymne.
(148) Dubris	X	X	Dover.
(1) Rhutupis Colonia	X	XV	Richborough.
(149) Regulbio	X	VIIII	Reculver.
(2) Contiopoli	X	X	Canterbury.
(3) Durelevo	XVIII	XII	Stone Chaple in Ospringe.
(150) Mado	XII	XVIII	On the bank of the Medway.
(151) Vagnaca	XVIII	VIIII	Barkfields in Southfleet.
(152) Novio Mago	XVIII	XV	Holwood Hill.
(5) Londinio	XV	XV	London.

This Iter leads from London to the south-west part of Hampshire, and from thence, skirting the Sussex and Kentish coasts, back to the capital.

At the first step the author gives forty-four miles as the distance between London and Silchester, instead of forty, as in the 12th Iter; hence we may deviate a little in settling the site of *Bibracte* or *Ad Pontes.* Of the next station we can merely offer a conjecture. As the country of the Attrebates and their capital *Calleva,* or Silchester, is by our author described as lying near the Thames, in distinction from that of the Segontiaci,† whose capital, *Vindomis,* was further distant from that river, and nearer the Kennet, one point only appears to suit the distances, which bears the proper relation to the neighbouring stations, and at the same time falls at the intersection of two known Roman roads. This is in the neighbourhood of St. Mary Bourne, and affords reason for considering Egbury Camp, or some spot near it, as the capital of the Segontiaci. For by following the Roman road called the Portway from Silchester, at the distance of fifteen miles is the

* *Stukeley,* X.

† Richard, b. 1, c. 6, sect. 28, describing the several nations whose territories were watered by the Thames in its course to the German Ocean, places the Attrebates between the Hedui and the Cassii, without even mentioning the Segontiaci : a proof that their territories did not approach the river.

rivulet near St. Mary Bourne, and not far from it, the point where
the Portway is intersected by the Roman road from Winchester to
Cirencester; and proceeding along this last we have another dis-
stance of twenty-one miles to Winchester. The road from Winchester by Otterbourne to Stoneham, and thence by the Green
Lane to Bittern, is well known, and the distance sufficiently exact.
But from thence, although traces of the road are occasionally dis-
coverable on Ridgeway, and to the north of Bursledon Hill, pointing towards Fareham and Portchester, yet the latter part is almost
totally unknown or lost. From Portchester it ran in the track of
the present turnpike to Chichester; and over the Arun not far
from Arundel; and then along the coast to Pevensey, the banks of
the Rother, Lymne, Dover, Richborough, Reculver, and Canterbury. There falling into the track of the first Iter, it went along
the Watling Street to the bank of the Medway, and passing that
river, proceeded by Barkfields in Southfleet, a station omitted
before, across the country with the ancient Watling Street, (by a
road now unknown,*) to Holwood Hill, the capital of the Regni,
and from thence to London.

Iter XVI.		Sites of the Stations.
(5) A Londinio Ceniam usque, sic :—		From London to the Fal.
	Corrected numbers.	
(139) Venta Belgarum		
m. p. XC	LXXX	Winchester.
(153) Brige XI	XI	Near Broughton.
(154) Sorbioduno VIII	VIIII	Old Sarum.
(155) Ventageladia XII	XV	Gussage Cow Down.
(156) Durnovaria VIIII	XXX	Dorchester.
(157) Moriduno XXXIII	XXX	Seaton.
(107) Isca Damnon XV	XXVIII	Exeter.
(158) Durio Amne ...	XXIII	On the Dart.
(159) Tamara ...	XXVI	On the Tamar.
(160) Voluba ...	XXVIII	On the Fowey.
(161) Cenia ...	XX	On the Fal.

* In Hasted's History of Kent is a passage which countenances the idea of
an ancient road having traversed the country in this line.

The exact route from London to Winchester not being defined, we may suppose that it ran as before, through Silchester, and from thence by St. Mary Bourne, as in the 15th Iter. From Winchester, as the road still exists leading to Old Sarum, the distance of eleven miles will probably give the site of *Brige*, although the station itself is not known ; and the nine following will lead us to Old Sarum. Pursuing the course of the road, which may be still traced quite to Dorchester, remains found on Gussage Cow Down point out the site of *Ventageladia ;* and the disagreement between the Itinerary and real distance from thence to Dorchester justifies us in supposing that some intermediate post has been omitted. The site of *Moridunum* is doubtful; some thinking it to be Eggardon, or the Hill of the Morini, with which the distance of nine miles would not disagree; while others, with more reason, prefer Seaton, the great port of the West, because the Foss leads from Ilchester directly to it. Intermediate stations have evidently been lost between this place and Exeter, as has also been the case between that place and the Dart, the Tamar, the Fowey, and the Fal. From Honiton the road is visible pointing to Exeter, as well as from Exeter to Totness, and according to the ingenious Borlase, even to Lostwithiel.

ITER XVII.			SITES OF THE STATIONS.
Ab Anderida [Eboracum] usque, sic :—			From East Bourne to York.
		Corrected numbers.	
(162) Sylva Anderida			
m. p. . .			East Bourne.
(152) Novio mago		XXXX	Holwood Hill.
(5) Londinio	XV	XV	London.
(163) Ad Fines *		XXVIII	Brougham.
(36) Durolisponte †		XXX	Godmanchester.
(37) Durnomago	XXX	XX	Castor, on the left bank of the Nen.
(38) Corisennis	XXX	XXV	Ancaster.
(39) Lindo	XXX	XXI	Lincoln.
(164) In Medio	XV	XV	
(165) Ab Abum	XV	XV	Winterton.
Unde transis in Maximam.			
(166) Ad Petuariam	VI	VI	Brough.
(43) Deinde Eboraco, ut supra (It. 5)			
m. p. XLVI		XXX	York.

* *Stuk.* XXX.
† It. 3. Duraliponte—Durnomago XX.—Isinnis XX.—Lindo XX.

. This Iter ran in the track of the British Ermyn Street, from Pevensey and East Bourne, which were perhaps the *Anderida Portus*, and *Anderida* of the 15th Iter, along the ridge of hills to Holwood Hill (already mentioned as the capital of the Rhemi), and from thence to London, but its traces are now so obscure as to be almost forgotten. Some think that from London it proceeded along the British Street, by the Green Lanes, Cheshunt, and to the west of Broxbourn to Ware; while others suppose that this Roman road went much straighter, and nearly in the course of the present turnpike through Ware to Broughing, a post at the confluence of the Rib and the Quin, where was probably the station *Ad Fines*, the boundary between the countries of the Iceni, the Cassii, and the Trinobantes. From hence the Roman road is so perfect by Caxton quite to Lincoln, that we fix the station of *Durnomagus* at the great camp near Castor, and the three others at Godmanchester, Ancaster, and Lincoln. From Lincoln the Roman road proceeds directly to the banks of the Humber, having, at the distance assigned in the Iter, the *Mansio in Medio*, and the post at Winterton; from whence six miles carry us across the river to Brough, or *Petuaria*, a post often confounded with the *Prætorium* of the 6th Iter. As there is a Roman road still existing from Brough towards Weighton and then over Barmby Moor to York, there can be little doubt in considering it as the course of this Iter. Should, however, the forty-six miles given in the Itinerary (which appears to have been an error arising from the mistake of the transcriber in confounding *Petuaria* and *Præturium*) be considered as correct, the course of the Iter may be supposed to have run from Brough by Londesborough and Millington, to the great road from Flamborough, and then to have turned with it to York, making exactly the forty-six miles of the Itinerary.

ITER XVIII.			SITES OF THE STATIONS.
(43) Ab Eboraco per medium insulæ Clausentum usque, sic :—			From York through the middle of the island to Bittern.
		Corrected numbers.	
(42) Legiolio m. p. XXI		XXI	Castleford.
(167) Ad Fines XVIII		XXIII	Temple Brough, on the bank of the Don.
(168) XVI		XVI	TaptonHill,nearChesterfield.
(169) XVI		XII	Camp near Penkridge.
(170) Derventione * XVI		XII	Little Chester.
(171) Ad Trivonam XII		XII	Berry Farm, in Branston.
(15) Etoceto † XII		XII	Wall.
(14) Manduesuedo XVI		XVI	Manceter.
(13) Benonnis XII		XII	High Cross.
(12) Tripontio XI		XI	Near Dove Bridge.
(11) Isannavaria XII		X	Burnt Walls.
(172) Brinavis XII		XII	Black Ground, near Chipping Norton.
(173) Ælia Castra XVI		XVI	Alcester, near Bicester.
(174) Dorocina XV		XVI	Dorchester.
(175) Tamesi VI		VI	On the Thames.
Vindomi ⎱ XV			
(122) *Calleva* ⎰		XX	Silchester.
(141) Clausento XXXXVI		XXXXV	Bittern, near Southampton.

This Iter proceeds from York in the same direction as the fourth to Castleford, where, bearing to the right to join the Ryknield Street, it continues with it through the several stations of Temple Brough on the Don, Chesterfield, Penkridge, Little Chester, and Branston, to Wall. Here diverging to the left with the Watling Street, it passed through Manceter, High Cross, and Dove Bridge, to Burnt Walls. It there quitted the known road, and bore across the country, by an unknown route, to Alcester, on the Akeman Street; but the considerable remains found at Black Ground, near Chipping Norton, would lead us to place the station of *Brinavis* there, if the Roman road did not make any material deviation between Burnt Walls and Alcester.

From Alcester the road runs plainly over Ottmoor, and indeed almost all the way to Dorchester. But from thence as we can discover no traces of a road, and as our next post appears to have been only six miles distant and on the Thames, if any reliance can be placed on the number, it may be the point where the Roman

---

* XVI.

† It. 2, inv. Etoceto.—Manduesuedo XIII.—Benonnis XII.—Tripontio Isanta Varia XII.

road from Wantage apparently passes that river opposite Monge-
well. The next distance of fifteen miles, being insufficient to lead
us by any road to *Vindomis*, if it were placed either at Silchester
or near St. Mary Bourne, it is more than probable that there is
some error in the name of the station; and as the following number of forty-six miles agrees with the distance in the 15th Iter of
the road from Silchester passing near Egbury to Bittern, we cannot
help supposing that the name of *Vindomis* has been inserted by
mistake for that of *Calleva*.

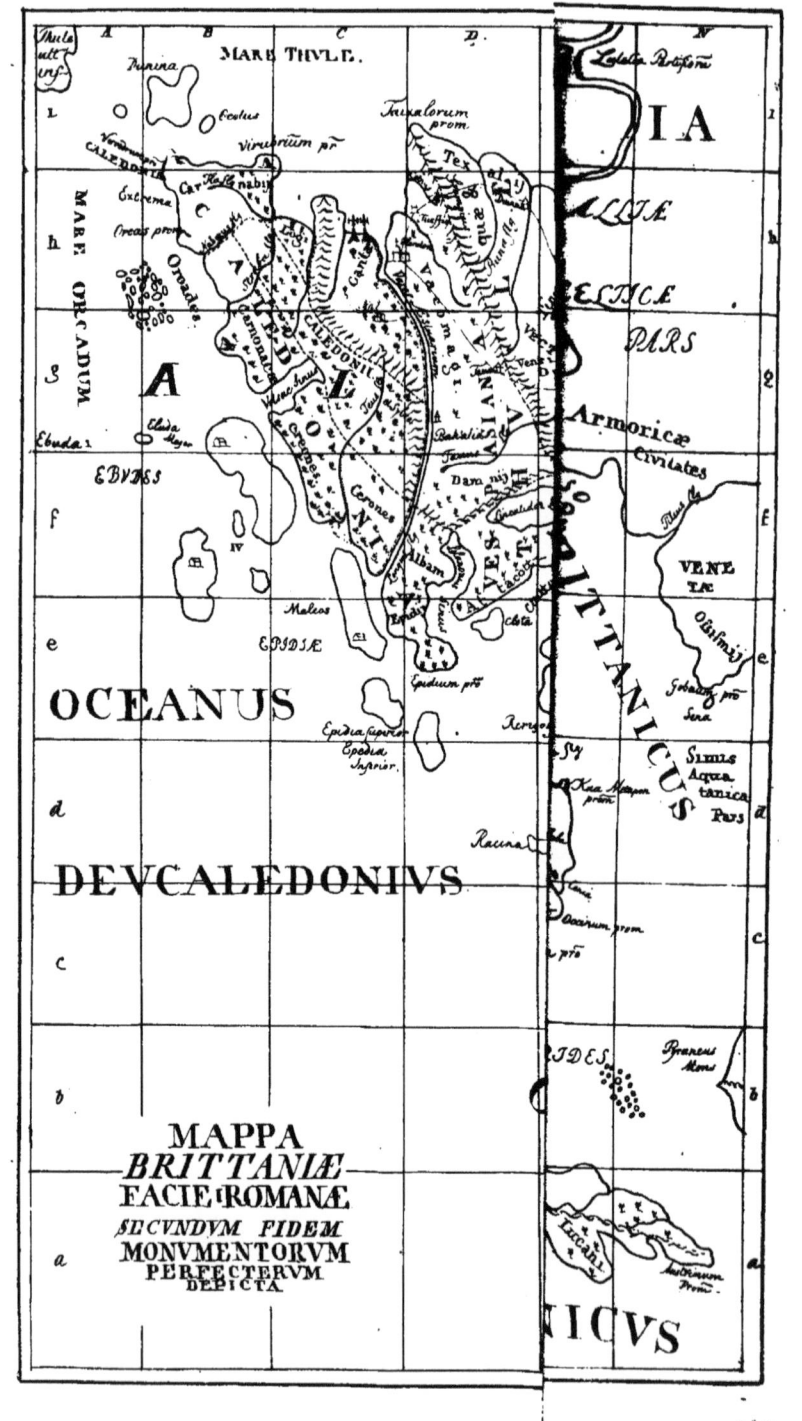

MAPPA
BRITTANIÆ
FACIE ROMANÆ
SECUNDUM FIDEM
MONUMENTORUM
PERFECTERUM
DEPICTA

INDEX TO THE MAP.

D.

Dabrona, river, *K b.*
Damnii, *D f, E e, F d.*
Damnonii, state of, *L e.*
Darabona, }
Darabouna, } river, *F c.*
Derbentio, town, *H g.*
————, river, *F f.*
Deva, colony, called Getica, *H f.*
——, river, *D g, E e f, G d, H f.*
Dimeciæ, *I e.*
Diva, river, *I e.*
Divanà, city, *D h.*
Dubana, river, *L b.*
Dubræ, city, }
——, port, } *K h.*
Dubrona, river, *K b.*
Dunina, islands, *A i.*
Dunum, city, *F d, H c.*
Durius, river, *L e a.*
Durnomagus, town under the Latian law, *I g.*
Durobris, Durobrobis, Duroprovæ, Durobrivæ, stipendiary town, *K h.*

E.

Eblana, town, *H c.*
Eblanæ, }
Eblani, } *H c.*
Eboracum, } municipal and me-
Eburacum, } tropolis, *G g.*
Ebudes, isles, *B f g.*
Ebuda prima, island, *A g.*
———— secunda, *A f.*
———— major, *B g.*
———— quarta, *B f.*
———— quinta, *B f.*
Ebudium, }
Ebudum, } prom., *B g.*
Edria, isle, *H d.*
Epiacum, town, *F g.*
Epidiæ, isles, *C e.*
Epidia inferior, *D d.*
———— superior, *C e.*
Epidii, *C e.*
Epidium, prom., *D e.*
Eriri, mount, *H e.*
Etocetum, town, *I f.*
Extremitas Caledoniæ, *B i.*

F.

Flavia Extrema, *I h.*
————, province, *H f, I g.*
Forum Dianæ, town, *I g.*
Fretum Britannicum, *K i, L h.*

G.

Gadeni, *E g.*
Galacum, }
Galgacum, } town, *F g.*
Gallia, *L M N f g h i.*
———— Belgica, *L i.*
———— Celtica, *M h.*
Garion, }
Garionis, } river, *I h.*
Gessoriacum, town, *L h.*
Glebon, Glevum colony, called Claudia, *K f.*
Gobaneum, }
Gobannium, } town, *I f.*
Gobœum, promontory, *N e.*
Grampius, mount., *D h.*

H.

Halangium, }
Holongum, } town, *L c.*
Hardinii, *G b.*
Hedui, region of, *K f.*
Helenis, }
Helenum, } prom., *M e.*
Herculea, isle, *K d.*
Horestii, *E g.*
Hybernia, *F—N a b c d.*

I.

Iberna, river, *M a.*
Ibernii, *M a.*
Iceni, *H g.*
Idmana, river, *I h.*
Jena, river, *E e.*
Ila, river, *B h.*
Isamnium, promontory, *G d.*
Isca, colony, metropolis, named Secunda, *K f.*
Isca, *L e.*
——, river, *I e, L e.*
——, stipendiary town, *L e.*
Isurium, city, *G g.*
Ituna, æstuary, *F f.*
——, river, *D h, F f.*
Itys, river, *C g.*

K.

Κριοῦ μέτωπον, promontory, *M d.*

L.

Laberus, town, *G d.*
Lelanonius, bay, *D f.*
Lemana, river, *L h.*
Lemanus, town, *K h.*
Libnius, river, *I a.*
Limnia, isle, *H d.*
Lindum, colony, *H g.*
Lindum, *E g.*

William Stevens, Printer, Bell Yard, Temple Bar.

BY THE REV. DR. GILES.

I. Classical.

1. A Greek-English and English-Greek Lexicon, to which is prefixed a Greek Grammar, for the use of Colleges and Schools, 2nd Edit. 8vo. Longman and Co. 1*l.* 1*s. cloth bds.* 1841
2. A Grammar of the Latin Language, 2nd Edit. 8vo. J. Bohn and W. Pickering, 6*s. bds.* 1836
3. Avieni, Rufi Festi, Opera, ex editionibus variis in unum collecta, 8vo. *bds.* J. Bohn 1839
4. Germanici Cæsaris, Inclyti ducis, poetæ elegantis Carmina, quæ extant, 8vo. *bds.* J. Bohn 1839
5. Antimachi Colophonii Reliquiæ, 8vo. *bds.* J. Bohn . 1838
6. Valerii Catonis Carmina, 8vo. *bds.* J. Bohn . . 1839
7. Severi Sancti Carmen de mortibus boum, 8vo. *bds.* J. Bohn 1839
8. Maximiani Elegiæ Sex, 8vo. *bds.* J. Bohn . . 1839
   (Of these minor Classical Authors only 100 copies have been printed.)
9. Ennii Poetæ fragmenta quæ extant, ed. sec. 8vo., prostant apud Librarios, (only 70 copies) 1841
10. Terentii Comœdiæ Sex, cum notis et scholiis omnibus, 8vo. 1838

II. Historical.

1. Venerable Bede's Ecclesiastical History of Britain, translated and revised from the translation of Stevens, with illustrations and facsimiles of MSS., 8vo. *half morocco.* J. Bohn 1840
2. The Minor Historical Works of Venerable Bede will shortly appear in the same form.
3. The Works of Gildas and Nennius, translated from the original, and with the former translations diligently compared, with facsimiles, 8vo. *half morocco.* J. Bohn . . 1841
4. Richard of Devizes, and Richard of Cirencester, translated from the Latin, to which is added the Latin Text of Richard of Cirencester, 8vo. *half morocco.* J. Bohn . . 1841